HYMNS
ANCIENT & MODERN
REVISED

HYMNS
ANCIENT & MODERN
REVISED

THE CANTERBURY PRESS NORWICH

*The Canterbury Press Norwich, St Mary's Works,
St Mary's Plain, Norwich, Norfolk NR3 3BH
The Canterbury Press Norwich is a publishing imprint of
Hymns Ancient & Modern Limited*

© **Compilation**
HYMNS ANCIENT AND MODERN LIMITED

New Imprint June 1982
Second impression January 1984
Third impression July 1984
Fourth impression February 1985
Fifth impression October 1985
Sixth impression September 1987
Seventh impression June 1988

ISBN 0 907547 04 4 (for Reference No. 67)
ISBN 0 907547 05 2 (for Reference No. 68)
ISBN 0 907547 13 3 (for Reference No. 500)

PRINTED AND BOUND IN GREAT BRITAIN BY
RICHARD CLAY LTD, BUNGAY, SUFFOLK

PREFACE

HYMNS ANCIENT AND MODERN was first published (in a form complete with music) in 1861. It was an attempt to consolidate the hymn-books, Anglican and others, which had appeared in the previous hundred years or more and had now become very numerous. It soon became something of a national institution. The Proprietors, a body of Church of England clergymen, found themselves almost embarrassed by the success of their undertaking. An appendix was added in 1868. A revised edition appeared in 1875, to which a Supplement was added in 1889. A new edition, published in 1904, did not succeed in replacing the old book, which with a Second Supplement (1916) has continued to be the most widely used Hymnal of the Church of England. The Standard Edition dates from 1922, when it was reset and many improvements were introduced.

The Proprietors, five in number, were appointed under a Trust Deed. They nominated Assessors to aid them. After certain deductions authorised by the Trust Deed, the whole of the profits on the book was paid to a body of Trustees who distributed them to charities in accordance with the instructions of the Proprietors. It was the custom of the Proprietors to make a donation to the Central Board of Finance of the Church of England a first charge on the sum available for charitable donations. The Rev. Sir Henry Baker was the first Chairman of the Proprietors. Among his successors, Bishop W. H. Frere and Sir Sydney Nicholson may be specially mentioned.

The Musical Editors have been as follows: Dr. W. H. Monk (helped by the Rev. Sir F. A. Gore-Ouseley) from 1861 to 1889; then Dr. C. Steggall for the 1889 Supplement. The music of the 1904 edition was edited by Mr. B. Luard Selby, the Supplement of 1916 by Sir Sydney Nicholson, who continued to be Musical Editor until his death in 1947. In the preparation of the edition now published Sir Sydney was assisted by Mr. G. H. Knight and Dr. J. Dykes Bower.

The shaping of Hymns Ancient and Modern Revised has been a task of much labour, and the Proprietors had a good hope that it will be welcomed by the large public for whom it is designed, as preserving the general tone and character which the book has always had and at the same time making it more serviceable both by what it adds and by what it omits.

The cumbrous device of two Supplements was inconvenient in itself and had made the book too large. It will be seen that the hymns are now arranged in one series of not much over 600 in all. In order to effect this reduction and to make room for new matter the Editors were obliged to leave out a good number of hymns. These soon fell into two distinct classes. The first was of those which had never really found favour. It was easy to cut them out, but there were not enough of them to meet the whole of the necessary reduction. The second class was of those which the Editors felt could well be spared, yet undoubtedly they were endeared to quite a number of congregations. Most of these had to go on the assumption that they were not likely to last much longer. They were bound in the end to be discarded, the Editors thought, and by a justifiable anticipation might be discarded now. Sometimes a favourite hymn may therefore seem to be missing, but the Editors believe that prevailing tendencies would have swept it away before long. They have tried to respect the strong power of association which operates in the minds of hymn-singers by preserving, where possible, the old numbers in the earlier part of the book. A few hymns which have recently become popular are absent owing to copyright difficulties.

Of the hymns to be found in this book which have not appeared in previous editions of Hymns Ancient and Modern, the greater number are old hymns which have been successfully resuscitated in one place or another and have won a wide acceptance and so have become such as no hymn-book could well omit. The Editors have brought in a certain number of new hymns, mainly to satisfy a particular need or occasion, or to match a good tune with fitting words.

The book does not always adhere to the original text of the hymns. The Editors of the earlier editions made alterations to meet the requirements of a hymn-singing congregation, and the present Editors see no reason to go back upon the practice of their predecessors. Many of the great Charles Wesley's hymns have hardly ever been sung as he originally wrote them. Not a few authors, including Dr. Neale, have agreed that for the purpose of a hymn-book the versions of their hymns in Hymns Ancient and Modern were, on the whole, improvements. The case for alteration has been considered on its merits, and in many hymns the author's text has been restored. In others, however, the emended text has been retained as more convenient and having the sanction of long usage.

The provision of hymns to be sung in Procession has been very much increased and made more methodical. On the other hand, from some hymns which seemed over-long for ordinary use one or more verses have been omitted where this appeared not to spoil the effect as a whole.

In concluding what has been the labour of many years, the Proprietors expressed a hope that in this new book the Church will find the same endearing and enduring qualities as in the old, the same heartfelt yet sober tone, so much in keeping with English-speaking Christianity. At the same time they believed that what is new in sense and sound will commend itself as a real augmentation of the rich treasury of hymns and hymn-tunes which are now employed in the divine praises and catholic teaching of the Christian Church. The new book does not aim at breaking fresh ground or exploiting novel ideas. The hope is that it may prove to be, as it was before, a consolidation of all that has been gained over many a long year since the wholesome practice of hymn-singing won an accepted place in Church, School and Home.

ACKNOWLEDGEMENTS

THANKS ARE DUE to those who have given permission for the use of their copyright hymns. The present owners, so far as they can be ascertained, are:

Mr Barclay Baron 500—Mrs Boutflower 404—T. & T. Clark 380—Miss M. Cropper 450—Girls' Friendly Society (and Miss Cropper) 434—Lord Gorell 428—The Mothers' Union 498—A. R. Mowbray & Co. Ltd 436—Novello & Co. Ltd 604—The Royal School of Church Music 297—St Christopher's College, Blackheath 438, 495—Mr C. R. Sedgwick 406—The S.P.C.K. 430, 440, 455, 460, 461, 492, 501, 585.

Also to the personal representatives of the authors for these:

150, 315, 380, 403, 496, 534.

The following belong to *Hymns Ancient and Modern Limited*:

10, 37, 84, 85, 115, 121, 145, 174, 260, 340, 388, 391, 402, 422, 423, 427, 465, 493, 494, 497, 511, 512, 519, 520, 522, 537, 538, 542, 547, 551, 556, 562, 564, 574, 586, 596, 598, 599, 600, 603, 608, 612, 618, 622, 627, 633.

Apologies are offered to any authors where names have been omitted from the above lists, through inadvertence or inability to trace; mistakes will be rectified as soon as possible.

June 1988

TABLE OF CONTENTS

COPYRIGHT AND GRANTS

For permission to print copyright hymns and tunes belonging to the Company, whether in permanent or temporary form, application should be made to the Publishers, HYMNS ANCIENT AND MODERN LIMITED, St Mary's Works, St Mary's Plain, Norwich, Norfolk, NR3 3BH. For other copyright hymns and tunes, application must be made to the respective owners.

Liberal grants of HYMNS ANCIENT AND MODERN are made by the Company to help parishes in the introduction of the book or in the renewal of existing supplies. An application form for a grant can be obtained from the Publishers.

EXPLANATION OF MARKS

† signifies a slight alteration of the author's original; ‡ a more extensive alteration; ⋆ indicates that these verses may be omitted if so desired; ‿ (phrasing sign) indicates that there should be no break between the end of a line and that which follows it.

HYMNS

MORNING

Jam lucis orto sidere

1 NOW that the daylight fills the sky,
   We lift our hearts to God on high,
   That he, in all we do or say,
   Would keep us free from harm to-day:

2 Would guard our hearts and tongues from strife;
   From anger's din would hide our life: [strife;
   From all ill sights would turn our eyes,
   Would close our ears from vanities:

3 Would keep our inmost conscience pure;
   Our souls from folly would secure;
   Would bid us check the pride of sense
   With due and holy abstinence.

4 So we, when this new day is gone,
   And night in turn is drawing on,
   With conscience by the world unstained
   Shall praise his name for victory gained.

5 All laud to God the Father be;
   All praise, eternal Son, to thee;
   All glory, as is ever meet,
   To God the holy Paraclete.

2   *St. Ambrose. Tr. Compilers† (1904)*

Splendor paternae gloriae

1 O SPLENDOUR of God's glory bright,
   Who bringest forth the light from Light;
   O Light, of light the fountain-spring;
   O Day, our days illumining;

2 Come, very Sun of truth and love,
Come in thy radiance from above,
And shed the Holy Spirit's ray
On all we think or do to-day.

3 Teach us to work with all our might;
Put Satan's fierce assaults to flight;
Turn all to good that seems most ill;
Help us our calling to fulfil.

4 O joyful be the livelong day,
Our thoughts as pure as morning ray,
Our faith like noonday's glowing height,
Our souls undimmed by shades of night.

5 All praise to God the Father be,
All praise, eternal Son, to thee,
Whom with the Spirit we adore
For ever and for evermore.

3
Bishop T. Ken†

1 AWAKE, my soul, and with the sun
Thy daily stage of duty run;
Shake off dull sloth, and joyful rise
To pay thy morning sacrifice.

2 Redeem thy mis-spent time that's past,
And live this day as if thy last;
Improve thy talent with due care;
For the great day thyself prepare.

3 Let all thy converse be sincere,
Thy conscience as the noon-day clear;
Think how all-seeing God thy ways
And all thy secret thoughts surveys.

4 Wake, and lift up thyself, my heart,
And with the angels bear thy part,
Who all night long unwearied sing
High praise to the eternal King.

PART 2

5 Glory to thee, who safe hast kept
And hast refreshed me whilst I slept;
Grant, Lord, when I from death shall wake,
I may of endless light partake.

6 Lord, I my vows to thee renew;
Disperse my sins as morning dew;
Guard my first springs of thought and will,
And with thyself my spirit fill.

7 Direct, control, suggest, this day,
All I design or do or say;
That all my powers, with all their might,
In thy sole glory may unite.

*The following Doxology should be used at
the end of either Part:*

8 Praise God, from whom all blessings flow,
Praise him, all creatures here below,
Praise him above, angelic host,
Praise Father, Son, and Holy Ghost.

4   *J. Keble†*

1 NEW every morning is the love
Our wakening and uprising prove;
Through sleep and darkness safely brought,
Restored to life and power and thought.

2 New mercies, each returning day,
Hover around us while we pray;
New perils past, new sins forgiven,
New thoughts of God, new hopes of heaven.

3 If on our daily course our mind
Be set to hallow all we find,
New treasures still, of countless price,
God will provide for sacrifice.

4 The trivial round, the common task,
  Will furnish all we need to ask,
  Room to deny ourselves, a road
  To bring us daily nearer God.

5 Only, O Lord, in thy dear love
  Fit us for perfect rest above;
  And help us, this and every day,
  To live more nearly as we pray.

5   *Sir H. W. Baker*

1 MY Father, for another night
  Of quiet sleep and rest,
  For all the joy of morning light,
  Thy holy name be blest.

2 Now with the new-born day I give
  Myself anew to thee,
  That as thou willest I may live,
  And what thou willest be.

3 Whate'er I do, things great or small,
  Whate'er I speak or frame,
  Thy glory may I seek in all,
  Do all in Jesus' name.

4 My Father, for his sake, I pray,
  Thy child accept and bless;
  And lead me by thy grace to-day
  In paths of righteousness.

6   *W. Bright*

mf 1 AT thy feet, O Christ, we lay
     Thine own gift of this new day;
     Doubt of what it holds in store
     Makes us crave thine aid the more;
     Lest it prove a time of loss,
     Mark it, Saviour, with thy Cross.

2 If it flow on calm and bright,
   Be thyself our chief delight;
p If it bring unknown distress,
   Good is all that thou canst bless;
   Only, while its hours begin,
   Pray we, keep them clear of sin.

mf 3 We in part our weakness know,
   And in part discern our foe;
   Well for us, before thine eyes
   All our danger open lies;
   Turn not from us, while we plead
   Thy compassions and our need.

4 Fain would we thy word embrace,
   Live each moment on thy grace,
   All our selves to thee consign,
   Fold up all our wills in thine,
   Think and speak and do and be
   Simply that which pleases thee.

5 Hear us, Lord, and that right soon;
   Hear, and grant the choicest boon
   That thy love can e'er impart,
   Loyal singleness of heart:
f So shall this and all our days,
   Christ our God, show forth thy praise.

7   *C. Wesley*

f 1 CHRIST, whose glory fills the skies,
   Christ, the true, the only Light,
   Sun of Righteousness, arise,
   Triumph o'er the shades of night;
   Dayspring from on high, be near;
   Daystar, in my heart appear.

p   2 Dark and cheerless is the morn
      Unaccompanied by thee;
  Joyless is the day's return,
     Till thy mercy's beams I see,
  Till they inward light impart,
  Glad my eyes, and warm my heart.

mf 3 Visit then this soul of mine,
     Pierce the gloom of sin and grief;
  Fill me, radiancy divine,
     Scatter all my unbelief;
f   More and more thyself display,
  Shining to the perfect day.

8
I. Watts

1 GOD of the morning, at whose voice‿
    The cheerful sun makes haste to rise,
  And like a giant doth rejoice
    To run his journey through the skies;

2 O, like the sun, may I fulfil‿
    The appointed duties of the day,
  With ready mind and active will
    March on, and keep my heavenly way.

3 Give me thy counsel for my guide,
    And then receive me to thy bliss:
  All my desires and hopes beside
    Are faint and cold, compared with this.

9
Tr. R. M. Moorsom

ἐξεγερθέντες τοῦ ὕπνου

mf 1   AWAKED from sleep we fall‿
    Before thee, God of love,
  And chant the praise the angels raise,
    O God of might, above:
  Holy, Holy, Holy! Thou art God adored!
p In thy pitying mercy show us mercy, Lord.

mf 2   As at thy call I rise,
        Shine on this mind and heart,
        And touch my tongue, that I among
          Thy choir may take my part:
    Holy, Holy, Holy! Trinity adored!
p   In thy pitying mercy show me mercy, Lord.

mf 3   The Judge will come with speed,
        And each man's deeds be known;
        Our trembling cry shall rise on high
          At midnight to thy throne:
    Holy, Holy, Holy! King of Saints adored!
p   In the hour of judgement show us mercy,
    Lord.

10   *Tr. C. S. Phillips*
           Nocte surgentes

1 LET hearts awaken, now the night is ended,
  And raise their morning psalm of adoration,
  In sweetest concert the Creator's glory
    Joyfully singing.

2 So, with the anthems of the blest uniting,
  May we find grace to win the courts celestial,
  And hymn the praise of heaven's high King
    Through life unending.   [eternal

3 Grant this, O Father, Son, and Holy Spirit,
  Trinity blessèd, who one Godhead sharest:
  Thine be the glory through the whole creation
    Now and for ever.

11 *Terce*   ♪ *St. Ambrose*
                Tr. Cardinal J. H. Newman‡
        Nunc Sancte nobis Spiritus

1 COME, Holy Ghost, who ever One
  Art with the Father and the Son,
  Come, Holy Ghost, our souls possess
  With thy full flood of holiness.

2 In will and deed, by heart and tongue,
    With all our powers, thy praise be sung;
    And love light up our mortal frame,
    Till others catch the living flame.

3 Almighty Father, hear our cry
    Through Jesus Christ our Lord most high,
    Who with the Holy Ghost and thee
    Doth live and reign eternally.

MID-DAY

12 *Sext*   ♪ *St. Ambrose. Tr. Compilers*
               Rector potens, verax Deus

1 O GOD of truth, O Lord of might,
    Who orderest time and change aright,
    Arraying morn with joyful gleams,
    And kindling noonday's fiery beams;

2 Quench thou on earth the flames of strife;
    From passion's heat preserve our life;
    Our bodies keep from perils free,
    And grant our souls true peace in thee.

3 Almighty Father, hear our cry
    Through Jesus Christ our Lord most high,
    Who with the Holy Ghost and thee
    Doth live and reign eternally.

13   *J. Ellerton*

1 BEHOLD us, Lord, a little space
        From daily tasks set free,
    And met within thy holy place
        To rest awhile with thee.

2 Around us rolls the ceaseless tide
        Of business, toil, and care;
    And scarcely can we turn aside
        For one brief hour of prayer.

3 Yet these are not the only walls
  Wherein thou may'st be sought:
On homeliest work thy blessing falls,
  In truth and patience wrought.

4 Thine is the loom, the forge, the mart,
  The wealth of land and sea;
The worlds of science and of art,
  Revealed and ruled by thee.

5 Then let us prove our heavenly birth
  In all we do and know;
And claim the kingdom of the earth
  For thee, and not thy foe.

6 Work shall be prayer, if all be wrought
  As thou wouldst have it done;
And prayer, by thee inspired and taught,
  Itself with work be one.

EVENING

14 *None*   *♭ St. Ambrose*

Tr. J. M. Neale and Compilers (1904)

Rerum Deus tenax vigor

1 O GOD, the world's sustaining force,
  Thyself unmoved, all motion's source,
  Who, from the morn till evening's ray,
  Dost through its changes guide the day;

2 O grant us light at eventide,
  That life may unimpaired abide,
  And that a holy death may be
  The door of immortality

3 Almighty Father, hear our cry
  Through Jesus Christ our Lord most high,
  Who with the Holy Ghost and thee
  Doth live and reign eternally.

15
⹁ St. Ambrose
Tr. J. M. Neale and Compilers

O Lux beata Trinitas

1 O TRINITY, most blessèd Light,
O Unity of sovereign might,
As now the fiery sun departs,
Shed thou thy beams within our hearts.

2 To thee our morning song of praise,
To thee our evening prayer we raise;
Thee may our souls for evermore
In lowly reverence adore.

3 All praise to God the Father be,
All praise, eternal Son, to thee,
Whom with the Spirit we adore,
For ever and for evermore.

16 *Compline*   *Tr. J. M. Neale*

Te lucis ante terminum

1 BEFORE the ending of the day,
Creator of the world, we pray,
That with thy wonted favour thou
Wouldst be our guard and keeper now.

2 From all ill dreams defend our eyes,
From nightly fears and fantasies;
Tread under foot our ghostly foe,
That no pollution we may know.

3 O Father, that we ask be done,
Through Jesus Christ thine only Son,
Who, with the Holy Ghost and thee,
Doth live and reign eternally.

17
                              ♭ St. Ambrose
                    Tr. J. Ellerton and F. J. A. Hort
                    Rerum Deus tenax vigor

mf 1 O STRENGTH and stay upholding all crea-
         tion,
       Who ever dost thyself unmoved abide,
       Yet day by day the light in due gradation
         From hour to hour through all its changes
         guide;

p 2 Grant to life's day a calm unclouded ending,
       An eve untouched by shadows of decay,
     The brightness of a holy death-bed blend-
         ing‿
       With dawning glories of the eternal day.

mf 3 Hear us, O Father, gracious and forgiving,
       Through Jesus Christ thy co-eternal Word,
     Who with the Holy Ghost by all things living
       Now and to endless ages art adored.

18
                    3rd cent. or carlier. Tr. J. Keble
                    φῶς ἱλαρὸν ἁγίας δόξης

1   HAIL, gladdening Light, of his pure glory
       poured
     Who is the immortal Father, heavenly, blest,
   Holiest of Holies, Jesus Christ our Lord!

2   Now we are come to the sun's hour of rest,
       The lights of evening round us shine,
     We hymn the Father, Son, and Holy Spirit divine.

3   Worthiest art thou at all times to be sung
       With undefilèd tongue,
     Son of our God, giver of life, alone:
   Therefore in all the world thy glories, Lord, they
       own.

19
G. Thring

mf 1 THE radiant morn hath passed away,
And spent too soon her golden store;
The shadows of departing day
⌣ Creep on once more.

2 Our life is but an autumn day,
Its glorious noon how quickly past!
Lead us, O Christ, thou living Way,
Safe home at last.

3 O by thy soul-inspiring grace
Uplift our hearts to realms on high;
Help us to look to that bright place
⌣ Beyond the sky,

4 Where light and life and joy and peace
In undivided empire reign,
And thronging angels never cease
⌣ Their deathless strain;

f 5 Where saints are clothed in spotless white,
And evening shadows never fall,
Where thou, eternal Light of Light,
Art Lord of all.

20
H. Twells

mf 1 AT even, ere the sun was set,
The sick, O Lord, around thee lay;
O in what divers pains they met!
O with what joy they went away!

2 Once more 'tis eventide, and we
⌣ Oppressed with various ills draw near;
What if thy form we cannot see?
We know and feel that thou art here.

3 O Saviour Christ, our woes dispel;
 For some are sick, and some are sad,
And some have never loved thee well,
 And some have lost the love they had;

4 And some have found the world is vain,
 Yet from the world they break not free;
And some have friends who give them pain,
 Yet have not sought a friend in thee;

5 And none, O Lord, have perfect rest,
 For none are wholly free from sin;
And they who fain would serve thee best
 Are conscious most of wrong within.

6 O Saviour Christ, thou too art Man;
 Thou hast been troubled, tempted, tried;
Thy kind but searching glance can scan
 The very wounds that shame would hide;

f 7 Thy touch has still its ancient power;
 No word from thee can fruitless fall:
mf Hear, in this solemn evening hour,
 And in thy mercy heal us all.

21   *Tr. J. M. Neale* ‡

τὴν ἡμέραν διελθών

1 THE day is past and over;
  All thanks, O Lord, to thee;
 I pray thee now that sinless
  The hours of dark may be:
O Jesu, keep me in thy sight,
And guard me through the coming night.

2 The joys of day are over;
  I lift my heart to thee,
 And ask thee that offenceless
  The hours of dark may be:
O Jesu, keep me in thy sight,
And guard me through the coming night.

3   The toils of day are over;
        I raise the hymn to thee,
    And ask that free from peril
       The hours of dark may be:
O Jesu, keep me in thy sight,
And guard me through the coming night.

4   Be thou my soul's preserver,
        For thou alone dost know‿
    How many are the perils
       Through which I have to go:
O loving Jesu, hear my call,
And guard and save me from them all.

22   *R. H. Robinson*

mf   1   HOLY Father, cheer our way
       With thy love's perpetual ray;
       Grant us every closing day
         Light at evening time.

2   Holy Saviour, calm our fears
       When earth's brightness disappears;
       Grant us in our latter years
         Light at evening time.

p   3   Holy Spirit, be thou nigh
       When in mortal pains we lie;
       Grant us, as we come to die,
         Light at evening time.

f   4   Holy, blessèd Trinity,
       Darkness is not dark with thee;
       Those thou keepest always see‿
         Light at evening time.

23 *Bishop T. Ken*

f 1 GLORY to thee, my God, this night
For all the blessings of the light;
Keep me, O keep me, King of Kings,
Beneath thy own almighty wings.

mf 2 Forgive me, Lord, for thy dear Son,
The ill that I this day have done,
That with the world, myself, and thee,
I, ere I sleep, at peace may be.

3 Teach me to live, that I may dread
The grave as little as my bed;
Teach me to die, that so I may
Rise glorious at the awful day.

4 O may my soul on thee repose,
And may sweet sleep mine eyelids close,
Sleep that may me more vigorous make
To serve my God when I awake.

5 When in the night I sleepless lie,
My soul with heavenly thoughts supply;
Let no ill dreams disturb my rest,
No powers of darkness me molest.

f 6 Praise God, from whom all blessings flow,
Praise him, all creatures here below,
Praise him above, angelic host,
Praise Father, Son, and Holy Ghost.

24 *J. Keble*

mf 1 SUN of my soul, thou Saviour dear,
It is not night if thou be near:
O may no earth-born cloud arise
To hide thee from thy servant's eyes.

p   2 When the soft dews of kindly sleep
My wearied eyelids gently steep,
Be my last thought, how sweet to rest
For ever on my Saviour's breast.

mf   3 Abide with me from morn till eve,
For without thee I cannot live;
Abide with me when night is nigh,
For without thee I dare not die.

4 If some poor wandering child of thine
Have spurned to-day the voice divine,
Now, Lord, the gracious work begin;
Let him no more lie down in sin.

5 Watch by the sick; enrich the poor
With blessings from thy boundless store;
Be every mourner's sleep to-night
Like infant's slumbers, pure and light.

f   6 Come near and bless us when we wake,
Ere through the world our way we take;
Till in the ocean of thy love
We lose ourselves in heaven above.

25
T. Kelly

1 THROUGH the day thy love has spared us;
Now we lay us down to rest;
Through the silent watches guard us,
Let no foe our peace molest:
Jesus, thou our guardian be;
Sweet it is to trust in thee.

2 Pilgrims here on earth and strangers,
Dwelling in the midst of foes,
Us and ours preserve from dangers;
In thine arms may we repose,
And, when life's sad day is past,
Rest with thee in heaven at last.

26

1 *Bishop R. Heber*
2 *Archbishop R. Whately*

1 GOD, that madest earth and heaven,
    Darkness and light;
Who the day for toil hast given,
    For rest the night;
May thine angel-guards defend us,
Slumber sweet thy mercy send us,
Holy dreams and hopes attend us,
    This livelong night.

2 Guard us waking, guard us sleeping,
    And, when we die,
May we in thy mighty keeping
    All peaceful lie:
When the last dread call shall wake us,
Do not thou our God forsake us,
But to reign in glory take us
    With thee on high.

27

H. F. Lyte

mf 1 ABIDE with me; fast falls the eventide:
The darkness deepens; Lord, with me abide:
When other helpers fail, and comforts flee,
Help of the helpless, O abide with me.

p 2 Swift to its close ebbs out life's little day;
Earth's joys grow dim, its glories pass away;
Change and decay in all around I see:
O thou who changest not, abide with me.

mf 3 I need thy presence every passing hour;
What but thy grace can foil the tempter's
        power?
Who like thyself my guide and stay can be?
Through cloud and sunshine, Lord, abide
    with me.

f 4 I fear no foe with thee at hand to bless;
       Ills have no weight, and tears no bitterness.
       Where is death's sting? Where, grave, thy
           victory?
       I triumph still, if thou abide with me.

p 5 Hold thou thy Cross before my closing eyes;
       Shine through the gloom, and point me to
           the skies:
f   Heaven's morning breaks, and earth's vain
           shadows flee;
       In life, in death, O Lord, abide with me.

28
F. W. Faber

mf 1 SWEET Saviour, bless us ere we go;
        Thy word into our minds instil,
        And make our lukewarm hearts to glow
          With lowly love and fervent will. [night,
f   Through life's long day and death's dark
        O gentle Jesus, be our Light.

p   2 The day is done, its hours have run,
          And thou hast taken count of all,
        The scanty triumphs grace hath won,
          The broken vow, the frequent fall.
f   Through life's long day, etc.

mf 3 Grant us, dear Lord, from evil ways‿
          True absolution and release;
        And bless us, more than in past days,
          With purity and inward peace.
f   Through life's long day, etc.

mf 4 Do more than pardon; give us joy,
          Sweet fear, and sober liberty,
        And loving hearts without alloy
          That only long to be like thee.
f   Through life's long day, etc.

p   5 For all we love, the poor, the sad,
        The sinful, unto thee we call;
mf   O let thy mercy make us glad:
        Thou art our Jesus, and our all.
f   Through life's long day, etc.

29   *C. Coffin. Tr. J. Chandler* ‡

                    Labente jam solis rota

p   1 AS now the sun's declining rays
        At eventide descend,
      So life's brief day is sinking down⌣
        To its appointed end.

    2 Lord, on the Cross thine arms were
        To draw thy people nigh: [stretched
      O grant us then that Cross to love,
        And in those arms to die.

f   3 All glory to the Father be,
        All glory to the Son,
      All glory, Holy Ghost, to thee,
        While endless ages run.

30   *c. 18th cent. Tr. E. Caswall*†

                    Sol praeceps rapitur

p   1 THE sun is sinking fast,
        The daylight dies;
      Let love awake, and pay⌣
        Her evening sacrifice.

    2 As Christ upon the Cross
        His head inclined,
      And to his Father's hands
        His parting soul resigned,

mf 3 So now herself my soul
    Would wholly give⌣
In his sacred charge,
    In whom all spirits live;

4 So now beneath his eye
    Would calmly rest,
Without a wish or thought
    Abiding in the breast,

5 Save that his will be done,
    Whate'er betide,
Dead to herself, and dead⌣
    In him to all beside.

f 6 Thus would I live; yet now⌣
    Not I, but he,
In all his power and love
    Henceforth alive in me.

7 One sacred Trinity!
    One Lord divine!
May I be ever his,
    And he for ever mine.

31 *At the end of Service*   *J. Ellerton*

mf 1 SAVIOUR, again to thy dear name we raise
With one accord our parting hymn of praise;
We stand to bless thee ere our worship cease;
p   Then, lowly kneeling, wait thy word of
    peace.

2 Grant us thy peace upon our homeward way;
With thee began, with thee shall end, the day:
Guard thou the lips from sin, the hearts from
    shame,
That in this house have called upon thy name.

3 Grant us thy peace, Lord, through the coming
    night;
f   Turn thou for us its darkness into light;
    From harm and danger keep thy children free,
    For dark and light are both alike to thee.

mf 4 Grant us thy peace throughout our earthly life,
    Our balm in sorrow, and our stay in strife;
p   Then, when thy voice shall bid our conflict
        cease,
    Call us, O Lord, to thine eternal peace.

32 *At the end of Service* W. Bright

mf 1 AND now the wants are told, that brought⌣
        Thy children to thy knee;
    Here lingering still, we ask for nought,
    But simply worship thee.

2 The hope of heaven's eternal days
    Absorbs not all the heart
    That gives thee glory, love, and praise,
    For being what thou art.

3 For thou art God, the One, the Same,
    O'er all things high and bright;
    And round us, when we speak thy name,
    There spreads a heaven of light.

p 4 O wondrous peace, in thought to dwell⌣
        On excellence divine;
    To know that nought in man can tell
    How fair thy beauties shine!

mf 5 O thou, above all blessing blest,
        O'er thanks exalted far,
    Thy very greatness is a rest
    To weaklings as we are;

6 For when we feel the praise of thee
   A task beyond our powers,
We say, 'A perfect God is he,
   And he is fully ours.'

f 7 All glory to the Father be,
   All glory to the Son,
All glory, Holy Ghost, to thee,
   While endless ages run.

33
J. Ellerton

mf 1 THE day thou gavest, Lord, is ended,
   The darkness falls at thy behest;
To thee our morning hymns ascended,
   Thy praise shall sanctify our rest.

2 We thank thee that thy Church unsleeping,
   While earth rolls onward into light,
Through all the world her watch is keeping,
   And rests not now by day or night.

3 As o'er each continent and island
   The dawn leads on another day,
The voice of prayer is never silent,
   Nor dies the strain of praise away.

4 The sun that bids us rest is waking
   Our brethren 'neath the western sky,
And hour by hour fresh lips are making
   Thy wondrous doings heard on high.

f 5 So be it, Lord; thy throne shall never,
   Like earth's proud empires, pass away;
Thy Kingdom stands, and grows for ever,
   Till all thy creatures own thy sway.

34

Yattendon Hymnal. Based on **Nun ruhen
alle Wälder,** *P. Gerhardt*

mf 1 THE duteous day now closeth,
Each flower and tree reposeth,
    Shade creeps o'er wild and wood:
Let us, as night is falling,
On God our Maker calling,
    Give thanks to him, the giver good.

2 Now all the heavenly splendour
Breaks forth in starlight tender
    From myriad worlds unknown;
And man, the marvel seeing,
Forgets his selfish being,
    For joy of beauty not his own.

3 His care he drowneth yonder,
Lost in the abyss of wonder;
    To heaven his soul doth steal:
This life he disesteemeth,
The day it is that dreameth,
    That doth from truth his vision seal.

p 4 Awhile his mortal blindness
May miss God's loving-kindness,
    And grope in faithless strife:
cr But when life's day is over
Shall death's fair night discover
    The fields of everlasting life.

35   *W. Romanis*

mf 1 ROUND me falls the night;
Saviour, be my light:
Through the hours in darkness shrouded
Let me see thy face unclouded;
    Let thy glory shine
    In this heart of mine.

p   2   Earthly work is done,
    Earthly sounds are none;
Rest in sleep and silence seeking,
Let me hear thee softly speaking;
    In my spirit's ear
    Whisper, 'I am near.'

mf   3   Blessèd, heavenly Light,
    Shining through earth's night;
Voice, that oft of love hast told me;
Arms, so strong to clasp and hold me;
    Thou thy watch wilt keep,
    Saviour, o'er my sleep.

36

I. Watts

mf   1   AND now another day is gone,
    I'll sing my Maker's praise,
My comforts every hour make known,
    His providence and grace.

p   2   I lay my body down to sleep;
    May angels guard my head,
And through the hours of darkness keep
    Their watch around my bed.

f   3   With cheerful heart I close my eyes,
    Since thou wilt not remove;
And in the morning let me rise
    Rejoicing in thy love.

37

c. 18th cent. Tr. C. S. Phillips

Sol praeceps rapitur

1   FAST sinks the sun to rest,
    Fast fall the shades of night;
Fain would the weary heart
    Keep love's frail flame alight,
End the day that fading dies
With an offering of sacrifice.

2   E'en as the Crucified,
        Calm in the hour of death,
Into his Father's hands
        Yielded his latest breath,
So my spirit would repose
Safe in God's mighty keeping close.

3   Meekly beneath his hand
        Lieth my helplessness,
Thinking and caring naught
        Save what he purposes,
And in utter calm abides,
Dead to self and to all besides.

4   Be it not I who live
        But God who lives in me,
Reigning and triumphing
        In love's sweet majesty;
May he mine for ever be,
God who One is in Trinity.

38 *For Festivals*   *J. Ellerton*

mf 1 OUR day of praise is done;
        The evening shadows fall;
But pass not from us with the sun,
        True Light that lightenest all.

f   2 Around the throne on high,
        Where night can never be,
The white-robed harpers of the sky
        Bring ceaseless hymns to thee.

p   3 Too faint our anthems here;
        Too soon of praise we tire:
mf   But O the strains how full and clear
        Of that eternal choir!

4 Yet, Lord, to thy dear will
 If thou attune the heart,
We in thine angels' music still
 May bear our lower part.

5 'Tis thine each soul to calm,
 Each wayward thought reclaim,
And make our life a daily psalm
 Of glory to thy name.

f   6 A little while, and then⌣
 Shall come the glorious end;
And songs of angels and of men
 In perfect praise shall blend.

SUNDAY

39   *Morning.*   18*th cent. Tr. Sir H. W. Baker* ‡
     Die parente temporum

f   1 ON this day, the first of days,
 God the Father's name we praise,
Who, creation's Lord and spring,
 Did the world from darkness bring.

2 On this day the eternal Son
 Over death his triumph won;
On this day the Spirit came
 With his gifts of living flame.

3 O that fervent love to-day
 May in every heart have sway,
Teaching us to praise aright
 God the source of life and light!

mf   4 Father, who didst fashion me
 Image of thyself to be,
Fill me with thy love divine.
 Let my every thought be thine.

5 Holy Jesus, may I be
Dead and risen here with thee,
And upon love's fire arise
Unto thee a sacrifice.

6 Thou who dost all gifts impart,
Shine, good Spirit, in my heart;
Best of gifts, thyself bestow;
Make me burn thy love to know.

7 God, the one God of my heart,
I am thine, and mine thou art;
Take me, blessèd One in Three,
Here I give myself to thee.

40

*Ascribed to Thomas à Kempis
Tr. J. M. Neale and Compilers*
En dies est dominica

1 AGAIN the Lord's own day is here,
The day to Christian people dear,
As, week by week, it bids them tell
How Jesus rose from death and hell.

2 For by his flock their Lord declared
His Resurrection should be shared;
And we who trust in him to save
With him are risen from the grave.

3 We, one and all, of him possessed,
Are with exceeding treasures blessed;
For all he did, and all he bare,
He gives us as our own to share.

4 Eternal glory, rest on high,
A blessèd immortality,
True peace and gladness, and a throne,
Are all his gifts, and all our own.

5 And therefore unto thee we sing,
O Lord of peace, eternal King;
Thy love we praise, thy name adore,
Both on this day and evermore.

41

Bishop Chr. Wordsworth†

1 O DAY of rest and gladness,
    O day of joy and light,
O balm of care and sadness,
    Most beautiful, most bright;
On thee the high and lowly
    Before the eternal throne
Sing Holy, Holy, Holy,
    To the great Three in One.

2 On thee, at the creation,
    The light first had its birth;
On thee for our salvation
    Christ rose from depths of earth;
On thee our Lord victorious
    The Spirit sent from heaven;
And thus on thee most glorious
    A triple light was given.

3 *To-day on weary nations
    The heavenly manna falls,
To holy convocations
    The silver trumpet calls,
Where Gospel-light is glowing
    With pure and radiant beams,
And living water flowing
    With soul-refreshing streams.

4 New graces ever gaining
    From this our day of rest,
We reach the rest remaining
    To spirits of the blest:
To Holy Ghost be praises,
    To Father, and to Son;
The Church her voice upraises
    To thee, blest Three in One.

42

J. Ellerton

f 1 THIS is the day of light:
Let there be light to-day;
O Dayspring, rise upon our night,
And chase its gloom away.

mf 2 This is the day of rest:
Our failing strength renew;
On weary brain and troubled breast ⌣
Shed thou thy freshening dew.

3 This is the day of peace:
Thy peace our spirits fill;
Bid thou the blasts of discord cease,
The waves of strife be still.

4 This is the day of prayer:
Let earth to heaven draw near;
Lift up our hearts to seek thee there,
Come down to meet us here.

f 5 This is the first of days:
Send forth thy quickening breath,
And wake dead souls to love and praise,
O vanquisher of death.

43

I. Watts†

f 1 THIS is the day the Lord hath made,
He calls the hours his own;
Let heaven rejoice, let earth be glad,
And praise surround the throne.

2 To-day he rose and left the dead,
And Satan's empire fell;
To-day the saints his triumph spread,
And all his wonders tell.

3 Hosanna to the anointed King,
To David's holy Son!
O help us, Lord, descend and bring ⌣
Salvation from thy throne.

mf 4 Blest be the Lord, who comes to men
With messages of grace;
Who comes, in God his Father's name,
To save our sinful race.

f 5 Hosanna in the highest strains
The Church on earth can raise;
The highest heavens in which he reigns
Shall give him nobler praise.

44 *Evening*   *Tr. Compilers*

Lucis Creator optime

mf 1 BLEST Creator of the light,
Making day with radiance bright,
Thou didst o'er the forming earth
Give the golden light its birth.

2 Shade of eve with morning ray
Took from thee the name of day;
Darkness now is drawing nigh;
Listen to our humble cry.

p 3 May we ne'er by guilt depressed
Lose the way to endless rest;
Nor with idle thoughts and vain
Bind our souls to earth again.

mf 4 Rather may we heavenward rise
Where eternal treasure lies;
Purified by grace within,
Hating every deed of sin.

5 Holy Father, hear our cry
Through thy Son our Lord most high.
f   Whom our thankful hearts adore
With the Spirit evermore.

ADVENT

45   *Tr. J. M. Neale and Compilers*

Conditor alme siderum

1 CREATOR of the starry height,
   Thy people's everlasting Light,
   Jesu, Redeemer of us all,
   Hear thou thy servants when they call.

2 Thou, sorrowing at the helpless cry
   Of all creation doomed to die,
   Didst come to save our fallen race
   By healing gifts of heavenly grace.

3 When earth was near its evening hour,
   Thou didst, in love's redeeming power,
   Like bridegroom from his chamber, come
   Forth from a Virgin-mother's womb.

4 At thy great name, exalted now,
   All knees in lowly homage bow;
   All things in heaven and earth adore,
   And own thee King for evermore.

5 To thee, O Holy One, we pray,
   Our Judge in that tremendous day,
   Ward off, while yet we dwell below,
   The weapons of our crafty foe.

6 To God the Father, God the Son,
   And God the Spirit, Three in One,
   Praise, honour, might, and glory be
   From age to age eternally.

46 *Tr. R. M. Moorsom*

ἰδοὺ ὁ Νυμφίος

f 1 'BEHOLD, the Bridegroom draweth nigh!'
Hear ye the oft-repeated cry?
  Go forth into the midnight dim;
mf For blest are they whom he shall find
With ready heart and watchful mind;
  Go forth, my soul, to him.

f 2 'Behold, the Bridegroom cometh by!'
The call is echoed from the sky:
  Go forth, ye servants, watch and wait;
mf The slothful cannot join his train;
No careless one may entrance gain:
  Awake, my soul, 'tis late.

p 3 The wise will plead with one accord,
'O Holy, Holy, Holy Lord,
  On us thy quickening grace bestow,
That none may reach the door too late,
When thou shalt enter at the gate
  And to thy Kingdom go.'

f 4 'Behold, the Bridegroom draweth near!'
The warning falls on every ear:
  That night of dread shall come to all:
Behold, my soul, thy lamp so dim,
Rise, rise the smoking flax to trim;
  Soon shalt thou hear his call.

47 *Tr. E. Caswall* ‡

Vox clara ecce intonat

f 1 HARK! a thrilling voice is sounding;
  'Christ is nigh,' it seems to say;
'Cast away the dreams of darkness,
  O ye children of the day!'

2 Wakened by the solemn warning,
 Let the earth-bound soul arise;
Christ, her Sun, all ill dispelling,
 Shines upon the morning skies.

mf 3 Lo, the Lamb, so long expected,
 Comes with pardon down from heaven;
Let us haste, with tears of sorrow,
 One and all to be forgiven;

4 That when next he comes with glory,
 And the world is wrapped in fear,
With his mercy he may shield us,
 And with words of love draw near.

f 5 Honour, glory, might, and blessing
 To the Father and the Son,
With the everlasting Spirit,
 While eternal ages run.

48   *C. Coffin. Tr. J. Chandler and Compilers*
     Instantis adventum Dei

1 THE advent of our King
 Our prayers must now employ,
And we must hymns of welcome sing
 In strains of holy joy.

2 The everlasting Son
 Incarnate deigns to be;
Himself a servant's form puts on,
 To set his servants free.

3 Daughter of Sion, rise
 To meet thy lowly King;
Nor let thy faithless heart despise
 The peace he comes to bring.

4 As Judge, on clouds of light,
 He soon will come again,
And his true members all unite
 With him in heaven to reign.

5   All glory to the Son
Who comes to set us free,
With Father, Spirit, ever One,
Through all eternity.

49   *Tr. J. M. Neale and Compilers*

Veni, veni, Emmanuel

1 O COME, O come, Emmanuel,
And ransom captive Israel,
That mourns in lonely exile here,
Until the Son of God appear.
      Rejoice! Rejoice! Emmanuel
      Shall come to thee, O Israel.

2 O come, thou Rod of Jesse, free
Thine own from Satan's tyranny;
From depths of hell thy people save,
And give them victory o'er the grave.
      Rejoice, etc.

3 O come, thou Dayspring, come and cheer
Our spirits by thine advent here;
Disperse the gloomy clouds of night,
And death's dark shadows put to flight.
      Rejoice, etc.

4 O come, thou Key of David, come,
And open wide our heavenly home;
Make safe the way that leads on high,
And close the path to misery.
      Rejoice, etc.

5 O come, O come, thou Lord of Might,
Who to thy tribes, on Sinai's height,
In ancient times didst give the law
In cloud and majesty and awe.
      Rejoice, etc.

50   *C. Coffin. Tr. J. Chandler and Compilers*
Jordanis oras praevia

1 ON Jordan's bank the Baptist's cry
   Announces that the Lord is nigh;
   Awake, and hearken, for he brings
   Glad tidings of the King of Kings.

2 Then cleansed be every breast from sin;
   Make straight the way for God within;
   Prepare we in our hearts a home,
   Where such a mighty guest may come.

3 For thou art our salvation, Lord,
   Our refuge, and our great reward;
   Without thy grace we waste away,
   Like flowers that wither and decay.

4 To heal the sick stretch out thine hand,
   And bid the fallen sinner stand;
   Shine forth, and let thy light restore
   Earth's own true loveliness once more.

5 All praise, eternal Son, to thee
   Whose advent doth thy people free,
   Whom with the Father we adore
   And Holy Ghost for evermore.

51   *C. Wesley and J. Cennick*

f 1 LO, he comes with clouds descending,
     Once for favoured sinners slain;
   Thousand thousand saints attending
     Swell the triumph of his train:
       Alleluia!
     Christ appears on earth to reign.

p 2 Every eye shall now behold him
     Robed in dreadful majesty;
   Those who set at naught and sold him,
     Pierced and nailed him to the Tree,
       Deeply wailing,
     Shall the true Messiah see.

mf 3 Those dear tokens of his Passion
          Still his dazzling body bears,
      Cause of endless exultation
          To his ransomed worshippers:
              With what rapture
          Gaze we on those glorious scars!

f 4 Yea, Amen, let all adore thee,
          High on thine eternal throne;
      Saviour, take the power and glory,
          Claim the kingdom for thine own:
              Alleluia!
          Thou shalt reign, and thou alone.

52   *John Milton*

1 THE Lord will come and not be slow,
       His footsteps cannot err;
   Before him righteousness shall go,
       His royal harbinger.

2 Truth from the earth, like to a flower,
       Shall bud and blossom then;
   And justice, from her heavenly bower,
       Look down on mortal men.

3 Rise, God, judge thou the earth in might,
       This wicked earth redress;
   For thou art he who shalt by right
       The nations all possess.

4 The nations all whom thou hast made
       Shall come, and all shall frame
   To bow them low before thee, Lord,
       And glorify thy name.

5 For great thou art, and wonders great
       By thy strong hand are done:
   Thou in thy everlasting seat
       Remainest God alone.

53
P. Doddridge†

f 1 HARK the glad sound! the Saviour comes,
      The Saviour promised long:
      Let every heart prepare a throne,
      And every voice a song.

     2 He comes, the prisoners to release
       In Satan's bondage held;
       The gates of brass before him burst,
       The iron fetters yield.

mf 3 He comes, the broken heart to bind,
      The bleeding soul to cure,
      And with the treasures of his grace
      To bless the humble poor.

f 4 Our glad Hosannas, Prince of Peace,
      Thy welcome shall proclaim;
      And heaven's eternal arches ring
      With thy belovèd name.

54
C. Wesley

mf 1 COME, thou long-expected Jesus,
      Born to set thy people free;
      From our fears and sins release us;
      Let us find our rest in thee.

     2 Israel's strength and consolation,
       Hope of all the earth thou art;
       Dear Desire of every nation,
       Joy of every longing heart.

f 3 Born thy people to deliver;
      Born a Child and yet a King;
      Born to reign in us for ever;
      Now thy gracious kingdom bring.

mf 4 By thy own eternal Spirit,
      Rule in all our hearts alone:
  By thy all-sufficient merit,
      Raise us to thy glorious throne.

55   *P. Nicolai. Tr. Frances E. Cox†*
                 Wachet auf

1 SLEEPERS, wake! the watch-cry pealeth,
  While slumber deep each eyelid sealeth:
    Awake, Jerusalem, awake!
  Midnight's solemn hour is tolling,
  And seraph-notes are onward rolling;
    They call on us our part to take.
      Come forth, ye virgins wise:
      The Bridegroom comes, arise!
        Alleluia!
    Each lamp be bright
    With ready light
  To grace the marriage feast to-night.

2 Zion hears the voice that singeth,
  With sudden joy her glad heart springeth,
    At once she wakes, she stands arrayed:
  Her Light is come, her Star ascending,
  Lo, girt with truth, with mercy blending,
    Her Bridegroom there, so long delayed.
      All hail! God's glorious Son,
      All hail! our joy and crown,
        Alleluia!
    The joyful call
    We answer all,
  And follow to the bridal hall.

3 Praise to him who goes before us!
  Let men and angels join in chorus,
    Let harp and cymbal add their sound.
  Twelve the gates, a pearl each portal—

We haste to join the choir immortal
　Within the Holy City's bound.
　　Ear ne'er heard aught like this,
　　Nor heart conceived such bliss.
　　　Alleluia!
　　We raise the song,
　　We swell the throng,
To praise thee ages all along.

56   *J. Anstice*

1 WHEN came in flesh the incarnate Word,
　　The heedless world slept on,
　And only simple shepherds heard
　　That God had sent his Son.

2 When comes the Saviour at the last,
　　From east to west shall shine
　The aweful pomp, and earth aghast
　　Shall tremble at the sign.

3 Lord, who could dare see thee descend
　　In state, unless he knew
　Thou art the sorrowing sinner's friend,
　　The gracious and the true?

4 Dwell in our hearts, O Saviour blest:
　　So shall thine advent's dawn
　'Twixt us and thee, our bosom-guest,
　　Be but the veil withdrawn.

The following hymns are suitable for this season:

227　O quickly come, dread Judge of all.
228　That day of wrath, that dreadful day.
229　Ye servants of the Lord.
262　Thy Kingdom come, O God.
263　Thy Kingdom come! on bended knee.

CHRISTMAS

57   *Sedulius. Tr. J. Ellerton*

A solis ortus cardine

f   1 FROM east to west, from shore to shore,
        Let every heart awake and sing⌣
    The holy Child whom Mary bore,
        The Christ, the everlasting King.

mf 2 Behold, the world's Creator wears⌣
        The form and fashion of a slave;
    Our very flesh our Maker shares,
        His fallen creature, man, to save.

    3 For this how wondrously he wrought!
        A maiden, in her lowly place,
    Became, in ways beyond all thought,
        The chosen vessel of his grace.

    4 She bowed her to the angel's word
        Declaring what the Father willed,
    And suddenly the promised Lord
        That pure and hallowed temple filled.

p   5 He shrank not from the oxen's stall,
        He lay within the manger bed,
    And he whose bounty feedeth all
        At Mary's breast himself was fed.

mf 6 And while the angels in the sky
        Sang praise above the silent field,
    To shepherds poor the Lord most high,
        The one great Shepherd, was revealed.

f   7 All glory for this blessèd morn
        To God the Father ever be;
    All praise to thee, O Virgin-born,
        All praise, O Holy Ghost, to thee.

58 *Prudentius. Tr. J. M. Neale* ‡
Corde natus ex Parentis

mf 1 OF the Father's love begotten
    Ere the worlds began to be,
He is Alpha and Omega,
    He the source, the ending he,
Of the things that are, that have been,
    And that future years shall see,
      Evermore and evermore.

2 O that birth for ever blessèd!
    When the Virgin, full of grace,
By the Holy Ghost conceiving,
    Bare the Saviour of our race,
And the Babe, the world's Redeemer,
    First revealed his sacred face,
      Evermore and evermore.

f 3 O ye heights of heaven, adore him;
    Angel hosts, his praises sing;
Powers, dominions bow before him,
    And extol our God and King;
Let no tongue on earth be silent,
    Every voice in concert ring,
      Evermore and evermore.

Note.—A longer version of this hymn will be found in the 'Processional' section (591)*.*

59 *18th cent. Tr. F. Oakeley* ‡
Adeste fideles

1 O COME, all ye faithful,
    Joyful and triumphant,
O come ye, O come ye to Bethlehem;
    Come and behold him,
    Born the King of Angels:
    O come, let us adore him,
    O come, let us adore him,
O come, let us adore him, Christ the Lord.

2   God of God,
Light of Light,
Lo, he abhors not the Virgin's womb;
Very God,
Begotten, not created:
O come, let us adore him, etc.

3   Sing, choirs of angels,
Sing in exultation,
Sing, all ye citizens of heaven above:
'Glory to God
In the highest:'
O come, let us adore him, etc.

4   Yea, Lord, we greet thee,
Born this happy morning;
Jesus, to thee be glory given;
Word of the Father,
Now in flesh appearing:
O come, let us adore him, etc.

Note.—A longer version of this hymn will be found in the 'Processional' section (**593**).

60   *C. Wesley and others*

1   HARK! the herald-angels sing
Glory to the new-born King,
Peace on earth, and mercy mild,
God and sinners reconciled.
Joyful, all ye nations, rise,
Join the triumph of the skies;
With the angelic host proclaim,
'Christ is born in Bethlehem.'
      Hark! the herald-angels sing
      Glory to the new-born King.

2 Christ, by highest heaven adored,
　Christ, the everlasting Lord,
　Late in time behold him come,
　Offspring of a Virgin's womb.
　Veiled in flesh the Godhead see!
　Hail, the incarnate Deity!
　Pleased as Man with man to dwell,
　Jesus, our Emmanuel.
　　　　Hark, etc.

3 Hail, the heaven-born Prince of Peace!
　Hail, the Sun of Righteousness!
　Light and life to all he brings,
　Risen with healing in his wings.
　Mild he lays his glory by,
　Born that man no more may die,
　Born to raise the sons of earth,
　Born to give them second birth.
　　　　Hark, etc.

61　　　　　　　　　　　　　　　　*J. Byrom* ‡

f 1 CHRISTIANS, awake! salute the happy
　　　morn,
　Whereon the Saviour of the world was born;
　Rise to adore the mystery of love,
　Which hosts of angels chanted from above:
　With them the joyful tidings first begun
　Of God incarnate and the Virgin's Son.

2 Then to the watchful shepherds it was told,
　Who heard the angelic herald's voice, 'Behold,
　I bring good tidings of a Saviour's birth
　To you and all the nations upon earth:
　This day hath God fulfilled his promised
　　word,
　This day is born a Saviour, Christ the Lord.'

3 He spake; and straightway the celestial choir
   In hymns of joy, unknown before, conspire;
   The praises of redeeming love they sang,
   And heaven's whole orb with Alleluias rang:
   God's highest glory was their anthem still,
   Peace upon earth, and unto men good will.

4 To Bethlehem straight the enlightened shep-
      herds ran,
   To see the wonder God had wrought for man,
   And found, with Joseph and the blessèd Maid,
   Her Son, the Saviour, in a manger laid:
   Then to their flocks, still praising God, re-
      turn,
   And their glad hearts with holy rapture burn.

PART 2

mf 5 O may we keep and ponder in our mind
   God's wondrous love in saving lost mankind;
   Trace we the Babe, who hath retrieved our
      loss,
   From his poor manger to his bitter Cross;
   Tread in his steps, assisted by his grace,
   Till man's first heavenly state again takes place.

f 6 Then may we hope, the angelic hosts among,
   To sing, redeemed, a glad triumphal song:
   He that was born upon this joyful day
   Around us all his glory shall display;
   Saved by his love, incessant we shall sing
   Eternal praise to heaven's almighty King.

62   *N. Tate*

mf 1 WHILE shepherds watched their flocks
      by night,
         All seated on the ground,
      The angel of the Lord came down,
         And glory shone around.

2 'Fear not,' said he (for mighty dread
    Had seized their troubled mind);
'Glad tidings of great joy I bring
    To you and all mankind.

3 'To you in David's town this day
    Is born of David's line
A Saviour, who is Christ the Lord;
    And this shall be the sign:

4 'The heavenly Babe you there shall find
    To human view displayed,
All meanly wrapped in swathing bands,
    And in a manger laid.'

5 Thus spake the seraph; and forthwith
    Appeared a shining throng
Of angels praising God, who thus
    Addressed their joyful song:

f 6 'All glory be to God on high,
    And to the earth be peace;
Good will henceforth from heaven to men
    Begin and never cease.'

63

C. Coffin
Tr. Bp. J. R. Woodford and Compilers
Jam desinant suspiria

f 1 GOD from on high hath heard!
    Let sighs and sorrows cease!
Lo, from the opening heaven descends
    To man the promised peace.

2 Hark! through the silent night
    Angelic voices swell;
Their joyful songs proclaim that God
    Is born on earth to dwell.

mf 3 See how the shepherd-band
    Speed on with eager feet;
Come to the hallowed cave with them
    The holy Babe to greet.

p   4   But O what sight appears
        Within that lowly door!
    A manger, stall, and swaddling clothes,
        A child, and mother poor!

mf 5   Art thou the Christ? the Son?
        The Father's Image bright?
    And see we him whose arm upholds‿
        Earth and the starry height?

f   6   Yea, faith can pierce the cloud
        Which veils thy glory now;
    We hail thee God, before whose throne‿
        The angels prostrate bow.

mf 7   Our sinful pride to cure
        With that pure love of thine,
    O be thou born within our hearts,
        Most holy Child divine.

64
                                    J. Montgomery

mf 1   ANGELS, from the realms of glory,
            Wing your flight o'er all the earth;
        Ye who sang creation's story,
            Now proclaim Messiah's birth:
f   Come and worship,
        Worship Christ, the new-born King.

mf 2   Shepherds, in the field abiding,
            Watching o'er your flocks by night,
        God with man is now residing,
            Yonder shines the infant Light:
f   Come and worship, etc.

mf 3   Sages, leave your contemplations;
            Brighter visions beam afar:
        Seek the great Desire of Nations;
            Ye have seen his natal star:
f   Come and worship, etc.

mf 4 Saints before the altar bending,
　　　Watching long in hope and fear,
　　Suddenly the Lord, descending,
　　　In his temple shall appear:
f　　　　Come and worship, etc.

mf 5 Though an infant now we view him,
　　　He shall fill his Father's throne,
　　Gather all the nations to him;
　　　Every knee shall then bow down:
f　　　　Come and worship, etc.

65　　　　　　　　　*Bishop Phillips Brooks*

p 1 O LITTLE town of Bethlehem,
　　　How still we see thee lie!
　　Above thy deep and dreamless sleep
　　　The silent stars go by:
mf　Yet in thy dark streets shineth
　　　The everlasting Light;
f　The hopes and fears of all the years
　　　Are met in thee to-night.

　　2 For Christ is born of Mary;
　　　And, gathered all above,
p　While mortals sleep, the angels keep⌣
　　　Their watch of wondering love.
f　O morning stars, together
　　　Proclaim the holy birth,
　　And praises sing to God the King,
　　　And peace to men on earth.

p 3 How silently, how silently,
　　　The wondrous gift is given!
　　So God imparts to human hearts
　　　The blessings of his heaven.
　　No ear may hear his coming;
　　　But in this world of sin,
　　Where meek souls will receive him, still⌣
　　　The dear Christ enters in.

mf   4 O holy Child of Bethlehem,
          Descend to us, we pray;
        Cast out our sin, and enter in:
          Be born in us to-day.
f   We hear the Christmas angels⌣
          The great glad tidings tell:
        O come to us, abide with us,
          Our Lord Emmanuel.

The last line of each verse may be repeated.

66

E. H. Sears

mf   1 IT came upon the midnight clear,
          That glorious song of old,
        From angels bending near the earth
          To touch their harps of gold:
        'Peace on the earth, good will to men,
          From heaven's all-gracious King!'
        The world in solemn stillness lay
          To hear the angels sing.

       2 Still through the cloven skies they come,
          With peaceful wings unfurled;
        And still their heavenly music floats
          O'er all the weary world:
        Above its sad and lowly plains
          They bend on hovering wing;
        And ever o'er its Babel-sounds
          The blessèd angels sing.

p   3 Yet with the woes of sin and strife
          The world has suffered long;
        Beneath the angel-strain have rolled
          Two thousand years of wrong;
        And man, at war with man, hears not
          The love-song which they bring:
        O hush the noise, ye men of strife,
          And hear the angels sing.

4*And ye, beneath life's crushing load,
　　Whose forms are bending low,
Who toil along the climbing way
　　With painful steps and slow,
Look, now! for glad and golden hours
　　Come swiftly on the wing;
O rest beside the weary road,
　　And hear the angels sing.

mf　5 For lo, the days are hastening on,
　　By prophet-bards foretold,
When, with the ever-circling years,
　　Comes round the age of gold;
f　When peace shall over all the earth
　　Its ancient splendours fling,
And the whole world give back the song
　　Which now the angels sing.

67   *Christina Rossetti*

1 IN the bleak mid-winter
　　Frosty wind made moan:
Earth stood hard as iron,
　　Water like a stone:
Snow had fallen, snow on snow,
　　Snow on snow,
In the bleak mid-winter,
　　Long ago.

2 Our God, heaven cannot hold him
　　Nor earth sustain;
Heaven and earth shall flee away
　　When he comes to reign:
In the bleak mid-winter
　　A stable-place sufficed
The Lord God Almighty,
　　Jesus Christ.

3 Enough for him, whom cherubim
    Worship night and day,
A breastful of milk,
    And a mangerful of hay:
Enough for him, whom angels ⌣
    Fall down before,
The ox and ass and camel
    Which adore.

4 Angels and archangels
    May have gathered there,
Cherubim and seraphim
    Thronged the air—
But only his mother
    In her maiden bliss
Worshipped the Belovèd
    With a kiss.

5 What can I give him,
    Poor as I am?
If I were a shepherd
    I would bring a lamb;
If I were a wise man
    I would do my part;
Yet what I can I give him—
    Give my heart.

68 *St. Germanus. Tr. J. M. Neale*†
μέγα καὶ παράδοξον θαῦμα

mf 1 A GREAT and mighty wonder,
    A full and holy cure!
The Virgin bears the Infant
    With virgin-honour pure:
f   Repeat the hymn again!
    'To God on high be glory,
    And peace on earth to men.'

mf 2 The Word becomes incarnate,
    And yet remains on high;
  And cherubim sing anthems
    To shepherds from the sky:
f   Repeat, etc.

3 While thus they sing your Monarch,
    Those bright angelic bands,
  Rejoice, ye vales and mountains,
    Ye oceans, clap your hands:
f   Repeat, etc.

mf 4 Since all he comes to ransom,
    By all be he adored,
  The infant born in Bethlem,
    The Saviour and the Lord:
f   Repeat, etc.

69   *T. Pestel*

1 BEHOLD, the great Creator makes
    Himself a house of clay,
A robe of virgin flesh he takes
  Which he will wear for ay.

2 Hark, hark! the wise eternal Word
    Like a weak infant cries;
In form of servant is the Lord,
    And God in cradle lies.

3 This wonder struck the world amazed,
    It shook the starry frame;
Squadrons of spirits stood and gazed,
    Then down in troops they came.

4 Glad shepherds ran to view this sight;
    A choir of angels sings,
And eastern sages with delight
    Adore this King of Kings.

5 Join then, all hearts that are not stone,
   And all our voices prove,
     To celebrate this Holy One,
       The God of peace and love.

70
Ben Jonson

1 I SING the birth was born to-night,
   The Author both of life and light:
     The angels so did sound it;
   And like the ravished shepherds said,
   Who saw the light and were afraid,
     Yet searched, and true they found it.

2 The Son of God, the eternal King,
   That did us all salvation bring,
     And freed the world from danger,
   He whom the whole world could not take,
   The Lord which heaven and earth did make,
     Was now laid in a manger.

3 The Father's wisdom willed it so,
   The Son's obedience knew no 'No,'
     Both wills were in one stature;
   And, as that wisdom hath decreed,
   The Word was now made flesh indeed,
     And took on him our nature.

4 What comfort by him do we win,
   Who made himself the price of sin,
     To make us heirs of glory!
   To see this Babe, all innocence,
   A martyr born in our defence—
     Can man forget this story?

71
C. Wesley†

1 TO us a Child of royal birth,
   Heir of the promises, is given;
   The invisible appears on earth,
     The Son of Man, the God of heaven.

2 A Saviour born, in love supreme,
    He comes our fallen souls to raise;
He comes his people to redeem,
    With all the fulness of his grace.

3 The Christ, by raptured seers foretold,
    Filled with the eternal Spirit's power,
Prophet, and Priest, and King behold,
    And Lord of all the worlds adore.

4 The Lord of Hosts, the God most high,
    Who quits his throne on earth to live,
With joy we welcome from the sky,
    With faith into our hearts receive.

NEW YEAR

72   *L. Tuttiett*

mf 1 FATHER, let me dedicate
        All this year to thee,
    In whatever worldly state
        Thou wilt have me be:
    Not from sorrow, pain, or care
        Freedom dare I claim;
    This alone shall be my prayer,
        'Glorify thy name.'

    2 Can a child presume to choose
        Where or how to live?
    Can a Father's love refuse
        All the best to give?
    More thou givest every day
        Than the best can claim,
    Nor withholdest aught that may
        Glorify thy name.

p 3 If thou callest to the cross,
        And its shadow come,
    Turning all my gain to loss,
        Shrouding heart and home;

mf   Let me think how thy dear Son
      To his glory came,
    And in deepest woe pray on,
     'Glorify thy name.'

   4 If in mercy thou wilt spare
      Joys that yet are mine;
    If on life, serene and fair,
     Brighter rays may shine;
f   Let my glad heart, while it sings,
      Thee in all proclaim,
    And, whate'er the future brings,
     Glorify thy name.

73   *H. Downton*†

mf 1 FOR thy mercy and thy grace,
      Faithful through another year,
    Hear our song of thankfulness;
     Jesu, our Redeemer, hear.

   2 In our weakness and distress,
      Rock of strength, be thou our stay;
    In the pathless wilderness
     Be our true and living Way.

p 3 Who of us death's awful road
      In the coming year shall tread,
    With thy rod and staff, O God,
     Comfort thou his dying bed.

mf 4 Keep us faithful, keep us pure,
      Keep us evermore thine own,
    Help, O help us to endure,
     Fit us for thy promised crown.

f 5 So within thy palace gate
      We shall praise on golden strings
    Thee the only potentate,
     Lord of Lords and King of Kings.

EPIPHANY

74   *Sedulius. Tr. Compilers*

Hostis Herodes impie

mf 1 HOW vain the cruel Herod's fear,
   When told that Christ the King is near!
   He takes not earthly realms away,
   Who gives the realms that ne'er decay.

2 The eastern sages saw from far
   And followed on his guiding star;
   By light their way to Light they trod,
   And by their gifts confessed their God.

3 Within the Jordan's sacred flood
   The heavenly Lamb in meekness stood;
   That he who knew no sin that day
   His people's sin might wash away.

4 And O what miracle divine,
   When water reddened into wine!
   He spake the word, and forth it flowed
   In streams that nature ne'er bestowed.

f 5 All glory, Jesu, be to thee
   For this thy glad Epiphany;
   Whom with the Father we adore
   And Holy Ghost for evermore.

75   *Bishop R. Heber*

f 1 BRIGHTEST and best of the sons of the
      morning,
   Dawn on our darkness, and lend us thine aid;
   Star of the east, the horizon adorning,
   Guide where our infant Redeemer is laid.

mf 2 Cold on his cradle the dew-drops are shining;
    Low lies his head with the beasts of the stall;
    Angels adore him in slumber reclining,
        Maker and Monarch and Saviour of all.

3 Say, shall we yield him, in costly devotion,
    Odours of Edom, and offerings divine,
    Gems of the mountain, and pearls of the
        ocean,
    Myrrh from the forest, or gold from the
        mine?

4 Vainly we offer each ample oblation,
    Vainly with gifts would his favour secure:
    Richer by far is the heart's adoration,
    Dearer to God are the prayers of the poor.

The first verse may be repeated at the end.

76   *Prudentius. Tr. E. Caswall and Compilers*
        O sola magnarum urbium

mf 1 EARTH has many a noble city;
    Bethlem, thou dost all excel:
    Out of thee the Lord from heaven
    Came to rule his Israel.

2 Fairer than the sun at morning
    Was the star that told his birth,
    To the world its God announcing
    Seen in fleshly form on earth.

3 Eastern sages at his cradle
    Make oblations rich and rare;
    See them give in deep devotion
    Gold and frankincense and myrrh.

4 Sacred gifts of mystic meaning:
    Incense doth their God disclose,
    Gold the King of Kings proclaimeth,
    Myrrh his sepulchre foreshows.

/ 5 Jesu, whom the Gentiles worshipped
At thy glad Epiphany,
Unto thee with God the Father
And the Spirit glory be.

77 *J. S. B. Monsell*

1 O WORSHIP the Lord in the beauty of holiness!
Bow down before him, his glory proclaim;
With gold of obedience, and incense of lowliness,
Kneel and adore him: the Lord is his name.

2 Low at his feet lay thy burden of carefulness:
High on his heart he will bear it for thee,
Comfort thy sorrows, and answer thy prayerful-
ness,
Guiding thy steps as may best for thee be.

3 Fear not to enter his courts in the slenderness
Of the poor wealth thou wouldst reckon as
thine:
Truth in its beauty, and love in its tenderness,
These are the offerings to lay on his shrine.

4. These, though we bring them in trembling and
fearfulness,
He will accept for the name that is dear;
Mornings of joy give for evenings of tearfulness,
Trust for our trembling and hope for our fear.

The first verse may be repeated at the end.

78 *J. B. de Santeuil*
Tr. J. Chandler and Compilers
Divine crescebas puer

mf 1 THE heavenly Child in stature grows,
And, growing, learns to die;
And still his early training shows⌣
His coming agony.

2　The Son of God his glory hides
　　　To dwell with parents poor;
　And he who made the heavens abides
　　　In dwelling-place obscure.

3　Those mighty hands that rule the sky
　　　No earthly toil refuse;
　The Maker of the stars on high
　　　An humble trade pursues.

4　He whom the choirs of angels praise,
　　　Bearing each dread decree,
　His earthly parents now obeys
　　　In glad humility.

f　5　For this thy lowliness revealed,
　　　Jesu, we thee adore,
　And praise to God the Father yield
　　　And Spirit evermore.

79　　　　　　　　　　*W. Chatterton Dix*

f　1　AS with gladness men of old
　　　Did the guiding star behold,
　As with joy they hailed its light,
　　　Leading onward, beaming bright;
　So, most gracious Lord, may we
　　　Evermore be led to thee.

mf　2　As with joyful steps they sped,
　　　Saviour, to thy lowly bed,
　There to bend the knee before
　　　Thee whom heaven and earth adore;
　So may we with willing feet
　　　Ever seek thy mercy-seat.

3　As they offered gifts most rare
　　　At thy cradle rude and bare,
　So may we with holy joy,
　　　Pure and free from sin's alloy,
　All our costliest treasures bring,
　　　Christ, to thee our heavenly King.

p 4 Holy Jesus, every day
Keep us in the narrow way,

mf And, when earthly things are past,
Bring our ransomed souls at last

f Where they need no star to guide,
Where no clouds thy glory hide.

5 In the heavenly country bright
Need they no created light;
Thou its light, its joy, its crown,
Thou its sun which goes not down;
There for ever may we sing
Alleluias to our King.

80 *J. Morrison and Compilers*

mf 1 THE people that in darkness sat
A glorious light have seen;
The light has shined on them who long
In shades of death have been.

2 To hail thee, Sun of Righteousness,
The gathering nations come;
They joy as when the reapers bear
Their harvest treasures home.

3 For thou their burden dost remove,
And break the tyrant's rod,
As in the day when Midian fell
Before the sword of God.

f 4 For unto us a Child is born,
To us a Son is given,
And on his shoulder ever rests
All power in earth and heaven.

5 His name shall be the Prince of Peace,
The everlasting Lord,
The Wonderful, the Counsellor,
The God by all adored.

6 His righteous government and power‿
   Shall over all extend;
On judgement and on justice based,
   His reign shall have no end.

mf 7 Lord Jesus, reign in us, we pray,
   And make us thine alone,
Who with the Father ever art
   And Holy Spirit One.

81   *Bishop Chr. Wordsworth*

mf 1 SONGS of thankfulness and praise,
Jesu, Lord, to thee we raise,
Manifested by the star
To the sages from afar;
Branch of royal David's stem
In thy birth at Bethlehem:
f   Anthems be to thee addrest,
God in Man made manifest.

mf 2 Manifest at Jordan's stream,
Prophet, Priest, and King supreme;
And at Cana wedding-guest
In thy Godhead manifest;
Manifest in power divine,
Changing water into wine:
f   Anthems be to thee addrest,
God in Man made manifest.

mf 3 Manifest in making whole
Palsied limbs and fainting soul;
Manifest in valiant fight,
Quelling all the devil's might;
Manifest in gracious will,
Ever bringing good from ill:
f   Anthems be to thee addrest,
God in Man made manifest.

mf 4*Sun and moon shall darkened be,
Stars shall fall, the heavens shall flee;
f Christ will then like lightning shine,
All will see his glorious sign;
All will then the trumpet hear,
All will see the Judge appear:
Thou by all wilt be confest,
God in Man made manifest.

mf 5 Grant us grace to see thee, Lord,
Mirrored in thy holy word;
May we imitate thee now,
And be pure, as pure art thou;
That we like to thee may be
At thy great Epiphany;
f And may praise thee, ever blest,
God in Man made manifest.

The following hymns are suitable for this season:

82 *For the week before Septuagesima*

Tr. J. M. Neale and Compiler

Alleluia, dulce carmen

f 1 ALLELUIA, song of sweetness,
  Voice of joy that cannot die;
 Alleluia is the anthem
  Ever dear to choirs on high:
 In the house of God abiding
  Thus they sing eternally.

2 Alleluia thou resoundest,
  True Jerusalem and free;
 Alleluia, joyful mother,
  All thy children sing with thee;
p But by Babylon's sad waters
  Mourning exiles now are we.

3 Alleluia cannot always͜
  Be our song while here below;
 Alleluia our transgressions͜
  Make us for awhile forgo;
 For the solemn time is coming
  When our tears for sin must flow.

mf 4 Therefore in our hymns we pray thee,
  Grant us, blessèd Trinity,
 At the last to keep thine Easter
  In our home beyond the sky,
f There to thee for ever singing
  Alleluia joyfully.

SEPTUAGESIMA

83 *C. Coffin. Tr. Compiler.*

Te laeta, mundi Conditor

mf 1 CREATOR of the world, to thee͜
  An endless rest of joy belongs;
 And heavenly choirs are ever free
  To sing on high their festal songs.

p 2 But we are fallen creatures here,
     Where pain and sorrow daily come;
     And how can we in exile drear
     Sing out, as they, sweet songs of home?

mf 3 O Father, who dost promise still
     That they who mourn shall blessèd be,
p   Help us to grieve for deeds of ill
     That banish us so long from thee:

     4 And, while we grieve, give faith to rest⏝
     In hope upon thy loving care;
mf Till thou restore us, with the blest,
     Their songs of praise in heaven to share.

*From Septuagesima Sunday to Lent the following
hymns are suitable:*

For Septuagesima:

LENT

84   *Tr. Compilers*

Audi, benigne Conditor

 1 O MAKER of the world, give ear;
   In pitying love vouchsafe to hear
   The prayers our contrite spirits raise
   In this our fast of forty days.

2 All hearts are open unto thee;
Thou knowest each infirmity;
Now, as we turn to seek thy face,
Pour down on us thy pardoning grace.

3 Help us to grow in self-control,
To make the body serve the soul:
So may thy loving-kindness bless
Our fast with fruits of holiness.

85

Tr. Bishop W. H. Frere

Jesu quadragenariae

1 JESU, who this our Lenten-tide
Of abstinence hast sanctified,
Be with thy Church in saving power
In this her penitential hour.

2 And, as thou dost forgive the past,
Thy sheltering arms around us cast,
That we may in thy grace remain
And fall not back to sins again.

3 Make, Lord, this Lenten discipline
An expiation for our sin;
And through these days ourselves prepare
The joys of Eastertide to share.

86

Sir R. Grant†

p 1 SAVIOUR, when in dust to thee
Low we bow the adoring knee;
When, repentant, to the skies
Scarce we lift our weeping eyes;
O by all thy pains and woe
Suffered once for man below,
Bending from thy throne on high,
Hear our solemn litany.

mf 2 By thy helpless infant years,
   By thy life of want and tears,
   By thy days of sore distress
   In the savage wilderness;
   By the dread mysterious hour
   Of the insulting tempter's power:
   Turn, O turn a favouring eye,
p   Hear our solemn litany.

mf 3*By the sacred griefs that wept
   O'er the grave where Lazarus slept;
   By the boding tears that flowed
   Over Salem's loved abode;
   By the mournful word that told
   Treachery lurked within thy fold:
   From thy seat above the sky
p   Hear our solemn litany.

   4 By thine hour of dire despair;
   By thine agony of prayer;
   By the Cross, the nail, the thorn,
   Piercing spear, and torturing scorn;
   By the gloom that veiled the skies
   O'er the dreadful Sacrifice:
   Listen to our humble cry,
   Hear our solemn litany.

   5 By thy deep expiring groan;
   By the sad sepulchral stone;
   By the vault whose dark abode
   Held in vain the rising God:
f   O, from earth to heaven restored,
   Mighty, re-ascended Lord,
mf   Listen, listen to the cry
p   Of our solemn litany.

87　　　　　　　　　　　　　　*J. S. B. Monsell*

p　1 SINFUL, sighing to be blest;
　　　　Bound, and longing to be free;
　　　Weary, waiting for my rest:
　　　　God, be merciful to me.

　　2 Goodness I have none to plead,
　　　　Sinfulness in all I see,
　　　I can only bring my need:
　　　　God, be merciful to me.

　　3*Broken heart and downcast eyes
　　　　Dare not lift themselves to thee;
　　　Yet thou canst interpret sighs:
　　　　God, be merciful to me.

　　4 From this sinful heart of mine
　　　　To thy bosom I would flee;
　　　I am not my own, but thine:
　　　　God, be merciful to me.

f　5 There is One beside the throne,
　　　　And my only hope and plea
　　　Are in him, and him alone:
mf　　　God, be merciful to me.

　　6 He my cause will undertake,
　　　　My interpreter will be;
　　　He's my all; and for his sake,
　　　　God, be merciful to me.

88　　　　　　　　　　　*Mrs. C. F. Alexander*

p　1 WHEN wounded sore the stricken heart
　　　　Lies bleeding and unbound,
　　　One only hand, a piercèd hand,
　　　　Can salve the sinner's wound.

2 When sorrow swells the laden breast,
   And tears of anguish flow,
One only heart, a broken heart,
   Can feel the sinner's woe.

3 When penitential grief has wept
   Over some foul dark spot,
One only stream, a stream of Blood,
   Can wash away the blot.

mf 4 'Tis Jesus' Blood that washes white,
   His hand that brings relief;
His heart is touched with all our joys,
   And feels for all our grief.

5 Lift up thy bleeding hand, O Lord,
   Unseal that cleansing tide:
We have no shelter from our sin
   But in thy wounded side.

89 *J. Byrom*

1 MY spirit longs for thee
   Within my troubled breast,
Though I unworthy be
   Of so divine a guest.

2 Of so divine a guest
   Unworthy though I be,
Yet has my heart no rest
   Unless it come from thee.

3 Unless it come from thee,
   In vain I look around;
In all that I can see
   No rest is to be found.

4 No rest is to be found
   But in thy blessèd love:
O let my wish be crowned,
   And send it from above!

90

C. Wesley†

1 STILL nigh me, O my Saviour, stand,
  And guard in fierce temptation's hour;
Hide in the hollow of thy hand,
  Show forth in me thy saving power;
Still be thine arm my sure defence:
Nor earth nor hell shall pluck me thence.

2 Still let thy love point out my way:
  How wondrous things thy love hath
Still lead me, lest I go astray;   [wrought!
  Direct my work, inspire my thought;
And, if I fall, soon may I hear
Thy voice, and know that Love is near.

3 In suffering be thy love my peace,
  In weakness be thy love my power;
And when the storms of life shall cease,
  Jesus, in that tremendous hour,
In death as life be thou my guide,
And save me, who for me hast died.

91

J. M. Neale†

p   1 CHRISTIAN, dost thou see them
       On the holy ground,
     How the troops of Midian
       Prowl and prowl around?
f   Christian, up and smite them,
       Counting gain but loss;
     Smite them by the merit
       Of the holy Cross.

p   2 Christian, dost thou feel them,
       How they work within,
     Striving, tempting, luring,
       Goading into sin?
f   Christian, never tremble;
       Never be down-cast;
     Smite them by the virtue
       Of the Lenten fast.

p 3 Christian, dost thou hear them,
  How they speak thee fair?
 'Always fast and vigil?
  Always watch and prayer?'
f Christian, answer boldly,
  'While I breathe I pray:'
 Peace shall follow battle,
  Night shall end in day.

mf 4 'Well I know thy trouble,
  O my servant true;
 Thou art very weary,
  I was weary too;
f But that toil shall make thee⌣
  Some day all mine own,
 And the end of sorrow⌣
  Shall be near my throne.'

92   *G. H. Smyttan and F. Pott*

mf 1 FORTY days and forty nights
  Thou wast fasting in the wild;
 Forty days and forty nights
  Tempted, and yet undefiled:

2 Sunbeams scorching all the day;
  Chilly dew-drops nightly shed;
 Prowling beasts about thy way;
  Stones thy pillow, earth thy bed.

3 Shall not we thy sorrows share,
  And from earthly joys abstain,
 Fasting with unceasing prayer,
  Glad with thee to suffer pain?

4 And if Satan, vexing sore,
  Flesh or spirit should assail,
 Thou, his vanquisher before,
  Grant we may not faint nor fail.

p 5 So shall we have peace divine;
  Holier gladness ours shall be;
 Round us too shall angels shine,
  Such as ministered to thee.

mf 6 Keep, O keep us, Saviour dear,
  Ever constant by thy side;
f   That with thee we may appear
  At the eternal Eastertide.

93   *J. Marckant ‡ (form in Supplement to*
            New Version, 1708)

1 O LORD, turn not thy face from me,
  Who lie in woeful state,
 Lamenting all my sinful life
  Before thy mercy-gate:

2 A gate which opens wide to those
  That do lament their sin;
 Shut not that gate against me, Lord,
  But let me enter in.

3 And call me not to strict account
  How I have sojourned here;
 For then my guilty conscience knows
  How vile I shall appear.

4 Mercy, good Lord, mercy I ask:
  This is my humble prayer;
 For mercy, Lord, is all my suit:
  O let thy mercy spare.

94   *I. Williams*

1 LORD, in this thy mercy's day,
  Ere it pass for ay away,
  On our knees we fall and pray.

2 Holy Jesu, grant us tears,
  Fill us with heart-searching fears,
  Ere that awful doom appears.

3 Lord, on us thy Spirit pour
  Kneeling lowly at the door,
  Ere it close for evermore.

4 By thy night of agony,
  By thy supplicating cry,
  By thy willingness to die;

5 By thy tears of bitter woe
  For Jerusalem below,
  Let us not thy love forgo.

6 Grant us 'neath thy wings a place,
  Lest we lose this day of grace
  Ere we shall behold thy face.

95 *Evening*   *Tr. Compilers* (1904)
                Christe, qui lux es et dies

mf 1 O CHRIST, who art the Light and Day,
  Thou drivest night and gloom away;
  O Light of Light, whose word doth show
  The light of heaven to us below.

2 All-holy Lord, in humble prayer
  We ask to-night thy watchful care;
  O grant us calm repose in thee,
  A quiet night from perils free.

3 Asleep though wearied eyes may be,
  Still keep the heart awake to thee;
  Let thy right hand outstretched above
  Guard those who serve the Lord they love.

4*Behold, O God our Shield, and quell⏜
   The crafts and subtleties of hell;
   Direct thy servants in all good,
   Whom thou hast purchased with thy Blood.

f   5 All praise to God the Father be,
   All praise, eternal Son, to thee,
   Whom with the Spirit we adore,
   For ever and for evermore.

The following hymns, and some of the hymns for Passiontide, are suitable for this season:

182	Father, hear the prayer we offer.
200	Lord Jesus, think on me.
210	Rock of ages, cleft for me.
211	Jesu, grant me this, I pray.
291	Oft in danger, oft in woe.
300	Be thou my guardian and my guide.
308	Christian, seek not yet repose.
320	O help us, Lord! each hour of need.
322	Out of the deep I call.
323	Forsaken once and thrice denied.
333	Take up thy cross, the Saviour said.
334	Lord, as to thy dear Cross we flee.
345	Approach, my soul, the mercy-seat.
348	Art thou weary, art thou languid.
349	Just as I am, without one plea.
586	Litany for Lent.

PASSIONTIDE

96 *Passion Sunday to Wednesday before Easter*
Bishop Venantius Fortunatus
Tr. J. M. Neale and Compilers

Vexilla Regis prodeunt

f　1　THE royal banners forward go,
　　　The Cross shines forth in mystic glow;
　　　Where he in flesh, our flesh who made,
　　　Our sentence bore, our ransom paid.

mf　2　There whilst he hung, his sacred side
　　　By soldier's spear was opened wide,
　　　To cleanse us in the precious flood
　　　Of water mingled with his blood.

f　3　Fulfilled is now what David told
　　　In true prophetic song of old,
　　　How God the heathen's King should be;
　　　For God is reigning from the Tree.

mf　4　O Tree of glory, Tree most fair,
　　　Ordained those holy limbs to bear,
　　　How bright in purple robe it stood,
　　　The purple of a Saviour's blood!

　　　5　Upon its arms, like balance true,
　　　He weighed the price for sinners due,
　　　The price which none but he could pay,
f　　And spoiled the spoiler of his prey.

　　　6　To thee, eternal Three in One,
　　　Let homage meet by all be done:
　　　As by the Cross thou dost restore,
　　　So rule and guide us evermore.

97 *Passion Sunday to Wednesday before Easter*
Bishop Venantius Fortunatus
Tr. J. M. Neale and Compilers

Pange lingua gloriosi praelium certaminis

1 SING, my tongue, the glorious battle,
　　Sing the last, the dread affray ;
O'er the Cross, the Victor's trophy,
　　Sound the high triumphal lay,
How, the pains of death enduring,
　　Earth's Redeemer won the day.

2 When at length the appointed fulness
　　Of the sacred time was come,
He was sent, the world's Creator,
　　From the Father's heavenly home,
And was found in human fashion,
　　Offspring of the Virgin's womb.

3 Now the thirty years are ended
　　Which on earth he willed to see,
Willingly he meets his Passion,
　　Born to set his people free ;
On the Cross the Lamb is lifted,
　　There the Sacrifice to be.

4 There the nails and spear he suffers,
　　Vinegar and gall and reed ;
From his sacred body piercèd
　　Blood and water both proceed :
Precious flood, which all creation
　　From the stain of sin hath freed.

PART 2

5 Faithful Cross, above all other,
　　One and only noble Tree,
None in foliage, none in blossom,
　　None in fruit thy peer may be ;
Sweet the wood, and sweet the iron,
　　And thy load, most sweet is he.

6 Bend, O lofty Tree, thy branches,
    Thy too rigid sinews bend;
And awhile the stubborn hardness,
    Which thy birth bestowed, suspend;
And the limbs of heaven's high Monarch
    Gently on thine arms extend.

7 Thou alone wast counted worthy
    This world's Ransom to sustain,
That a shipwrecked race for ever
    Might a port of refuge gain,
With the sacred Blood anointed
    Of the Lamb for sinners slain.

*The following Doxology may be sung at
the end of either Part:*

8 Praise and honour to the Father,
    Praise and honour to the Son,
Praise and honour to the Spirit,
    Ever Three and ever One:
One in might, and One in glory,
    While eternal ages run.

98   *Palm Sunday.*   *St. Theodulph of Orleans*
                               Tr. J. M. Neale ‡
            Gloria, laus et honor

f   1 ALL glory, laud, and honour
      To thee, Redeemer, King,
    To whom the lips of children
      Made sweet Hosannas ring.

mf   2 Thou art the King of Israel,
      Thou David's royal Son,
    Who in the Lord's name comest,
      The King and blessèd one.
    f   All glory, etc.

mf 3 The company of angels
  Are praising thee on high,
And mortal men and all things⌣
  Created make reply.
  f All glory, etc.

mf 4 The people of the Hebrews
  With palms before thee went:
Our praise and prayer and anthems
  Before thee we present.
  f All glory, etc.

mf 5 To thee before thy Passion
  They sang their hymns of praise:
To thee now high exalted
  Our melody we raise.
  f All glory, etc.

mf 6 Thou didst accept their praises:
  Accept the prayers we bring,
Who in all good delightest,
  Thou good and gracious King.
  f All glory, etc.

Note.—A longer version of this hymn will be found in the 'Processional' section (597).

99 *Palm Sunday*   *H. H. Milman* ‡

 1 RIDE on! ride on in majesty!
  Hark! all the tribes Hosanna cry!
  O Saviour meek, pursue thy road
  With palms and scattered garments strowed.

 2 Ride on! ride on in majesty!
  In lowly pomp ride on to die:
  O Christ, thy triumphs now begin
  O'er captive death and conquered sin.

3 Ride on! ride on in majesty!
  The wingèd squadrons of the sky
  Look down with sad and wondering eyes
  To see the approaching Sacrifice.

4 Ride on! ride on in majesty!
  The last and fiercest strife is nigh:
  The Father on his sapphire throne
  Awaits his own anointed Son.

5 Ride on! ride on in majesty!
  In lowly pomp ride on to die;
  Bow thy meek head to mortal pain,
  Then take, O God, thy power, and reign.

100   *Holy Week*   *W. H. Draper*

mf 1 LORD, through this Holy Week of our sal-
  vation
  Which thou hast won for us who went
  astray,
  In all the conflict of thy sore temptation
  We would continue with thee day by day.

2 We would not leave thee, though our weak
  endurance
  Make us unworthy here to take our part;
  Yet give us strength to trust the sweet assurance
  That thou, O Lord, art greater than our
  heart.

3 Thou didst forgive thine own who slept for
  sorrow,
  Thou didst have pity: O have pity now,
  And let us watch through each sad eve and
  morrow
  With thee, in holy prayer and solemn vow.

p   4 Along that sacred way where thou art lead-
ing,
  Which thou didst take to save our souls
  from loss,
  Let us go also, till we see thee pleading
  In all-prevailing prayer upon thy Cross;

mf   5 Until thou see thy bitter travail's ending,
  The world redeemed, the will of God
  complete,
  And, to thy Father's hands thy soul com-
  mending,
  Thou lay the work he gave thee at his feet.

101

Bishop R. Mant

1 SEE the destined day arise!
  See, a willing sacrifice,
  Jesus, to redeem our loss,
  Hangs upon the shameful Cross!

2 Jesu, who but thou had borne,
  Lifted on that Tree of scorn,
  Every pang and bitter throe,
  Finishing thy life of woe?

3 Who but thou had dared to drain,
  Steeped in gall, that cup of pain,
  And with tender body bear
  Thorns and nails and piercing spear?

4 Thence the cleansing water flowed,
  Mingled from thy side with blood:
  Sign to all attesting eyes
  Of the finished Sacrifice.

5 Holy Jesu, grant us grace
  In that Sacrifice to place
  All our trust for life renewed,
  Pardoned sin, and promised good.

102   *S. Crossman*

1 MY song is love unknown,
      My Saviour's love to me,
Love to the loveless shown,
      That they might lovely be.
            O who am I,
                  That for my sake
                  My Lord should take
            Frail flesh, and die?

2 He came from his blest throne,
      Salvation to bestow;
But men made strange, and none
      The longed-for Christ would know.
            But O, my Friend,
                  My Friend indeed,
                  Who at my need
            His life did spend!

3 Sometimes they strew his way,
      And his sweet praises sing;
Resounding all the day
      Hosannas to their King.
            Then 'Crucify!'
                  Is all their breath,
                  And for his death
            They thirst and cry.

4*Why, what hath my Lord done?
      What makes this rage and spite?
He made the lame to run,
      He gave the blind their sight.
            Sweet injuries!
                  Yet they at these
                  Themselves displease,
            And 'gainst him rise.

5 They rise, and needs will have
　　My dear Lord made away;
A murderer they save,
　　The Prince of Life they slay
　　　Yet cheerful he
　　　　To suffering goes,
　　　　That he his foes
　From thence might free.

6*In life, no house, no home
　　My Lord on earth might have;
In death, no friendly tomb
　　But what a stranger gave.
　　　What may I say?
　　　　Heaven was his home;
　　　　But mine the tomb
　Wherein he lay.

7 Here might I stay and sing.
　　No story so divine;
Never was love, dear King,
　　Never was grief like thine!
　　　This is my Friend,
　　　　In whose sweet praise
　　　　I all my days
　Could gladly spend.

103　　　　　　　　*J. Bridaine. Tr. T. B. Pollock.*
　　　　　Est-ce vous que je vois?

mf 1 MY Lord, my Master, at thy feet adoring,
　　　I see thee bowed beneath thy load of
　　　　woe;
　For me, a sinner, is thy life-blood pouring:
　　　For thee, my Saviour, scarce my tears will
　　　　flow.

2 Thine own disciple to the Jews has sold thee,
　　　With friendship's kiss and loyal word he
　　　　came;
　　How oft of faithful love my lips have told
　　　　thee,
　　　While thou hast seen my falsehood and my
　　　　shame!

3 With taunts and scoffs they mock what seems
　　　thy weakness,
　　　With blows and outrage adding pain to
　　　　pain;
　　Thou art unmoved and steadfast in thy
　　　　meekness:
　　　When I am wronged how quickly I com-
　　　　plain!

p 4 My Lord, my Saviour, when I see thee wear-
　　　　ing
　　　Upon thy bleeding brow the crown of
　　　　thorn,
　　Shall I for pleasure live, or shrink from bear-
　　　　ing
　　　Whate'er my lot may be of pain or scorn?

mf 5 O Victim of thy love! O pangs most healing!
　　　O saving Death! O wounds that I adore!
　　O shame most glorious! Christ, before thee
　　　　kneeling,
　　　I pray thee keep me thine for evermore.

104   18th cent. Tr. E. Caswall ‡
　　　　　Quicumque certum quaeritis

1 ALL ye who seek for sure relief
　　　In trouble and distress,
　　Whatever sorrow vex the mind,
　　　Or guilt the soul oppress,

2 Jesus, who gave himself for you
　　Upon the Cross to die,
Opens to you his sacred heart:
　　O to that heart draw nigh.

3 Ye hear how kindly he invites;
　　Ye hear his words so blest:
'All ye that labour come to me,
　　And I will give you rest.'

4 O Jesus, joy of saints on high,
　　Thou hope of sinners here,
Attracted by those loving words
　　To thee we lift our prayer.

5 Wash thou our wounds in that dear Blood
　　Which from thy heart doth flow;
A new and contrite heart on all⁀
　　Who cry to thee bestow.

105　　　　*St. Bonaventura. Tr. F. Oakeley* ‡
　　　　　　　In passione Domini

p　1 IN the Lord's atoning grief
　　Be our rest and sweet relief;
Store we deep in heart's recess
All the shame and bitterness:

　2 Thorns and cross and nails and lance,
Wounds, our rich inheritance,
Vinegar and gall and reed,
And the cry his soul that freed.

mf　3 May these all our spirits fill,
And with love's devotion thrill;
In our souls plant virtue's root,
And mature its glorious fruit.

4 Crucified, we thee adore;
   Thee with all our hearts implore,
Us with all thy saints unite
   In the realms of heavenly light.

5 Christ, by coward hands betrayed,
   Christ, for us a captive made,
Christ, upon the bitter Tree
   Slain for man, be praise to thee.

106   17th cent. Tr. E. Caswall†

O Deus, ego amo te

mf 1 MY God, I love thee, not because
   I hope for heaven thereby,
Nor yet because who love thee not
   Are lost eternally.

2 Thou, O my Jesus, thou didst me
   Upon the Cross embrace;
For me didst bear the nails and spear,
   And manifold disgrace,

p 3 And griefs and torments numberless,
   And sweat of agony;
Yea, death itself—and all for me
   Who was thine enemy.

mf 4 Then why, O blessèd Jesu Christ,
   Should I not love thee well?
Not for the sake of winning heaven,
   Nor of escaping hell;

5 Not from the hope of gaining aught,
   Not seeking a reward;
But as thyself hast lovèd me,
   O ever-loving Lord.

f 6 So would I love thee, dearest Lord,
     And in thy praise will sing;
     Solely because thou art my God,
     And my most loving King.

107   *18th cent. Tr. E. Caswall†*

Viva! Viva! Gesù

f 1 GLORY be to Jesus,
     Who, in bitter pains,
     Poured for me the life-blood
     From his sacred veins.

mf 2 Grace and life eternal
     In that Blood I find;
     Blest be his compassion
     Infinitely kind.

    3 Blest through endless ages
     Be the precious stream,
     Which from endless torments
     Did the world redeem.

    4 Abel's blood for vengeance
     Pleaded to the skies;
     But the Blood of Jesus
     For our pardon cries.

    5 Oft as it is sprinkled
     On our guilty hearts,
     Satan in confusion
     Terror-struck departs;

f 6 Oft as earth exulting
     Wafts its praise on high,
     Angel-hosts rejoicing
     Make their glad reply.

    7 Lift ye then your voices;
     Swell the mighty flood;
     Louder still and louder
     Praise the precious Blood.

108

I. Watts ‡

mf 1 WHEN I survey the wondrous Cross
        On which the Prince of Glory died,
    My richest gain I count but loss,
        And pour contempt on all my pride.

    2 Forbid it, Lord, that I should boast
        Save in the Cross of Christ my God;
    All the vain things that charm me most,
        I sacrifice them to his Blood.

p   3 See from his head, his hands, his feet,
        Sorrow and love flow mingling down;
    Did e'er such love and sorrow meet,
        Or thorns compose so rich a crown?

f   4 Were the whole realm of nature mine,
        That were an offering far too small;
    Love so amazing, so divine,
        Demands my soul, my life, my all.

109

Bishop W. Walsham How

    1 LORD Jesu, when we stand afar,
        And gaze upon thy holy Cross,
    In love of thee and scorn of self,
        O may we count the world as loss!

    2 When we behold thy bleeding wounds,
        And the rough way that thou hast trod,
    Make us to hate the load of sin
        That lay so heavy on our God.

    3 O holy Lord, uplifted high,
        With outstretched arms, in mortal woe,
    Embracing in thy wondrous love
        The sinful world that lies below,

4 Give us an ever-living faith,
　　To gaze beyond the things we see;
And in the mystery of thy Death
　　Draw us and all men unto thee.

110 *J. Montgomery*

1 GO to dark Gethsemane,
　　Ye that feel the tempter's power,
Your Redeemer's conflict see,
　　Watch with him one bitter hour;
Turn not from his griefs away:
Learn of Jesus Christ to pray.

2 Follow to the judgement-hall,
　　View the Lord of Life arraigned;
O the wormwood and the gall!
　　O the pangs his soul sustained!
Shun not suffering, shame, or loss:
Learn of him to bear the cross.

3 Calvary's mournful mountain climb;
　　There, adoring at his feet,
Mark that miracle of time,
　　God's own Sacrifice complete;
'It is finished!' hear him cry:
Learn of Jesus Christ to die.

111 *P. Gerhardt. Based on* Salve caput
　　cruentatum. *Tr. Sir H. W. Baker* ‡
　　O Haupt voll Blut und Wunden

mf 1 O SACRED head, surrounded
　　By crown of piercing thorn!
O bleeding head, so wounded,
　　So shamed and put to scorn!
Death's pallid hue comes o'er thee,
　　The glow of life decays;
Yet angel-hosts adore thee,
　　And tremble as they gaze.

p 2 Thy comeliness and vigour
    Is withered up and gone,
And in thy wasted figure
    I see death drawing on.
O agony and dying!
    O love to sinners free!
Jesu, all grace supplying,
    Turn thou thy face on me.

mf 3 In this thy bitter Passion,
    Good Shepherd, think of me
With thy most sweet compassion,
    Unworthy though I be:
Beneath thy Cross abiding
    For ever would I rest,
In thy dear love confiding,
    And with thy presence blest.

112 *Evening   Prudentius. Tr. Compilers* (1889)
        Ades Pater supreme

mf 1 FATHER most high, be with us,
    Unseen, thy goodness showing,
And Christ the Word incarnate,
    And Spirit grace bestowing.

f 2 O Trinity, O Oneness
    Of light and power exceeding;
O God of God eternal,
    O God, from Both proceeding!

mf 3 While daylight hours are passing
    We live and work before thee;
Now, ere we rest in slumber,
    We gather to adore thee.

    4 Our Christian name and calling
    Of our new birth remind us;
The Spirit's gifts and sealing
    To firm obedience bind us.

f 5 Begone, ye powers of evil
          With snares and wiles unholy!
        Disturb not with your temptings
          The spirits of the lowly.

6 Depart! for Christ is present,
          Beside us, yea, within us;
        Away! his sign (ye know it)
          The victory shall win us.

p 7 Awhile the body resteth;
          The spirit, wakeful ever,
        Abideth in communion‿
          With Christ, who sleepeth never.

f 8 To God, the eternal Father,
          To Christ our sure salvation,
        To God, the Holy Spirit,
          Be endless adoration.

The following hymns are suitable:

212 Behold the Lamb of God.
213 Jesu, meek and lowly.
214 There is a green hill far away.
215 We sing the praise of him who died.

MAUNDY THURSDAY

The following hymns are suitable:

110 Go to dark Gethsemane.
383 Now, my tongue, the mystery telling.
384 The heavenly Word, proceeding forth.
402 O thou, who at thy Eucharist didst pray.

GOOD FRIDAY

113   *F. W. Faber* ‡

p   1 O COME and mourn with me awhile;
  O come ye to the Saviour's side;
  O come, together let us mourn:
  Jesus, our Lord, is crucified.

 2 Have we no tears to shed for him,
  While soldiers scoff and Jews deride?
  Ah, look how patiently he hangs:
  Jesus, our Lord, is crucified.

 3 How fast his hands and feet are nailed;
  His throat with parching thirst is dried;
  His failing eyes are dimmed with blood:
  Jesus, our Lord, is crucified.

 4 Seven times he spake, seven words of love;
  And all three hours his silence cried
  For mercy on the souls of men:
  Jesus, our Lord, is crucified.

mf 5 O love of God! O sin of man!
  In this dread act your strength is tried;
  And victory remains with love:
  Jesus, our Lord, is crucified.

HYMNS ON THE SEVEN WORDS FROM THE CROSS
**'Father, forgive them, for they know not
what they do.'**

114   *Mrs. C. F. Alexander* †

 1 'FORGIVE them, O my Father,
  They know not what they do:'
  The Saviour spake in anguish,
  As the sharp nails went through.

2 No word of anger spake he
    To them that shed his blood,
But prayer and tenderest pity
    Large as the love of God.

3 For me was that compassion,
    For me that tender care;
I need his wide forgiveness
    As much as any there.

4 It was my pride and hardness
    That hung him on the Tree;
Those cruel nails, O Saviour,
    Were driven in by me.

5 And often I have slighted
    Thy gentle voice that chid:
Forgive me too, Lord Jesus;
    I knew not what I did.

6 O depth of sweet compassion!
    O love divine and true!
Save thou the souls that slight thee,
    And know not what they do.

Or

115   *Ada R. Greenaway*

p 1 O WORD of pity, for our pardon pleading,
    Breathed in the hour of loneliness and pain;
mf   O voice, which through the ages interceding
    Calls us to fellowship with God again!

p 2 O word of comfort, through the silence steal-
      ing,
    As the dread act of sacrifice began;
  O infinite compassion, still revealing
    The infinite forgiveness won for man!

mf 3 O word of hope to raise us nearer heaven,
    When courage fails us and when faith is
      dim!
    The souls for whom Christ prays to Christ
      are given,
      To find their pardon and their joy in him.

4 O Intercessor, who art ever living
    To plead for dying souls that they may live,
    Teach us to know our sin which needs for-
      giving,
      Teach us to know the love which can for-
      give.

**'Verily I say unto thee, To-day shalt thou be
with me in Paradise.'**

116
Archbishop W. D. Maclagan

1 'LORD, when thy Kingdom comes, remember
      me!'
    Thus spake the dying lips to dying ears:
    O faith, which in that darkest hour could see
      The promised glory of the far-off years!

2 No kingly sign declares that glory now,
    No ray of hope lights up that awful hour;
    A thorny crown surrounds the bleeding brow,
      The hands are stretched in weakness, not in
      power.

3 Hark! through the gloom the dying Saviour saith,
    'Thou too shalt rest in Paradise to-day:'
    O words of love to answer words of faith!
    O words of hope for those who live to pray!

4 Lord, when with dying lips my prayer is said,
    Grant that in faith thy Kingdom I may see;
    And, thinking on thy Cross and bleeding head,
      May breathe my parting words, 'Remember
      me.'

5*Remember me, but not my shame or sin:
    Thy cleansing Blood hath washed them all
        away;
Thy precious Death for me did pardon win;
    Thy Blood redeemed me in that awful day.

6 Remember me; and, ere I pass away,
    Speak thou the assuring word that sets us
        free,
And make thy promise to my heart, 'To-day⌣
    Thou too shalt rest in Paradise with me.'

Or

117   *T. Haweis* ‡

mf 1 O THOU, from whom all goodness flows,
      I lift my heart to thee;
    In all my sorrows, conflicts, woes,
p   Good Lord, remember me.

mf 2 When on my aching burdened heart
      My sins lie heavily,
    Thy pardon grant, thy peace impart:
p   Good Lord, remember me.

mf 3 When trials sore obstruct my way,
      And ills I cannot flee,
    Then let my strength be as my day:
p   Good Lord, remember me.

mf 4 If worn with pain, disease, and grief,
      This feeble spirit be,
    Grant patience, rest, and kind relief:
p   Good Lord, remember me.

mf 5 And O, when in the hour of death
      I bow to thy decree,
    Jesu, receive my parting breath:
p   Good Lord, remember me.

'Woman, behold thy son . . . Behold thy mother.'

118   *Ascribed to Jacopone da Todi*
                    Tr. E. Caswall and Compilers

Stabat Mater dolorosa

mf 1 AT the Cross her station keeping
          Stood the mournful Mother weeping,
              Where he hung, the dying Lord;
          For her soul, of joy bereavèd,
          Bowed with anguish, deeply grievèd,
              Felt the sharp and piercing sword.

p   2 O how sad and sore distressèd
          Now was she, that Mother blessèd
              Of the Sole-begotten One!
          Deep the woe of her affliction,
          When she saw the Crucifixion
              Of her ever-glorious Son.

mf 3 Who, on Christ's dear Mother gazing
          Pierced by anguish so amazing,
              Born of woman, would not weep?
          Who, on Christ's dear Mother thinking
          Such a cup of sorrow drinking,
              Would not share her sorrows deep?

p   4 For his people's sins chastisèd,
          She beheld her Son despisèd,   [twined;
              Scourged, and crowned with thorns en-
          Saw him then from judgement taken,
          And in death by all forsaken,
              Till his spirit he resigned.

mf 5 O good Jesu, let me borrow
          Something of thy Mother's sorrow,
              Fount of love, Redeemer kind,
          That my heart fresh ardour gaining,
          And a purer love attaining,
              May with thee acceptance find.

'My God, my God, why hast thou forsaken me?'

119   *J. Ellerton*

1 THRONED upon the awful Tree,
   King of grief, I watch with thee;
   Darkness veils thine anguished face,
   None its lines of woe can trace,
   None can tell what pangs unknown
   Hold thee silent and alone:

2 Silent through those three dread hours,
   Wrestling with the evil powers,
   Left alone with human sin,
   Gloom around thee and within,
   Till the appointed time is nigh,
   Till the Lamb of God may die.

3 Hark that cry that peals aloud
   Upward through the whelming cloud!
   Thou, the Father's only Son,
   Thou, his own Anointed One,
   Thou dost ask him (can it be?)
   'Why hast thou forsaken me?'

4 Lord, should fear and anguish roll
   Darkly o'er my sinful soul,
   Thou, who once wast thus bereft
   That thine own might ne'er be left,
   Teach me by that bitter cry
   In the gloom to know thee nigh.

'I thirst.'

120   *Mrs. C. F. Alexander*

1 HIS are the thousand sparkling rills
   That from a thousand fountains burst,
   And fill with music all the hills;
       And yet he saith, 'I thirst.'

2 All fiery pangs on battle-fields,
  On fever beds where sick men toss,
Are in that human cry he yields
    To anguish on the Cross.

3 But more than pains that racked him then
  Was the deep longing thirst divine
That thirsted for the souls of men:
    Dear Lord! and one was mine.

4 O Love most patient, give me grace;
  Make all my soul athirst for thee:
That parched dry lip, that fading face,
    That thirst, were all for me.

Or

121
               Ada R. Greenaway

mf 1   O PERFECT God, thy love
    As perfect Man did share
Here upon earth each form of ill
    Thy fellow-men must bear.

2   Now from the Tree of scorn
    We hear thy voice again;
Thou who didst take our mortal flesh
    Hast felt our mortal pain.

p 3   Thy body suffers thirst,
    Parched are thy lips and dry:
How poor the offering man can bring
    Thy thirst to satisfy!

mf 4   O Saviour, by thy thirst
    Borne on the Cross of shame,
Grant us in all our sufferings here
    To glorify thy name;

5   That through each pain and grief
    Our souls may onward move
To gain more likeness to thy life,
    More knowledge of thy love.

'It is finished.'

122   *Sir H. W. Baker*

1   O PERFECT life of love!
      All, all is finished now;
  All that he left his throne above
    To do for us below.

2   No work is left undone
      Of all the Father willed;
  His toil, his sorrows, one by one,
    The scripture have fulfilled.

3   No pain that we can share
      But he has felt its smart;
  All forms of human grief and care
    Have pierced that tender heart.

4   And on his thorn-crowned head,
      And on his sinless soul,
  Our sins in all their guilt were laid,
    That he might make us whole.

5   In perfect love he dies;
      For me he dies, for me:
  O all-atoning Sacrifice,
    I cling by faith to thee.

6   In every time of need,
      Before the judgement-throne,
  Thy works, O Lamb of God, I'll plead,
    Thy merits, not my own.

7   Yet work, O Lord, in me
      As thou for me hast wrought;
  And let my love the answer be
    To grace thy love has brought.

'Father, into thy hands I commend my spirit.'

123   *Mrs. E. S. Alderson*

1 AND now, belovèd Lord, thy soul resigning
   Into thy Father's arms with conscious will,
Calmly, with reverend grace, thy head inclining,
   Thy throbbing brow and labouring breast
    grow still.

2 Freely thy life thou yieldest, meekly bending
   E'en to the last beneath our sorrows' load,
Yet, strong in death, in perfect peace commend-
   Thy spirit to thy Father and thy God. [ing

3 Sweet Saviour, in mine hour of mortal anguish,
   When earth grows dim, and round me falls the
    night,
O breathe thy peace, as flesh and spirit languish;
   At that dread eventide let there be light.

4 To thy dear Cross turn thou mine eyes in dying;
   Lay but my fainting head upon thy breast;
Those outstretched arms receive my latest sigh-
    ing—
And then, O then, thine everlasting rest.

Or

  30 The sun is sinking fast.
  37 Fast sinks the sun to rest.

GOOD FRIDAY EVENING AND
EASTER EVEN

124   *Archbishop W. D. Maclagan*
            (Revised version by the author, 1902)

p 1 IT is finished! blessèd Jesus,
     Thou hast breathed thy latest sigh,
    Teaching us the sons of Adam
     How the Son of God can die.

2 Lifeless lies the piercèd body,
   Resting in its rocky bed;
Thou hast left the Cross of anguish
   For the mansions of the dead.

mf 3 In the hidden realms of darkness
   Shines a light unseen before,
When the Lord of dead and living
   Enters at the lowly door.

4 Lo, in spirit, rich in mercy
   Comes he from the world above,
Preaching to the souls in prison
   Tidings of his dying love.

5 Lo, the heavenly light around him,
   As he draws his people near;
All amazed they come rejoicing
   At the gracious words they hear.

6 Patriarch and priest and prophet
   Gather round him as he stands,
In adoring faith and gladness
   Hearing of the piercèd hands.

7 There in lowliest joy and wonder
   Stands the robber at his side,
Reaping now the blessèd promise
   Spoken by the Crucified.

p 8 Jesus, Lord of dead and living,
   Let thy mercy rest on me;
Grant me too, when life is finished,
   Rest in Paradise with thee.

125

I. Gregory Smith

1 BY Jesus' grave on either hand,
While night is brooding o'er the land,
The sad and silent mourners stand.

2 At last the weary life is o'er,
The agony and conflict sore
Of him who all our sufferings bore.

3 Deep in the rock's sepulchral shade
The Lord by whom the worlds were made,
The Saviour of mankind, is laid.

4 O hearts bereaved and sore distressed,
Here is for you a place of rest;
Here leave your griefs on Jesus' breast.

126   *Johann Rist. Tr. W. Douglas*

1 O SORROW deep!
Who would not weep
With heartfelt pain and sighing?
God the Father's only Son
In the tomb is lying.

2 O Jesus blest,
My help and rest,
With tears I pray thee, hear me:
Now, and even unto death,
Dearest Lord, be near me.

127   *T. Whytehead‡*

1 RESTING from his work to-day
In the tomb the Saviour lay;
Still he slept, from head to feet
Shrouded in the winding-sheet,
Lying in the rock alone,
Hidden by the sealèd stone.

2 Late at even there was seen
Watching long the Magdalene;
Early, ere the break of day,
Sorrowful she took her way
To the holy garden glade,
Where her buried Lord was laid.

3 So with thee, till life shall end,
   I would solemn vigil spend;
   Let me hew thee, Lord, a shrine
   In this rocky heart of mine,
   Where in pure embalmèd cell
   None but thou may ever dwell.

4 Myrrh and spices will I bring,
   True affection's offering;
   Close the door from sight and sound
   Of the busy world around;
   And in patient watch remain
   Till my Lord appear again.

EASTER

128

St. Fulbert of Chartres
Tr. R. Campbell and Compilers
Chorus novae Jerusalem

f 1 YE choirs of new Jerusalem,
     Your sweetest notes employ,
   The Paschal victory to hymn
     In strains of holy joy.

2 For Judah's Lion bursts his chains,
     Crushing the serpent's head;
   And cries aloud through death's domains
     To wake the imprisoned dead.

3 Devouring depths of hell their prey
     At his command restore;
   His ransomed hosts pursue their way
     Where Jesus goes before.

4 Triumphant in his glory now
     To him all power is given;
   To him in one communion bow
     All saints in earth and heaven.

mf 5 While we his soldiers praise our King,
    His mercy we implore,
  Within his palace bright to bring
    And keep us evermore.

f 6 All glory to the Father be,
    All glory to the Son,
  All glory, Holy Ghost, to thee,
    While endless ages run. Alleluia! Amen.

Note.—In verse 2, lines 1–2, Christ, *'the lion that
is of the tribe of Judah'* (Rev. 5. 5), is portrayed as
fulfilling the promise of redemption in Gen. 3. 15.

129
           Tr. J. M. Neale and Compilers
           Ad cenam Agni providi

  1 THE Lamb's high banquet called to share,
    Arrayed in garments white and fair,
    The Red Sea past, we fain would sing
    To Jesus our triumphant King.

  2 Upon the altar of the Cross
    His body hath redeemed our loss:
    And, tasting of his precious Blood,
    In him we live anew to God.

  3 Now Christ our Passover is slain,
    The Lamb of God without a stain;
    His flesh, the true unleavened bread,
    For us is freely offerèd.

  4 Christ rises conqueror from the grave,
    From death returning, strong to save;
    With his right hand the tyrant chains,
    And Paradise for man regains.

  5 All praise be thine, O risen Lord,
    From death to endless life restored;
    All praise to God the Father be
    And Holy Ghost eternally.

Another Office Hymn for Eastertide is:
602 Light's glittering morn bedecks the sky.

130

J. Tisserand
Tr. J. M. Neale and Compilers

O filii et filiae

f 1 ALLELUIA! Alleluia! Alleluia!
O sons and daughters, let us sing!
The King of Heaven, the glorious King,
O'er death to-day rose triumphing.
                  Alleluia!

mf 2 That Easter morn, at break of day,
The faithful women went their way
To seek the tomb where Jesus lay.
                  Alleluia!

     3 An angel clad in white they see,
Who sat, and spake unto the three,
'Your Lord doth go to Galilee.'
                  Alleluia!

p 4 That night the apostles met in fear;
Amidst them came their Lord most dear,
And said, 'My peace be on all here.'
                  Alleluia!

mf 5 When Thomas first the tidings heard,
How they had seen the risen Lord,
He doubted the disciples' word.
                  Alleluia!

p 6 'My piercèd side, O Thomas, see;
My hands, my feet I show to thee;
Not faithless, but believing be.'
                  Alleluia!

mf 7 No longer Thomas then denied;
He saw the feet, the hands, the side;
f   'Thou art my Lord and God,' he cried.
                  Alleluia!

mf 8 How blest are they who have not seen,
    And yet whose faith hath constant been!
    For they eternal life shall win.
                      Alleluia!

f 9 On this most holy day of days,
    To God your hearts and voices raise
    In laud and jubilee and praise.
                      Alleluia!

131
Jane E. Leeson

1 CHRIST the Lord is risen to-day!
Christians, haste your vows to pay;
Offer ye your praises meet
At the Paschal Victim's feet.
For the sheep the Lamb hath bled,
Sinless in the sinner's stead:
'Christ is risen!' to-day we cry;
Now he lives no more to die.

2 Christ, the Victim undefiled,
Man to God hath reconciled;
Whilst in strange and awful strife
Met together death and life.
Christians, on this happy day
Haste with joy your vows to pay:
'Christ is risen!' to-day we cry;
Now he lives no more to die.

3 Christ, who once for sinners bled,
Now the First-born from the dead,
Throned in endless might and power,
Lives and reigns for evermore.
Hail, eternal hope on high!
Hail, thou King of victory!
Hail, thou Prince of Life adored!
Help and save us, gracious Lord.

132   *St. John of Damascus. Tr. J. M. Neale*‡
ἀναστάσεως ἡμέρα

f   1 THE day of Resurrection!
    Earth, tell it out abroad;
    The Passover of gladness,
      The Passover of God!
    From death to life eternal,
      From earth unto the sky,
    Our God hath brought us over
      With hymns of victory.

mf   2 Our hearts be pure from evil,
    That we may see aright
    The Lord in rays eternal
      Of Resurrection-light;
    And, listening to his accents,
      May hear so calm and plain
    His own 'All hail,' and, hearing,
      May raise the victor strain.

f   3 Now let the heavens be joyful,
    And earth her song begin,
    The round world keep high triumph,
      And all that is therein;
    Let all things seen and unseen
      Their notes of gladness blend,
    For Christ the Lord is risen,
      Our joy that hath no end.

133   *St. John of Damascus*
Tr. J. M. Neale and Compilers
αἴσωμεν πάντες λαοί

1 COME, ye faithful, raise the strain
    Of triumphant gladness!
    God hath brought his Israel
      Into joy from sadness;
    Loosed from Pharaoh's bitter yoke
      Jacob's sons and daughters;
    Led them with unmoistened foot
      Through the Red Sea waters.

2 'Tis the spring of souls to-day;
 Christ hath burst his prison,
And from three days' sleep in death
 As a sun hath risen:
All the winter of our sins,
 Long and dark, is flying
From his light, to whom we give
 Laud and praise undying.

3 Now the queen of seasons, bright
 With the day of splendour,
With the royal feast of feasts,
 Comes its joy to render;
Comes to glad Jerusalem,
 Who with true affection
Welcomes in unwearied strains
 Jesu's Resurrection.

4 Alleluia now we cry
 To our King immortal,
Who triumphant burst the bars
 Of the tomb's dark portal;
Alleluia, with the Son
 God the Father praising;
Alleluia yet again
 To the Spirit raising.

134 *Lyra Davidica* (1708), *and the Supplement*
          (1816)

1 JESUS Christ is risen to-day,

        Alleluia!

Our triumphant holy day,

        Alleluia!

Who did once, upon the Cross,

        Alleluia!

Suffer to redeem our loss.

        Alleluia!

2 Hymns of praise then let us sing,
                    Alleluia!
Unto Christ, our heavenly King,
                    Alleluia!
Who endured the Cross and grave,
                    Alleluia!
Sinners to redeem and save.
                    Alleluia!

3 But the pains that he endured,
                    Alleluia!
Our salvation have procured;
                    Alleluia!
Now above the sky he's King,
                    Alleluia!
Where the angels ever sing.
                    Alleluia!

135   ? *17th cent. Tr. F. Pott‡*
                    Finita jam sunt praelia

f 1 ALLELUIA! Alleluia! Alleluia!
The strife is o'er, the battle done;
Now is the Victor's triumph won;
O let the song of praise be sung:
                    Alleluia!

2 Death's mightiest powers have done their
                    worst,
And Jesus hath his foes dispersed;
Let shouts of praise and joy outburst:
                    Alleluia!

3 On the third morn he rose again
Glorious in majesty to reign;
O let us swell the joyful strain:
                    Alleluia!

p 4 Lord, by the stripes which wounded thee
From death's dread sting thy servants free,
f   That we may live, and sing to thee
                    Alleluia!

136

M. Weisse. Tr. Catherine Winkworth†
Christus ist erstanden

f 1 CHRIST the Lord is risen again!
Christ hath broken every chain!
Hark! angelic voices cry,
Singing evermore on high,
Alleluia!

mf 2 He who gave for us his life,
Who for us endured the strife,
Is our Paschal Lamb to-day;
f We too sing for joy, and say
Alleluia!

mf 3 He who bore all pain and loss
Comfortless upon the Cross,
f Lives in glory now on high,
Pleads for us, and hears our cry:
Alleluia!

4*He whose path no records tell,
Who descended into hell,
Who the strong man armed hath bound,
Now in highest heaven is crowned.
Alleluia!

mf 5 He who slumbered in the grave
f Is exalted now to save;
Now through Christendom it rings
That the Lamb is King of Kings.
Alleluia!

mf 6 Now he bids us tell abroad
How the lost may be restored,
How the penitent forgiven,
How we too may enter heaven.
Alleluia!

7 Thou, our Paschal Lamb indeed,
Christ, thy ransomed people feed;
Take our sins and guilt away:
f Let us sing by night and day
Alleluia!

137

Bishop Chr. Wordsworth

f 1 ALLELUIA! Alleluia!
Hearts to heaven and voices raise;
Sing to God a hymn of gladness,
Sing to God a hymn of praise:
He who on the Cross a Victim
For the world's salvation bled,
Jesus Christ, the King of Glory,
Now is risen from the dead.

2 Christ is risen, Christ the first-fruits
Of the holy harvest field,
Which will all its full abundance
At his second coming yield;
Then the golden ears of harvest
Will their heads before him wave,
Ripened by his glorious sunshine,
From the furrows of the grave.

mf 3 Christ is risen, we are risen;
Shed upon us heavenly grace,
Rain, and dew, and gleams of glory
From the brightness of thy face;
That we, with our hearts in heaven,
Here on earth may fruitful be,
And by angel-hands be gathered,
And be ever, Lord, with thee.

f 4 Alleluia! Alleluia!
Glory be to God on high;
Alleluia to the Saviour,
Who has gained the victory;
Alleluia to the Spirit,
Fount of love and sanctity;
Alleluia! Alleluia!
To the Triune Majesty.

138

Victimae Paschali

1 CHRISTIANS, to the Paschal Victim
Offer your thankful praises!

2 A Lamb the sheep redeemeth:
Christ, who only is sinless,
Reconcileth sinners to the Father.

3 Death and life have contended
In that combat stupendous:
The Prince of Life, who died, reigns immortal.

4 Speak, Mary, declaring
What thou sawest wayfaring:

5 'The tomb of Christ, who is living,
The glory of Jesus' Resurrection;

6 Bright angels attesting,
The shroud and napkin resting.

7 Yea, Christ my hope is arisen:
To Galilee he goes before you.'

8*Happy they who hear the witness,
Mary's word believing
Above the tales of Jewry deceiving.

9 Christ indeed from death is risen,
Our new life obtaining:
Have mercy, Victor King, ever reigning!

R. Campbell

139

Based on Ad regias Agni dapes

1 AT the Lamb's high feast we sing
Praise to our victorious King,
Who hath washed us in the tide
Flowing from his piercèd side;
Praise we him, whose love divine
Gives his sacred Blood for wine,
Gives his Body for the feast,
Christ the Victim, Christ the Priest.

2 Where the Paschal blood is poured,
  Death's dark angel sheaths his sword;
  Israel's hosts triumphant go
  Through the wave that drowns the foe.
  Praise we Christ, whose Blood was shed,
  Paschal Victim, Paschal Bread;
  With sincerity and love
  Eat we manna from above.

3 Mighty Victim from the sky,
  Hell's fierce powers beneath thee lie;
  Thou hast conquered in the fight,
  Thou hast brought us life and light.
  Now no more can death appal,
  Now no more the grave enthral:
  Thou hast opened Paradise,
  And in thee thy saints shall rise.

4 Easter triumph, Easter joy,
  Sin alone can this destroy;
  From sin's power do thou set free
  Souls new-born, O Lord, in thee.
  Hymns of glory and of praise,
  Risen Lord, to thee we raise;
  Holy Father, praise to thee,
  With the Spirit, ever be.

140

C. F. Gellert
Tr. Frances E. Cox and others
Jesus lebt

1 JESUS lives! thy terrors now
    Can no more, O death, appal us;
  Jesus lives! by this we know
      Thou, O grave, canst not enthral us.
                    Alleluia!
2 Jesus lives! henceforth is death
    But the gate of life immortal:
  This shall calm our trembling breath,
    When we pass its gloomy portal.
                    Alleluia!

3 Jesus lives! for us he died;
   Then, alone to Jesus living,
Pure in heart may we abide,
   Glory to our Saviour giving.
                    Alleluia!

4 Jesus lives! our hearts know well
   Naught from us his love shall sever;
Life nor death nor powers of hell
   Tear us from his keeping ever.
                    Alleluia!

5 Jesus lives! to him the throne
   Over all the world is given:
May we go where he is gone,
   Rest and reign with him in heaven.
                    Alleluia!

141   *C. Wesley*

1 LOVE'S redeeming work is done;
Fought the fight, the battle won:
Lo, our Sun's eclipse is o'er!
Lo, he sets in blood no more!

2 Vain the stone, the watch, the seal!
Christ has burst the gates of hell;
Death in vain forbids his rise;
Christ has opened Paradise.

3 Lives again our glorious King;
Where, O death, is now thy sting?
Dying once, he all doth save;
Where thy victory, O grave?

4 Soar we now where Christ has led,
Following our exalted Head;
Made like him, like him we rise;
Ours the cross, the grave, the skies.

5 Hail the Lord of earth and heaven!
   Praise to thee by both be given:
Thee we greet triumphant now;
   Hail, the Resurrection thou!

142

T. Kelly‡

1 THE Lord is risen indeed!
   Now is his work performed;
Now is the mighty captive freed,
   And death's strong castle stormed.

2 The Lord is risen indeed!
   Then hell has lost his prey;
With him is risen the ransomed seed
   To reign in endless day.

3 The Lord is risen indeed!
   He lives, to die no more;
He lives, the sinner's cause to plead,
   Whose curse and shame he bore.

4 The Lord is risen indeed!
   Attending angels, hear!
Up to the courts of heaven with speed
   The joyful tidings bear.

5 Then take your golden lyres,
   And strike each cheerful chord;
Join, all ye bright celestial choirs,
   To sing our risen Lord.

143

Mrs. C. F. Alexander

1 HE is risen, he is risen!
   Tell it with a joyful voice;
He has burst his three days' prison;
   Let the whole wide earth rejoice.
Death is conquered, man is free,
Christ has won the victory.

2 Come, ye sad and fearful-hearted,
  With glad smile and radiant brow;
Lent's long shadows have departed,
  All his woes are over now,
And the Passion that he bore:
  Sin and pain can vex no more.

3 Come, with high and holy hymning
  Chant our Lord's triumphant lay;
Not one darksome cloud is dimming
  Yonder glorious morning ray,
Breaking o'er the purple east:
  Brighter far our Easter-feast.

The following hymns are suitable for this season:

222 Come, ye faithful, raise the anthem.
279 Light's abode, celestial Salem.
602 Light's glittering morn bedecks the sky.

ROGATIONTIDE

144
               J. Keble

1 LORD, in thy name thy servants plead,
  And thou hast sworn to hear:
Thine is the harvest, thine the seed,
  The fresh and fading year.

2 Our hope, when autumn winds blew wild,
  We trusted, Lord, with thee;
And still, now spring has on us smiled,
  We wait on thy decree.

3 The former and the latter rain,
  The summer sun and air,
The green ear, and the golden grain,
  All thine, are ours by prayer.

4 Thine too by right, and ours by grace,
  The wondrous growth unseen,
The hopes that soothe, the fears that brace,
  The love that shines serene.

5 So grant the precious things brought forth
    By sun and moon below,
That thee in thy new heaven and earth
    We never may forgo.

See also **606** To thee our God we fly.

ASCENSIONTIDE

145   *Tr. Compilers† (1904)*
Aeterne Rex altissime

1 O THOU eternal King most high,
  Whose Blood has brought salvation nigh,
  The bonds of death are burst by thee,
  And love has won the victory.

2 Ascending to the Father's throne
  Thou tak'st the kingdom as thine own;
  While awestruck angels contemplate
  The wondrous change of man's estate.

3 Be thou our joy, O mighty Lord,
  As thou wilt be our great reward;
  Let all our glory be in thee
  Both now and through eternity.

146   *Tr. J. Chandler and Compilers*
Jesu, nostra redemptio

1 JESU, our hope, our heart's desire,
    Thy work of grace we sing;
  Redeemer of the world art thou,
    Its Maker and its King.

2 How vast the mercy and the love
    Which laid our sins on thee,
  And led thee to a cruel death,
    To set thy people free!

3 But now the bonds of death are burst,
   The ransom has been paid;
And thou art on thy Father's throne,
   In glorious robes arrayed.

4 O may thy mighty love prevail
   Our sinful souls to spare!
O may we stand around thy throne,
   And see thy glory there!

5 Jesu, our only joy be thou,
   As thou our prize wilt be;
In thee be all our glory now
   And through eternity.

6 All praise to thee who art gone up
   Triumphantly to heaven;
All praise to God the Father's name
   And Holy Ghost be given.

147   *C. Wesley, T. Cotterill, and Compilers*

f 1 HAIL the day that sees him rise,
               Alleluia!
To his throne above the skies;
               Alleluia!
Christ, the Lamb for sinners given,
               Alleluia!
Enters now the highest heaven.
               Alleluia!

2 There for him high triumph waits;
               Alleluia!
Lift your heads, eternal gates!
               Alleluia!
He hath conquered death and sin;
               Alleluia!
Take the King of Glory in!
               Alleluia!

3 Lo, the heaven its Lord receives,
                    Alleluia!
  Yet he loves the earth he leaves;
                    Alleluia!
  Though returning to his throne,
                    Alleluia!
  Still he calls mankind his own.
                    Alleluia!

mf 4 See! he lifts his hands above;
                    Alleluia!
  See! he shews the prints of love;
                    Alleluia!
  Hark! his gracious lips bestow,
                    Alleluia!
  Blessings on his Church below.
                    Alleluia!

5 Still for us he intercedes,
                    Alleluia!
  His prevailing Death he pleads;
                    Alleluia!
  Near himself prepares our place,
                    Alleluia!
  He the first-fruits of our race.
                    Alleluia!

6 Lord, though parted from our sight,
                    Alleluia!
  Far above the starry height,
                    Alleluia!
f Grant our hearts may thither rise,
                    Alleluia!
  Seeking thee above the skies.
                    Alleluia!

Note.—*A longer form of this hymn will be found in the 'Processional' section* (**610**).

148

Bishop Chr. Wordsworth

f 1 SEE the Conqueror mounts in triumph,
  See the King in royal state
Riding on the clouds his chariot
  To his heavenly palace gate;
Hark! the choirs of angel voices
  Joyful Alleluias sing,
And the portals high are lifted
  To receive their heavenly King.

mf 2 Who is this that comes in glory,
  With the trump of jubilee?
Lord of battles, God of armies,
  He has gained the victory;
He who on the Cross did suffer,
f He who from the grave arose,
He has vanquished sin and Satan,
  He by death has spoiled his foes.

3 He has raised our human nature
  On the clouds to God's right hand;
There we sit in heavenly places,
  There with him in glory stand:
Jesus reigns, adored by angels;
  Man with God is on the throne;
Mighty Lord, in thine Ascension
  We by faith behold our own.

mf 4*See him who is gone before us
  Heavenly mansions to prepare,
See him who is ever pleading
  For us with prevailing prayer,
See him who with sound of trumpet
  And with his angelic train,
Summoning the world to judgement,
  On the clouds will come again.

f 5 Glory be to God the Father;
        Glory be to God the Son,
     Dying, risen, ascending for us,
        Who the heavenly realm has won;
     Glory to the Holy Spirit:
        To One God in Persons Three
     Glory both in earth and heaven,
        Glory, endless glory be.

149   *Mrs. E. Toke*

f 1 THOU art gone up on high,
        To mansions in the skies;
     And round thy throne unceasingly
        The songs of praise arise:
p   But we are lingering here,
        With sin and care oppressed;
     Lord, send thy promised Comforter,
        And lead us to thy rest.

mf 2 Thou art gone up on high;
        But thou didst first come down,
     Through earth's most bitter misery
        To pass unto thy crown;
     And girt with griefs and fears
        Our onward course must be;
     But only let this path of tears
        Lead us at last to thee.

f 3 Thou art gone up on high;
        But thou shalt come again,
     With all the bright ones of the sky
        Attendant in thy train.
     Lord, by thy saving power
        So make us live and die,
     That we may stand in that dread hour
        At thy right hand on high.

150

F. B. Macnutt

1 LET all the multitudes of light,
    Their songs in concert raising,
With earth's triumphal hymns unite,
    The risen Saviour praising.
Ye heavens, his festival proclaim!
Our King returneth whence he came,
    With victory amazing.

2 For us he bore the bitter Tree,
    To death's dark realm descending;
Our foe he slew, and set us free,
    Man's ancient bondage ending.
No more the tyrant's chains oppress;
O conquering Love, thy name we bless,
    With thee to heaven ascending.

3 Jesus, to thee be endless praise,
    For this thy great salvation;
O holy Father, thine always
    Be thanks and adoration;
Spirit of life and light, to thee
Eternal praise and glory be:
    One God of all creation!

*The following hymns are suitable for this
season:*

204   Where high the heavenly temple stands.
216   Rejoice! the Lord is King.
217   All hail the power of Jesus' name.
218   The head that once was crowned with thorns.
224   Crown him with many crowns.
225   At the name of Jesus.

WHITSUNTIDE

151   *Tr. J. Ellerton and Compilers†* (1904)
Beata nobis gaudia

1 O JOY, because the circling year
Hath brought our day of blessing here!
The day when first the light divine
Upon the Church began to shine.

2 Like unto quivering tongues of flame
Upon each one the Spirit came:
Tongues, that the earth might hear their call,
And fire, that love might burn in all.

3 Thus unto all was spread abroad
The wonder of the works of God;
They knew the prophet's word fulfilled,
And owned the work which God had willed.

4 Of old in every hallowed breast
Thou camest in thy grace to rest:
O grant us now from sin release,
And in our time, good Lord, give peace.

152   *? Archbishop Rabanus Maurus*
            Tr. Yattendon Hymnal
Veni, creator Spiritus

1 COME, O Creator Spirit, come,
And make within our hearts thy home;
To us thy grace celestial give,
Who of thy breathing move and live.

2 O Paraclete, that name is thine,
Of God most high the gift divine;
The well of life, the fire of love,
Our soul's anointing from above.

3 Thou dost appear in sevenfold dower
The sign of God's almighty power;
The Father's promise, making rich
With saving truth our earthly speech.

4 Our senses with thy light inflame,
Our hearts to heavenly love reclaim;
Our bodies' poor infirmity
With strength perpetual fortify.

5 Our mortal foe afar repel,
Grant us henceforth in peace to dwell;
And so to us, with thee for guide,
No ill shall come, no harm betide.

6 May we by thee the Father learn,
And know the Son, and thee discern,
Who art of Both; and thus adore
In perfect faith for evermore.

Note.—'*Paraclete*' *in verse* 2, *line* 1, *is the English
form of* '*Parakletos,*' *a title of the Holy Spirit used by
St. John and translated* '*Comforter*' (*or* '*Advocate*').

153   *Foundling Hospital Collection*† (1774)

1 SPIRIT of mercy, truth, and love,
O shed thine influence from above,
And still from age to age convey
The wonders of this sacred day.

2 In every clime, by every tongue,
Be God's surpassing glory sung;
Let all the listening earth be taught
The acts our great Redeemer wrought.

3 Unfailing comfort, heavenly guide,
Still o'er thy holy Church preside;
Still let mankind thy blessings prove,
Spirit of mercy, truth, and love.

154   *J. Keble*

f   1 WHEN God of old came down from heaven,
         In power and wrath he came;
      Before his feet the clouds were riven,
         Half darkness and half flame:

p   2 But, when he came the second time,
         He came in power and love;
      Softer than gale at morning prime
         Hovered his holy Dove.

f   3 The fires, that rushed on Sinai down
         In sudden torrents dread,
      Now gently light, a glorious crown,
         On every sainted head.

      4 And as on Israel's awestruck ear
         The voice exceeding loud,
      The trump that angels quake to hear,
         Thrilled from the deep, dark cloud;

      5 So, when the Spirit of our God
         Came down his flock to find,
      A voice from heaven was heard abroad,
         A rushing, mighty wind.

mf 6 It fills the Church of God; it fills
         The sinful world around:
      Only in stubborn hearts and wills
         No place for it is found.

p   7 Come, Lord, come Wisdom, Love, and
              Power,
         Open our ears to hear;
      Let us not miss the accepted hour:
         Save, Lord, by love or fear.

155

F. C. Burkitt

1 OUR Lord, his Passion ended,
   Hath gloriously ascended,
   Yet though from him divided,
   He leaves us not unguided;
       All his benefits to crown
       He hath sent his Spirit down,
       Burning like a flame of fire
       His disciples to inspire.

2 God's Spirit is directing;
   No more they sit expecting;
   But forth to all the nation
   They go with exultation;
       That which God in them hath wrought
       Fills their life and soul and thought;
       So their witness now can do
       Work as great in others too.

3 The centuries go gliding,
   But still we have abiding
   With us that Spirit Holy
   To make us brave and lowly—
       Lowly, for we feel our need:
       God alone is strong indeed;
       Brave, for with the Spirit's aid
       We can venture unafraid.

4 O Lord of every nation,
   Fill us with inspiration!
   We know our own unfitness,
   Yet for thee would bear witness.
       By thy Spirit now we raise
       To the heavenly Father praise:
       Holy Spirit, Father, Son,
       Make us know thee, ever One.

156 *(Other occasions also)*

ʔ *Archbishop Stephen Langton*
Tr. E. Caswall *and Compilers*

Veni, Sancte Spiritus

1 COME, thou Holy Spirit, come,
  And from thy celestial home
    Shed a ray of light divine;
  Come, thou Father of the poor,
  Come, thou source of all our store,
    Come, within our bosoms shine:

2 Thou of comforters the best,
  Thou the soul's most welcome guest,
    Sweet refreshment here below;
  In our labour rest most sweet,
  Grateful coolness in the heat,
    Solace in the midst of woe.

3 O most blessèd Light divine,
  Shine within these hearts of thine,
    And our inmost being fill;
  Where thou art not, man hath naught,
  Nothing good in deed or thought,
    Nothing free from taint of ill.

4 Heal our wounds; our strength renew;
  On our dryness pour thy dew;
    Wash the stains of guilt away;
  Bend the stubborn heart and will;
  Melt the frozen, warm the chill;
    Guide the steps that go astray.

5 On the faithful, who adore
  And confess thee, evermore
    In thy sevenfold gifts descend:
  Give them virtue's sure reward,
  Give them thy salvation, Lord,
    Give them joys that never end.

157 (*Other occasions also*)

Bishop J. Cosin
Based on Veni, creator Spiritus

mf 1 COME, Holy Ghost, our souls inspire,
   And lighten with celestial fire;
   Thou the anointing Spirit art,
   Who dost thy sevenfold gifts impart.

2 Thy blessèd unction from above
   Is comfort, life, and fire of love;
   Enable with perpetual light
   The dulness of our blinded sight.

3 Anoint and cheer our soilèd face
   With the abundance of thy grace:
   Keep far our foes, give peace at home;
   Where thou art guide no ill can come.

4 Teach us to know the Father, Son,
   And thee, of Both, to be but One;
   That through the ages all along
   This may be our endless song,

   'Praise to thy eternal merit,
   Father, Son, and Holy Spirit.'

The following hymns are suitable for this season:

TRINITY SUNDAY

158   *Before 10th cent. Tr. A. E. Alston*
                           O Pater sancte

1 FATHER most holy, merciful and loving,
  Jesu, Redeemer, ever to be worshipped,
  Life-giving Spirit, Comforter most gracious,
          God everlasting;

2 Three in a wondrous Unity unbroken,
  One perfect Godhead, love that never faileth,
  Light of the angels, succour of the needy,
          Hope of all living;

3 All thy creation serveth its Creator,
  Thee every creature praiseth without ceasing;
  We too would sing thee psalms of true devotion:
          Hear, we beseech thee.

4 Lord God Almighty, unto thee be glory,
  One in three Persons, over all exalted.
  Thine, as is meet, be honour, praise and blessing
          Now and for ever.

159   *F. W. Faber*

1 MOST ancient of all mysteries,
        Before thy throne we lie;
  Have mercy now, most merciful,
        Most holy Trinity.

2 When heaven and earth were yet unmade,
        When time was yet unknown,
  Thou in thy bliss and majesty
        Didst live and love alone.

3 Thou wast not born; there was no fount
        From which thy being flowed;
  There is no end which thou canst reach:
        But thou art simply God.

4 How wonderful creation is,
  The work which thou didst bless!
  And O what then must thou be like,
  Eternal loveliness!

5 Most ancient of all mysteries,
  Low at thy throne we lie;
  Have mercy now, most merciful,
  Most holy Trinity.

The following hymns are suitable:

GENERAL HYMNS

160
Bishop R. Heber

mf 1 HOLY, Holy, Holy! Lord God Almighty!
  Early in the morning our song shall rise to
    thee;
  Holy, Holy, Holy! merciful and mighty!
  God in three Persons, blessèd Trinity!

2 Holy, Holy, Holy! all the saints adore thee,
  Casting down their golden crowns around
    the glassy sea;
  Cherubim and seraphim falling down before
    thee,
  Which wert and art and evermore shalt be.

p 3 Holy, Holy, Holy! though the darkness hide
    thee,
  Though the eye of sinful man **thy** glory
    may not see,
mf Only thou art holy, there is none beside thee
  Perfect in power, in love, and purity.

4 Holy, Holy, Holy! Lord God Almighty!
f   All thy works shall praise thy name in earth
        and sky and sea;
    Holy, Holy, Holy! merciful and mighty!
    God in three Persons, blessèd Trinity!

161
Bishop R. Mant†

mf 1 BRIGHT the vision that delighted
     Once the sight of Judah's seer;
    Sweet the countless tongues united
     To entrance the prophet's ear.

2 Round the Lord in glory seated
    Cherubim and seraphim
    Filled his temple, and repeated
     Each to each the alternate hymn:

f 3 'Lord, thy glory fills the heaven;
    Earth is with its fulness stored;
    Unto thee be glory given,
     Holy, Holy, Holy, Lord.'

4 Heaven is still with glory ringing,
    Earth takes up the angels' cry,
    'Holy, Holy, Holy,' singing,
    'Lord of Hosts, the Lord most high.'

mf 5 With his seraph train before him,
    With his holy Church below,
    Thus unite we to adore him,
     Bid we thus our anthem flow:

f 6 'Lord, thy glory fills the heaven;
    Earth is with its fulness stored;
    Unto thee be glory given,
     Holy, Holy, Holy, Lord.'

*Note.—This hymn is based on the account of
Isaiah's vision in Is. 6.*

162 *St. Patrick's Breastplate*

Ascribed to St. Patrick
Tr. Mrs. C. F. Alexander

Atompuịp moụị

f   1 I BIND unto myself to-day
        The strong name of the Trinity,
      By invocation of the same,
        The Three in One, and One in Three.

mf 2 I bind this day to me for ever,
        By power of faith, Christ's Incarnation,
        His Baptism in the Jordan river,
          His Death on Cross for my salvation:
f   His bursting from the spicèd tomb,
          His riding up the heavenly way,
          His coming at the day of doom,
            I bind unto myself to-day.

mf 3*I bind unto myself the power
        Of the great love of cherubim;
        The sweet 'Well done!' in judgement hour;
        The service of the seraphim,
      Confessors' faith, apostles' word,
        The patriarchs' prayers, the prophets'
          scrolls,
p   All good deeds done unto the Lord,
        And purity of virgin souls.

mf 4*I bind unto myself to-day
        The virtues of the star-lit heaven,
        The glorious sun's life-giving ray,
          The whiteness of the moon at even,
f   The flashing of the lightning free,
          The whirling winds' tempestuous
            shocks,
      The stable earth, the deep salt sea
        Around the old eternal rocks.

mf 5 I bind unto myself to-day
  The power of God to hold and lead,
His eye to watch, his might to stay,
  His ear to hearken to my need;
mp The wisdom of my God to teach,
  His hand to guide, his shield to ward,
The word of God to give me speech,
  His heavenly host to be my guard.

mf 6*Against the demon snares of sin,
  The vice that gives temptation force,
The natural lusts that war within,
  The hostile men that mar my course—
p Or few or many, far or nigh,
  In every place, and in all hours,
Against their fierce hostility
  I bind to me these holy powers.

7*Against all Satan's spells and wiles,
  Against false words of heresy,
Against the knowledge that defiles,
  Against the heart's idolatry,
Against the wizard's evil craft,
  Against the death-wound and the burn-
    ing,
The choking wave, the poisoned shaft,
  Protect me, Christ, till thy returning.

PART 2

8 Christ be with me, Christ within me,
  Christ behind me, Christ before me,
Christ beside me, Christ to win me,
  Christ to comfort and restore me,
Christ beneath me, Christ above me,
  Christ in quiet, Christ in danger,
Christ in hearts of all that love me,
  Christ in mouth of friend and stranger.

Doxology to either part

9 I bind unto myself the name,
 The strong name of the Trinity,
By invocation of the same,
 The Three in One, and One in Three,
Of whom all nature hath creation,
 Eternal Father, Spirit, Word.
Praise to the Lord of my salvation:
 Salvation is of Christ the Lord.

163   *G. Rorison†*

1 THREE in One, and One in Three,
 Ruler of the earth and sea,
 Hear us, while we lift to thee‿
  Holy chant and psalm.

2 Light of lights! with morning shine;
 Lift on us thy light divine;
 And let charity benign
  Breathe on us her balm.

3 Light of lights! when falls the even,
 Let it close on sin forgiven;
 Fold us in the peace of heaven;
  Shed a holy calm.

4 Three in One and One in Three,
 Dimly here we worship thee;
 With the saints hereafter we‿
  Hope to bear the palm.

164   *E. Cooper†*

1 FATHER of heaven, whose love profound
 A ransom for our souls hath found,
 Before thy throne we sinners bend,
 To us thy pardoning love extend.

2 Almighty Son, incarnate Word,
Our Prophet, Priest, Redeemer, Lord,
Before thy throne we sinners bend,
To us thy saving grace extend.

3 Eternal Spirit, by whose breath
The soul is raised from sin and death,
Before thy throne we sinners bend,
To us thy quickening power extend.

4 Thrice Holy! Father, Spirit, Son;
Mysterious Godhead, Three in One,
Before thy throne we sinners bend,
Grace, pardon, life to us extend.

165 *Ps.* 90   *I. Watts*†

f 1 O GOD, our help in ages past,
Our hope for years to come,
Our shelter from the stormy blast,
And our eternal home;

mf 2 Beneath the shadow of thy throne
Thy saints have dwelt secure;
Sufficient is thine arm alone,
And our defence is sure.

3 Before the hills in order stood,
Or earth received her frame,
From everlasting thou art God,
To endless years the same.

p 4 A thousand ages in thy sight
Are like an evening gone;
Short as the watch that ends the night
Before the rising sun.

5*Time, like an ever-rolling stream,
    Bears all its sons away;
They fly forgotten, as a dream
    Dies at the opening day.

f 6 O God, our help in ages past,
    Our hope for years to come,
Be thou our guard while troubles last,
    And our eternal home.

166 *Ps.* 100   *W. Kethe, Day's Psalter* (1561)

f 1 ALL people that on earth do dwell,
    Sing to the Lord with cheerful voice;
Him serve with fear, his praise forth tell,
    Come ye before him, and rejoice.

mf 2 The Lord, ye know, is God indeed;
    Without our aid he did us make;
We are his folk, he doth us feed,
    And for his sheep he doth us take.

f 3 O enter then his gates with praise,
    Approach with joy his courts unto;
Praise, laud, and bless his name always,
    For it is seemly so to do.

mf 4 For why? the Lord our God is good;
    His mercy is for ever sure;
His truth at all times firmly stood,
    And shall from age to age endure.

5 To Father, Son, and Holy Ghost,
    The God whom heaven and earth adore,
From men and from the angel-host
    Be praise and glory evermore.

167 *Ps. 104*

Sir R. Grant†
Based on W. Kethe (1561)

f 1 O WORSHIP the King all glorious above;
O gratefully sing his power and his love;
Our Shield and Defender, the Ancient of
    Days,
Pavilioned in splendour and girded with
    praise.

2 O tell of his might, O sing of his grace,
Whose robe is the light, whose canopy space;
His chariots of wrath the deep thunder clouds
    form,
And dark is his path on the wings of the
    storm.

mf 3*The earth with its store of wonders untold,
Almighty, thy power hath founded of old;
Hath stablished it fast by a changeless decree,
And round it hath cast, like a mantle, the sea.

4 Thy bountiful care what tongue can recite?
It breathes in the air, it shines in the light;
It streams from the hills, it descends to the
    plain,
And sweetly distils in the dew and the rain.

p 5 Frail children of dust and feeble as frail,
In thee do we trust, nor find thee to fail;
Thy mercies how tender, how firm to the end!
Our Maker, Defender, Redeemer, and Friend.

6 O measureless Might, ineffable Love,
While angels delight to hymn thee above,
Thy ransomed creation, though feeble their
    lays,
With true adoration shall sing to thy praise.

168   J. Keble

mf   1   THERE is a book, who runs may read,
            Which heavenly truth imparts,
          And all the lore its scholars need,
            Pure eyes and Christian hearts.
          The works of God above, below,
            Within us and around,
          Are pages in that book, to show
            How God himself is found.

       2   The glorious sky, embracing all,
            Is like the Maker's love,
          Wherewith encompassed, great and small
            In peace and order move.
          The moon above, the Church below,
            A wondrous race they run;
          But all their radiance, all their glow,
            Each borrows of its sun.

       3*The Saviour lends the light and heat
            That crown his holy hill;
          The saints, like stars, around his seat
            Perform their courses still.
          The dew of heaven is like thy grace,
            It steals in silence down;
          But where it lights, the favoured place
            By richest fruits is known.

f   4   One name, above all glorious names,
            With its ten thousand tongues
          The everlasting sea proclaims,
            Echoing angelic songs.
          The raging fire, the roaring wind,
            Thy boundless power display;
          But in the gentler breeze we find
            Thy Spirit's viewless way.

mf 5 Two worlds are ours: 'tis only sin‿
    Forbids us to descry
The mystic heaven and earth within,
    Plain as the sea and sky.
Thou who hast given me eyes to see
    And love this sight so fair,
Give me a heart to find out thee,
    And read thee everywhere.

169
F. W. Faber

mf 1 MY God, how wonderful thou art,
    Thy majesty how bright,
How beautiful thy mercy-seat,
    In depths of burning light!

p 2 How dread are thine eternal years,
    O everlasting Lord,
By prostrate spirits day and night
    Incessantly adored!

mf 3 How wonderful, how beautiful,
    The sight of thee must be,
Thine endless wisdom, boundless power,
    And aweful purity!

p 4 O how I fear thee, living God,
    With deepest, tenderest fears,
And worship thee with trembling hope,
    And penitential tears!

mf 5 Yet I may love thee too, O Lord,
    Almighty as thou art,
For thou hast stooped to ask of me‿
    The love of my poor heart.

  6 No earthly father loves like thee,
    No mother, e'er so mild,
Bears and forbears as thou hast done‿
    With me thy sinful child.

7 Father of Jesus, love's reward,
  What rapture will it be,
  Prostrate before thy throne to lie,
  And gaze and gaze on thee!

170   *J. Addison*

1 THE spacious firmament on high,
  With all the blue ethereal sky,
  And spangled heavens, a shining frame,
  Their great Original proclaim.
  The unwearied sun from day to day
  Does his Creator's power display,
  And publishes to every land
  The works of an almighty hand.

2 Soon as the evening shades prevail
  The moon takes up the wondrous tale,
  And nightly to the listening earth
  Repeats the story of her birth;
  Whilst all the stars that round her burn,
  And all the planets in their turn,
  Confirm the tidings, as they roll,
  And spread the truth from pole to pole.

3 What though in solemn silence all
  Move round the dark terrestrial ball;
  What though nor real voice nor sound
  Amid their radiant orbs be found;
  In reason's ear they all rejoice,
  And utter forth a glorious voice,
  For ever singing as they shine,
  'The hand that made us is divine.'

171   *F. S. Pierpoint†*

mf 1 FOR the beauty of the earth,
        For the beauty of the skies,
        For the love which from our birth
        Over and around us lies,
f   Lord of all, to thee we raise
        This our grateful hymn of praise.

mf 2 For the beauty of each hour
  Of the day and of the night,
 Hill and vale, and tree and flower,
  Sun and moon and stars of light,
f Lord of all, etc.

mf 3 For the joy of human love,
  Brother, sister, parent, child,
 Friends on earth, and friends above,
  Pleasures pure and undefiled,
f Lord of all, etc.

mf 4 For each perfect gift of thine,
  To our race so freely given,
 Graces human and divine,
  Flowers of earth and buds of heaven.
f Lord of all, etc.

 5 For thy Church which evermore
  Lifteth holy hands above,
 Offering up on every shore
  Her pure sacrifice of love,
 Lord of all, etc.

172
*W. H. Draper. Based on St. Francis
of Assisi's Canticle of the Sun*

f 1 ALL creatures of our God and King,
 Lift up your voice and with us sing
  Alleluia, alleluia!
 Thou burning sun with golden beam,
 Thou silver moon with softer gleam,
  O praise him, O praise him,
  Alleluia, alleluia, alleluia!

 2 Thou rushing wind that art so strong,
 Ye clouds that sail in heaven along,
  O praise him, alleluia!
 Thou rising morn, in praise rejoice,
 Ye lights of evening, find a voice;
  O praise him, etc.

mf 3 Thou flowing water, pure and clear,
 Make music for thy Lord to hear,
  Alleluia, alleluia!
 Thou fire so masterful and bright,
 That givest man both warmth and light.
  O praise him, etc.

4*Dear mother earth, who day by day
 Unfoldest blessings on our way,
  O praise him, alleluia!
 The flowers and fruits that in thee grow,
 Let them his glory also show;
  O praise him, etc.

5 And all ye men of tender heart,
 Forgiving others, take your part,
  O sing ye alleluia!
 Ye who long pain and sorrow bear,
 Praise God and on him cast your care;
  O praise him, etc.

p 6*And thou, most kind and gentle death,
 Waiting to hush our latest breath,
  O praise him, alleluia!
 Thou leadest home the child of God,
 And Christ our Lord the way hath trod;
  O praise him, etc.

f 7 Let all things their Creator bless,
 And worship him in humbleness;
  O praise him, alleluia!
 Praise, praise the Father, praise the Son,
 And praise the Spirit, Three in One;
  O praise him, etc.

173   *Bishop R. Heber*

1 I PRAISED the earth, in beauty seen,
   With garlands gay of various green;
   I praised the sea, whose ample field
   Shone glorious as a silver shield—
   And earth and ocean seemed to say,
   'Our beauties are but for a day.'

2 I praised the sun, whose chariot rolled
   On wheels of amber and of gold;
   I praised the moon, whose softer eye
   Gleamed sweetly through the summer sky—
   And moon and sun in answer said,
   'Our days of light are numberèd.'

3 O God, O good beyond compare,
   If thus thy meaner works are fair,
   If thus thy beauties gild the span
   Of ruined earth and sinful man,
   How glorious must the mansion be
   Where thy redeemed shall dwell with thee!

174   *C. A. Alington*

1 LORD of beauty, thine the splendour
     Shewn in earth and sky and sea,
   Burning sun and moonlight tender,
     Hill and river, flower and tree:
   Lest we fail our praise to render
     Touch our eyes that they may see.

2 Lord of wisdom, whom obeying
     Mighty waters ebb and flow,
   While unhasting, undelaying,
     Planets on their courses go:
   In thy laws thyself displaying,
     Teach our minds thyself to know.

3 Lord of life, alone sustaining
    All below and all above,
  Lord of love, by whose ordaining
    Sun and stars sublimely move:
  In our earthly spirits reigning,
    Lift our hearts that we may love.

4 Lord of beauty, bid us own thee,
    Lord of truth, our footsteps guide,
  Till as Love our hearts enthrone thee,
    And, with vision purified,
  Lord of all, when all have known thee,
    Thou in all art glorified.

175   *J. Conder*

1 THE Lord is King! lift up thy voice,
  O earth, and all ye heavens, rejoice;
  From world to world the joy shall ring,
  'The Lord omnipotent is King!'

2 The Lord is King! who then shall dare
  Resist his will, distrust his care,
  Or murmur at his wise decrees,
  Or doubt his royal promises?

3 He reigns! ye saints, exalt your strains;
  Your God is King, your Father reigns;
  And he is at the Father's side,
  The Man of love, the Crucified.

4*Alike pervaded by his eye
  All parts of his dominion lie:
  This world of ours and worlds unseen,
  And thin the boundary between.

5 One Lord one empire all secures;
  He reigns, and life and death are yours;
  Through earth and heaven one song shall
  'The Lord omnipotent is King!'   [ring,

176   *W. Cowper*

1 SOMETIMES a light surprises
    The Christian while he sings:
It is the Lord who rises
    With healing in his wings;
When comforts are declining,
    He grants the soul again
A season of clear shining
    To cheer it after rain.

2 In holy contemplation
    We sweetly then pursue
The theme of God's salvation,
    And find it ever new:
Set free from present sorrow,
    We cheerfully can say,
E'en let the unknown morrow
    Bring with it what it may,

3 It can bring with it nothing
    But he will bear us through;
Who gives the lilies clothing
    Will clothe his people too:
Beneath the spreading heavens
    No creature but is fed;
And he who feeds the ravens
    Will give his children bread.

4 Though vine nor fig-tree neither
    Their wonted fruit should bear,
Though all the fields should wither,
    Nor flocks nor herds be there;
Yet, God the same abiding,
    His praise shall tune my voice;
For, while in him confiding,
    I cannot but rejoice.

177   *J. Addison*

mf 1 WHEN all thy mercies, O my God,
          My rising soul surveys,
       Transported with the view, I'm lost‿
          In wonder, love, and praise.

     2 Unnumbered comforts to my soul
          Thy tender care bestowed,
       Before my infant heart conceived
          From whom those comforts flowed.

p 3 When in the slippery paths of youth
          With heedless steps I ran,
mf   Thine arm unseen conveyed me safe,
          And led me up to man.

     4*Ten thousand thousand precious gifts
          My daily thanks employ,
       And not the least a cheerful heart
          Which tastes those gifts with joy.

f 5 Through every period of my life
          Thy goodness I'll pursue,
       And after death in distant worlds
          The glorious theme renew.

     6 Through all eternity to thee‿
          A joyful song I'll raise;
       For O, eternity's too short
          To utter all thy praise.

178 *Ps. 23*   *George Herbert*

mf 1 THE God of love my Shepherd is,
          And he that doth me feed;
       While he is mine and I am his,
          What can I want or need?

2 He leads me to the tender grass,
　　Where I both feed and rest;
　Then to the streams that gently pass:
　　In both I have the best.

3 Or if I stray, he doth convert,
　　And bring my mind in frame,
　And all this not for my desert,
　　But for his holy name.

p 4 Yea, in death's shady black abode
　　Well may I walk, not fear;
　For thou art with me, and thy rod
　　To guide, thy staff to bear.

mf 5 Surely thy sweet and wondrous love
　　Shall measure all my days;
f 　And, as it never shall remove,
　　So neither shall my praise.

179 *Ps. 23*　　　　　　　　　　　*J. Addison*

mf 1 THE Lord my pasture shall prepare,
　And feed me with a shepherd's care;
　His presence shall my wants supply,
　And guard me with a watchful eye;
　My noonday walks he shall attend,
　And all my midnight hours defend.

p 2 When in the sultry glebe I faint,
　Or on the thirsty mountain pant,
　To fertile vales and dewy meads
　My weary wandering steps he leads,
　Where peaceful rivers, soft and slow,
　Amid the verdant landscape flow.

mf 3 Though in a bare and rugged way
　Through devious lonely wilds I stray,
　Thy bounty shall my pains beguile;
　The barren wilderness shall smile
　With sudden greens and herbage crowned
　And streams shall murmur all around.

p   4 Though in the paths of death I tread,
       With gloomy horrors overspread,
mf   My steadfast heart shall fear no ill,
       For thou, O Lord, art with me still:
       Thy friendly crook shall give me aid,
       And guide me through the dreadful shade.

180
Anne Steele†

1 FATHER, whate'er of earthly bliss
     Thy sovereign will denies,
Accepted at thy throne of grace
     Let this petition rise:

2 Give me a calm and thankful heart,
     From every murmur free;
The blessings of thy grace impart,
     And let me live to thee.

3 Let the sweet hope that thou art mine
     My path of life attend;
Thy presence through my journey shine,
     And crown my journey's end.

181
W. Cowper

1 GOD moves in a mysterious way
     His wonders to perform;
He plants his footsteps in the sea,
     And rides upon the storm.

2 Deep in unfathomable mines
     Of never-failing skill
He treasures up his bright designs,
     And works his sovereign will.

3 Ye fearful saints, fresh courage take;
     The clouds ye so much dread
Are big with mercy, and shall break
     In blessings on your head.

4 Judge not the Lord by feeble sense,
    But trust him for his grace;
Behind a frowning providence
    He hides a smiling face.

5 His purposes will ripen fast,
    Unfolding every hour;
The bud may have a bitter taste,
    But sweet will be the flower.

6 Blind unbelief is sure to err,
    And scan his work in vain;
God is his own interpreter,
    And he will make it plain.

182   *Mrs. L. M. Willis* (1864)

1 FATHER, hear the prayer we offer:
    Not for ease that prayer shall be,
But for strength that we may ever
    Live our lives courageously.

2 Not for ever in green pastures
    Do we ask our way to be;
But the steep and rugged pathway
    May we tread rejoicingly.

3 Not for ever by still waters
    Would we idly rest and stay;
But would smite the living fountains
    From the rocks along our way.

4 Be our strength in hours of weakness,
    In our wanderings be our guide;
Through endeavour, failure, danger,
    Father, be thou at our side.

183

M. Luther. Tr. T. Carlyle

Ein' feste Burg

1 A SAFE stronghold our God is still,
   A trusty shield and weapon;
He'll keep us clear from all the ill
   That hath us now o'ertaken.
      The ancient prince of hell
      Hath risen with purpose fell;
      Strong mail of craft and power
      He weareth in this hour;
   On earth is not his fellow.

2 With force of arms we nothing can,
   Full soon were we down-ridden;
But for us fights the proper Man,
   Whom God himself hath bidden.
      Ask ye, Who is this same?
      Christ Jesus is his name,
      The Lord Sabaoth's Son;
      He, and no other one,
   Shall conquer in the battle.

3 And were this world all devils o'er,
   And watching to devour us,
We lay it not to heart so sore;
   Not they can overpower us.
      And let the prince of ill
      Look grim as e'er he will,
      He harms us not a whit;
      For why?—his doom is writ;
   A word shall quickly slay him.

4 God's word, for all their craft and force,
   One moment will not linger,
But, spite of hell, shall have its course;
   'Tis written by his finger.
      And though they take our life,
      Goods, honour, children, wife,
      Yet is their profit small;
      These things shall vanish all:
   The City of God remaineth!

184   *J. G. Whittier*

1 DEAR Lord and Father of mankind,
     Forgive our foolish ways!
Re-clothe us in our rightful mind,
     In purer lives thy service find,
     In deeper reverence praise.

2 In simple trust like theirs who heard,
     Beside the Syrian sea,
The gracious calling of the Lord,
Let us, like them, without a word
     Rise up and follow thee.

3 *O Sabbath rest by Galilee!
     O calm of hills above,
Where Jesus knelt to share with thee
     The silence of eternity,
     Interpreted by love!

4 Drop thy still dews of quietness,
     Till all our strivings cease;
Take from our souls the strain and stress,
And let our ordered lives confess
     The beauty of thy peace.

5 Breathe through the heats of our desire
     Thy coolness and thy balm;
Let sense be dumb, let flesh retire;
Speak through the earthquake, wind, and
     O still small voice of calm!   [fire,

185   *Cardinal J. H. Newman*

f   1 PRAISE to the Holiest in the height,
     And in the depth be praise:
In all his words most wonderful,
     Most sure in all his ways.

mf 2 O loving wisdom of our God!
  When all was sin and shame,
  A second Adam to the fight
  And to the rescue came.

3 O wisest love! that flesh and blood,
  Which did in Adam fail,
  Should strive afresh against the foe,
  Should strive and should prevail;

4 And that a higher gift than grace
  Should flesh and blood refine,
  God's presence and his very self,
  And essence all-divine.

5 O generous love! that he, who smote
  In Man for man the foe,
  The double agony in Man
  For man should undergo;

p 6 And in the garden secretly,
  And on the Cross on high,
  Should teach his brethren, and inspire
  To suffer and to die.

f 7 Praise to the Holiest in the height,
  And in the depth be praise:
  In all his words most wonderful,
  Most sure in all his ways.

186
         Cardinal J. H. Newman

1 FIRMLY I believe and truly
  God is Three and God is One;
  And I next acknowledge duly
  Manhood taken by the Son.

2 And I trust and hope most fully
  In that Manhood crucified;
  And each thought and deed unruly
  Do to death, as he has died.

3 Simply to his grace and wholly
    Light and life and strength belong,
And I love supremely, solely,
    Him the Holy, him the Strong.

4 And I hold in veneration,
    For the love of him alone,
Holy Church as his creation,
    And her teachings as his own.

5 Adoration ay be given,
    With and through the angelic host,
To the God of earth and heaven,
    Father, Son, and Holy Ghost.

187
          Ascribed to Thomas à Kempis
                    Tr. B. Webb‡

O amor quam ecstaticus

mf 1 O LOVE, how deep, how broad, how high!
    It fills the heart with ecstasy,
    That God, the Son of God, should take
    Our mortal form for mortals' sake.

2 He sent no angel to our race
    Of higher or of lower place,
    But wore the robe of human frame
    Himself, and to this lost world came.

3 For us he was baptized, and bore
    His holy fast, and hungered sore;
    For us temptations sharp he knew;
    For us the tempter overthrew.

p 4 For us to wicked men betrayed,
    Scourged, mocked, in purple robe arrayed,
    He bore the shameful Cross and death;
    For us at length gave up his breath.

f 5 For us he rose from death again,
    For us he went on high to reign,
    For us he sent his Spirit here,
    To guide, to strengthen, and to cheer.

6 To him whose boundless love has won
   Salvation for us through his Son,
   To God the Father, glory be
   Both now and through eternity.

188
                        c. 12th cent. Tr. J. M. Neale
                                 and Compilers

Jesu dulcis memoria

1 JESU! the very thought is sweet;
   In that dear name all heart-joys meet;
   But O, than honey sweeter far
   The glimpses of his presence are.

2 No word is sung more sweet than this,
   No sound is heard more full of bliss,
   No thought brings sweeter comfort nigh,
   Than Jesus, Son of God most high.

3 Jesu, the hope of souls forlorn,
   How good to them for sin that mourn!
   To them that seek thee, O how kind!
   But what art thou to them that find?

4 No tongue of mortal can express,
   No pen can write, the blessedness:
   He only who hath proved it knows
   What bliss from love of Jesus flows.

5*O Jesu, King of wondrous might!
   O Victor, glorious from the fight!
   Sweetness that may not be exprest,
   And altogether loveliest!

6 Abide with us, O Lord, to-day,
   Fulfil us with thy grace, we pray;
   And with thine own true sweetness feed
   Our souls from sin and darkness freed.

189   *c. 12th cent. Tr. E. Caswall*‡

Jesu dulcis memoria

1 JESU, the very thought of thee
  With sweetness fills the breast;
But sweeter far thy face to see,
  And in thy presence rest.

2 No voice can sing, no heart can frame,
  Nor can the memory find,
A sweeter sound than Jesu's name,
  The Saviour of mankind.

3 O hope of every contrite heart,
  O joy of all the meek,
To those who ask how kind thou art,
  How good to those who seek!

4 But what to those who find? Ah, this
  Nor tongue nor pen can show;
The love of Jesus, what it is
  None but his loved ones know.

5 Jesu, our only joy be thou,
  As thou our prize wilt be;
In thee be all our glory now,
  And through eternity.

PART 2

6 O Jesu, King most wonderful,
  Thou Conqueror renowned,
Thou sweetness most ineffable,
  In whom all joys are found!

7 When once thou visitest the heart,
  Then truth begins to shine,
Then earthly vanities depart,
  Then kindles love divine.

8 Thee, Jesu, may our voices bless,
    Thee may we love alone,
And ever in our lives express
    The image of thine own.

9 Abide with us, and let thy light
    Shine, Lord, on every heart;
Dispel the darkness of our night,
    And joy to all impart.

10 Jesu, our love and joy, to thee,
    The Virgin's holy Son,
All might and praise and glory be
    While endless ages run.

190
        c. 15*th cent. Tr. J. M. Neale*
        and Compilers

Gloriosi Salvatoris

1 TO the name of our salvation
    Laud and honour let us pay,
Which for many a generation
    Hid in God's foreknowledge lay,
But with holy exultation
    We may sing aloud to-day.

2 Jesus is the name we treasure,
    Name beyond what words can tell;
Name of gladness, name of pleasure,
    Ear and heart delighting well;
Name of sweetness passing measure,
    Saving us from sin and hell.

3*'Tis the name for adoration,
    Name for songs of victory,
Name for holy meditation
    In this vale of misery,
Name for joyful veneration
    By the citizens on high.

4 'Tis the name that whoso preacheth
 Speaks like music to the ear;
Who in prayer this name beseecheth
 Sweetest comfort findeth near;
Who its perfect wisdom reacheth
 Heavenly joy possesseth here.

5 Jesus is the name exalted
 Over every other name;
In this name, whene'er assaulted,
 We can put our foes to shame:
Strength to them who else had halted,
 Eyes to blind, and feet to lame.

6 Therefore we in love adoring
 This most blessèd name revere,
Holy Jesu, thee imploring
 So to write it in us here,
That hereafter heavenward soaring
 We may sing with angels there.

191   *18th cent. Tr. J. Chandler*
            and Compilers

Victis sibi cognomina

1 CONQUERING kings their titles take
From the foes they captive make:
 Jesus, by a nobler deed,
 From the thousands he hath freed.

2 Yes, none other name is given
Unto mortals under heaven,
 Which can make the dead arise,
 And exalt them to the skies.

3 That which Christ so hardly wrought,
That which he so dearly bought,
 That salvation, brethren, say,
 Shall we madly cast away?

4 Rather gladly for that name
   Bear the cross, endure the shame:
   Joyfully for him to die
   Is not death but victory.

5 Jesu, who dost condescend
   To be called the sinner's friend,
   Hear us, as to thee we pray,
   Glorying in thy name to-day.

6 Glory to the Father be,
   Glory, holy Son, to thee
   Glory to the Holy Ghost,
   From the saints and angel-host.

192
                                    J. Newton†

1 HOW sweet the name of Jesus sounds
   In a believer's ear!
   It soothes his sorrows, heals his wounds,
   And drives away his fear.

2 It makes the wounded spirit whole,
   And calms the troubled breast;
   'Tis manna to the hungry soul,
   And to the weary rest.

3 Dear name! the rock on which I build,
   My shield and hiding-place,
   My never-failing treasury filled
   With boundless stores of grace.

4 Jesus! my Shepherd, Brother, Friend,
   My Prophet, Priest, and King,
   My Lord, my Life, my Way, my End,
   Accept the praise I bring.

5 Weak is the effort of my heart,
   And cold my warmest thought;
   But when I see thee as thou art,
   I'll praise thee as I ought.

6 Till then I would thy love proclaim
    With every fleeting breath;
And may the music of thy name
    Refresh my soul in death.

193   *C. Wesley*

mf 1 JESU, lover of my soul,
        Let me to thy bosom fly,
    While the gathering waters roll,
        While the tempest still is high:
    Hide me, O my Saviour, hide,
        Till the storm of life is past;
    Safe into the haven guide,
        O receive my soul at last.

p 2 Other refuge have I none;
        Hangs my helpless soul on thee;
    Leave, ah, leave me not alone,
        Still support and comfort me.
    All my trust on thee is stayed,
        All my help from thee I bring;
    Cover my defenceless head
        With the shadow of thy wing.

f 3 Plenteous grace with thee is found,
        Grace to cleanse from every sin;
    Let the healing streams abound;
        Make and keep me pure within:
    Thou of life the fountain art;
        Freely let me take of thee;
    Spring thou up within my heart,
        Rise to all eternity.

194   *G. R. Prynne*

p 1 JESU, meek and gentle,
        Son of God most high,
    Pitying, loving Saviour,
        Hear thy children's cry.

2 Pardon our offences,
    Loose our captive chains,
      Break down every idol
        Which our soul detains.

mf 3 Give us holy freedom,
    Fill our hearts with love,
      Draw us, holy Jesus,
        To the realms above.

4 Lead us on our journey,
    Be thyself the Way
      Through terrestrial darkness
        To celestial day.

p 5 Jesu, meek and gentle,
    Son of God most high,
      Pitying, loving Saviour,
        Hear thy children's cry.

95   *C. Wesley†*

1 O LOVE divine, how sweet thou art!
  When shall I find my longing heart
    All taken up by thee?
 I thirst, I faint and die to prove
 The greatness of redeeming love,
  The love of Christ to me.

2 Stronger his love than death or hell;
  Its riches are unsearchable:
    The first-born sons of light
 Desire in vain its depth to see;
 They cannot reach the mystery,
  The length and breadth and height.

3*God only knows the love of God;
  O that it now were shed abroad
    In this poor stony heart!
 For love I sigh, for love I pine;
 This only portion, Lord, be mine,
  Be mine this better part.

4 For ever would I take my seat
With Mary at the Master's feet:
    Be this my happy choice;
My only care, delight, and bliss,
My joy, my heaven on earth, be this,
    To hear the Bridegroom's voice.

196
C. Wesle

1 O FOR a thousand tongues to sing
    My dear Redeemer's praise,
The glories of my God and King,
    The triumphs of his grace!

2 Jesus! the name that charms our fears,
    That bids our sorrows cease;
'Tis music in the sinner's ears,
    'Tis life and health and peace.

3 He speaks; and, listening to his voice,
    New life the dead receive,
The mournful broken hearts rejoice,
    The humble poor believe.

4 Hear him, ye deaf; his praise, ye dumb,
    Your loosened tongues employ;
Ye blind, behold your Saviour come;
    And leap, ye lame, for joy!

5 My gracious Master and my God,
    Assist me to proclaim
And spread through all the earth abroad
    The honours of thy name.

197   Ps. 23
Sir H. W. Bake

mf 1 THE King of love my Shepherd is,
        Whose goodness faileth never;
    I nothing lack if I am his
        And he is mine for ever.

2 Where streams of living water flow
   My ransomed soul he leadeth,
   And where the verdant pastures grow
   With food celestial feedeth.

3 Perverse and foolish oft I strayed,
   But yet in love he sought me,
   And on his shoulder gently laid,
   And home rejoicing brought me.

p 4 In death's dark vale I fear no ill
      With thee, dear Lord, beside me;
      Thy rod and staff my comfort still,
      Thy Cross before to guide me.

mf 5 Thou spread'st a table in my sight;
       Thy unction grace bestoweth;
       And O what transport of delight
       From thy pure chalice floweth!

f 6 And so through all the length of days
      Thy goodness faileth never:
      Good Shepherd, may I sing thy praise
      Within thy house for ever.

198   18th cent. *Tr. E. Caswall and Compilers*
                    Summi Parentis Filio

mf 1 TO Christ, the Prince of Peace,
         And Son of God most high,
      The Father of the world to come,
         We lift our joyful cry.

p 2 Deep in his heart for us
        The wound of love he bore,
      That love which he enkindles still
        In hearts that him adore.

mf 3 O Jesu, Victim blest,
         What else but love divine
      Could thee constrain to open thus
         That sacred heart of thine?

4 O wondrous fount of love,
O well of waters free,
O heavenly flame, refining fire,
O burning charity!

p 5 Hide us in thy dear heart,
Jesu, our Saviour blest,
mf So shall we find thy plenteous grace,
And heaven's eternal rest.

199

Bishop G. W. Doane

mf 1 THOU art the Way: by thee alone‿
From sin and death we flee;
And he who would the Father seek
Must seek him, Lord, by thee.

2 Thou art the Truth: thy word alone‿
True wisdom can impart;
Thou only canst inform the mind
And purify the heart.

f 3 Thou art the Life: the rending tomb‿
Proclaims thy conquering arm;
And those who put their trust in thee
Nor death nor hell shall harm.

mf 4 Thou art the Way, the Truth, the Life:
Grant us that Way to know,
That Truth to keep, that Life to win,
Whose joys eternal flow.

200

Bishop Synesius of Cyrene
Tr. A. W. Chatfield†
μνώεο Χριστέ

1 LORD Jesus, think on me,
And purge away my sin;
From earthborn passions set me free,
And make me pure within.

2   Lord Jesus, think on me
        With many a care opprest;
    Let me thy loving servant be,
        And taste thy promised rest.

3   Lord Jesus, think on me,
        Nor let me go astray;
    Through darkness and perplexity
        Point thou the heavenly way.

4   Lord Jesus, think on me,
        That, when the flood is past,
    I may the eternal brightness see,
        And share thy joy at last.

201   *Cento from* Jesu, dulcis memoria
                                        Tr. E. Caswall
                 Amor, Jesu dulcissime

1   JESU, thy mercies are untold
        Through each returning day;
    Thy love exceeds a thousandfold
        Whatever we can say:

2   That love which in thy Passion drained
        For us thy precious Blood;
    That love whereby the saints have gained
        The vision of their God.

3   'Tis thou hast loved us from the womb,
        Pure source of all our bliss,
    Our only hope of life to come,
        Our happiness in this.

4   Lord, grant us, while on earth we stay,
        Thy love to feel and know;
    And, when from hence we pass away,
        To us thy glory show.

202

H. Collins†

mf 1 JESU, my Lord, my God, my all,
Hear me, blest Saviour, when I call;
Hear me, and from thy dwelling-place
Pour down the riches of thy grace.
    Jesu, my Lord, I thee adore,
    O make me love thee more and more.

p 2 Jesu, too late I thee have sought:
mf How can I love thee as I ought?
And how extol thy matchless fame,
The glorious beauty of thy name?
    Jesu, my Lord, etc.

p 3 Jesu, what didst thou find in me,
That thou hast dealt so lovingly?
f How great the joy that thou hast brought,
So far exceeding hope or thought!
mf   Jesu, my Lord, etc.

f 4 Jesu, of thee shall be my song,
To thee my heart and soul belong;
All that I have or am is thine,
And thou, blest Saviour, thou art mine.
mf   Jesu, my Lord, etc.

203

J. Scheffler. Tr. Catherine Winkworth†
Liebe, die du mich zum Bilde

mf 1 O LOVE, who formedst me to wear⌣
The image of thy Godhead here;
Who soughtest me with tender care
    Through all my wanderings wild and
O Love, I give myself to thee,   [drear:
Thine ever, only thine to be.

2 O Love, who ere life's earliest dawn
On me thy choice hast gently laid;
O Love, who here as Man wast born,
    And wholly like to us wast made:
O Love, etc.

p 3 O Love, who once in time wast slain,
  Pierced through and through with bitter
    woe;
  O Love, who wrestling thus didst gain
  That we eternal joy might know:
mf O Love, etc.

f 4 O Love, who once shalt bid me rise
  From out this dying life of ours;
  O Love, who once o'er yonder skies
  Shalt set me in the fadeless bowers:
  O Love, etc.

204
            M. Bruce

nf 1 WHERE high the heavenly temple stands,
  The house of God not made with hands,
  A great High Priest our nature wears,
  The guardian of mankind appears.

  2 He who for men their surety stood,
  And poured on earth his precious Blood,
  Pursues in heaven his mighty plan,
  The Saviour and the Friend of man.

  3 Though now ascended up on high,
  He bends on earth a brother's eye;
  Partaker of the human name,
  He knows the frailty of our frame.

  4 In every pang that rends the heart
  The Man of Sorrows had a part;
  He sympathizes with our grief,
  And to the sufferer sends relief.

nf 5 With boldness therefore at the throne
  Let us make all our sorrows known;
  And ask the aid of heavenly power
  To help us in the evil hour.

205

C. Wesley†

mf 1 LOVE divine, all loves excelling,
　　　Joy of heaven, to earth come down,
　　Fix in us thy humble dwelling,
　　　All thy faithful mercies crown.
　　Jesu, thou art all compassion,
　　　Pure unbounded love thou art;
　　Visit us with thy salvation,
　　　Enter every trembling heart.

2 Come, almighty to deliver,
　　　Let us all thy grace receive;
　　Suddenly return, and never,
　　　Never more thy temple leave.
　　Thee we would be always blessing,
　　　Serve thee as thy hosts above;
　　Pray, and praise thee, without ceasing,
　　　Glory in thy perfect love.

f 3 Finish then thy new creation:
　　　Pure and spotless let us be;
　　Let us see thy great salvation,
　　　Perfectly restored in thee;
　　Changed from glory into glory,
　　　Till in heaven we take our place,
　　Till we cast our crowns before thee,
　　　Lost in wonder, love, and praise.

206

Count N. L. Zinzendorf
Tr. Jane L. Borthwick

Jesu, geh' voran

mf 1 JESUS, still lead on,
　　　Till our rest be won,
　　And, although the way be cheerless,
　　We will follow calm and fearless;
　　　Guide us by thy hand
　　　To our fatherland.

p 2 If the way be drear,
  If the foe be near,
 Let not faithless fears o'ertake us,
 Let not faith and hope forsake us;
  For, through many a foe,
  To our home we go.

mf 3 Jesus, still lead on,
  Till our rest be won;
 Heavenly leader, still direct us,
 Still support, console, protect us,
  Till we safely stand
  In our fatherland.

207

S. C. Lowry

1 SON of God, eternal Saviour,
 Source of life and truth and grace,
Son of Man, whose birth incarnate
 Hallows all our human race,
Thou, our Head, who, throned in glory,
 For thine own dost ever plead,
Fill us with thy love and pity;
 Heal our wrongs, and help our need.

2 As thou, Lord, hast lived for others,
 So may we for others live;
Freely have thy gifts been granted,
 Freely may thy servants give:
Thine the gold and thine the silver,
 Thine the wealth of land and sea,
We but stewards of thy bounty,
 Held in solemn trust for thee.

3 Come, O Christ, and reign among us,
 King of love, and Prince of Peace;
Hush the storm of strife and passion,
 Bid its cruel discords cease;
By thy patient years of toiling,
 By thy silent hours of pain,
Quench our fevered thirst of pleasure,
 Shame our selfish greed of gain.

4 Son of God, eternal Saviour,
    Source of life and truth and grace,
Son of Man, whose birth incarnate
    Hallows all our human race,
Thou who prayedst, thou who willest,
    That thy people should be one,
Grant, O grant our hope's fruition:
    Here on earth thy will be done.

208   *J. G. Whittier*

1 IMMORTAL love for ever full,
    For ever flowing free,
For ever shared, for ever whole,
    A never-ebbing sea!

2 Our outward lips confess the name
    All other names above;
Love only knoweth whence it came
    And comprehendeth love.

3 We may not climb the heavenly steeps
    To bring the Lord Christ down;
In vain we search the lowest deeps,
    For him no depths can drown:

4 But warm, sweet, tender, even yet
    A present help is he;
And faith has still its Olivet,
    And love its Galilee.

5 The healing of his seamless dress
    Is by our beds of pain;
We touch him in life's throng and press,
    And we are whole again.

6*Through him the first fond prayers are said
    Our lips of childhood frame;
The last low whispers of our dead
    Are burdened with his name.

7 Alone, O Love ineffable,
 Thy saving name is given;
To turn aside from thee is hell,
 To walk with thee is heaven.

209   *Sir E. Denny†*

mf 1 LIGHT of the lonely pilgrim's heart,
 Star of the coming day,
Arise, and with thy morning beams
 Chase all our griefs away.

f 2 Come, blessèd Lord, bid every shore⌣
 And answering island sing
The praises of thy royal name,
 And own thee as their King.

3 Bid the whole world, responsive now⌣
 To the bright world above,
Break forth in rapturous strains of joy
 In answer to thy love.

mf 4 Jesus, thy fair creation groans—
 The air, the earth, the sea—
In unison with all our hearts,
 And calls aloud for thee.

5 Thine was the Cross, with all its fruits⌣
 Of grace and peace divine:
f Be thine the crown of glory now,
 The palm of victory thine.

210   *A. M. Toplady†*

mf 1 ROCK of ages, cleft for me,
 Let me hide myself in thee;
Let the water and the blood,
From thy riven side which flowed,
Be of sin the double cure:
Cleanse me from its guilt and power.

2 Not the labours of my hands
Can fulfil thy law's demands;
Could my zeal no respite know,
Could my tears for ever flow,
All for sin could not atone:
Thou must save, and thou alone.

p   3 Nothing in my hand I bring,
Simply to thy Cross I cling;
Naked, come to thee for dress;
Helpless, look to thee for grace;
Foul, I to the fountain fly;
Wash me, Saviour, or I die.

4 While I draw this fleeting breath,
When my eyelids close in death,
When I soar through tracts unknown,
See thee on thy judgement throne;
mf   Rock of ages, cleft for me,
Let me hide myself in thee.

211   *17th cent. Tr. Sir H. W. Baker†*

Dignare me, O Jesu, rogo te

1 JESU, grant me this, I pray,
Ever in thy heart to stay;
Let me evermore abide
Hidden in thy wounded side.

2 If the world or Satan lay
Tempting snares about my way,
I am safe when I abide
In thy heart and wounded side.

3 If the flesh, more dangerous still,
Tempt my soul to deeds of ill,
Naught I fear when I abide
In thy heart and wounded side.

4 Death will come one day to me;
  Jesu, cast me not from thee:
  Dying let me still abide
  In thy heart and wounded side.

212   *M. Bridges and Compilers*

mf 1 BEHOLD the Lamb of God!
p   O thou for sinners slain,
        Let it not be in vain
          That thou hast died:
mf   Thee for my Saviour let me take,
        My only refuge let me make
          Thy piercèd side.

     2 Behold the Lamb of God!
       All hail, incarnate Word,
       Thou everlasting Lord,
         Saviour most blest!
       Fill us with love that never faints,
       Grant us with all thy blessèd saints
         Eternal rest.

     3 Behold the Lamb of God!
f   Worthy is he alone
       To sit upon the throne
         Of God above;
       One with the Ancient of all Days,
       One with the Comforter in praise,
         All Light and Love.

213   *H. Collins*

mf 1 JESU, meek and lowly,
       Saviour, pure and holy,
       On thy love relying
       Hear me humbly crying.

     2 Prince of life and power,
       My salvation's tower,
p   On the Cross I view thee
       Calling sinners to thee.

mf 3 There behold me gazing,
At the sight amazing;
Bending low before thee,
Helpless I adore thee.

p 4 By thy red wounds streaming
With thy life-blood gleaming,
Blood for sinners flowing,
Pardon free bestowing;

mf 5 By that fount of blessing,
Thy dear love expressing,
All my aching sadness
Turn thou into gladness.

6 Lord, in mercy guide me,
Be thou e'er beside me;
In thy ways direct me,
'Neath thy wings protect me.

214
Mrs. C. F. Alexander

mf 1 THERE is a green hill far away,
Without a city wall,
p Where the dear Lord was crucified,
Who died to save us all.

mf 2 We may not know, we cannot tell,
What pains he had to bear,
But we believe it was for us
He hung and suffered there.

3 He died that we might be forgiven,
He died to make us good,
That we might go at last to heaven,
Saved by his precious Blood.

4 There was no other good enough
To pay the price of sin;
He only could unlock the gate
Of heaven, and let us in.

5 O dearly, dearly has he loved,
  And we must love him too,
  And trust in his redeeming Blood,
  And try his works to do.

215 *T. Kelly*

1 WE sing the praise of him who died,
  Of him who died upon the Cross;
  The sinner's hope let men deride,
  For this we count the world but loss.

2 Inscribed upon the Cross we see
  In shining letters, 'God is love;'
  He bears our sins upon the Tree;
  He brings us mercy from above.

3 The Cross! it takes our guilt away;
  It holds the fainting spirit up;
  It cheers with hope the gloomy day,
  And sweetens every bitter cup.

4 It makes the coward spirit brave,
  And nerves the feeble arm for fight;
  It takes its terror from the grave,
  And gilds the bed of death with light:

5 The balm of life, the cure of woe,
  The measure and the pledge of love,
  The sinner's refuge here below,
  The angels' theme in heaven above.

216 *C. Wesley*

f 1 REJOICE! the Lord is King!
  Your Lord and King adore;
  Mortals, give thanks and sing,
  And triumph evermore:
  Lift up your heart, lift up your voice;
  Rejoice, again I say, rejoice.

mf 2 Jesus, the Saviour, reigns,
  The God of truth and love;
  When he had purged our stains,
   He took his seat above:
f Lift up your heart, etc.

mf 3 His kingdom cannot fail;
  He rules o'er earth and heaven;
  The keys of death and hell
   Are to our Jesus given:
f Lift up your heart, etc.

mf 4 He sits at God's right hand
  Till all his foes submit,
  And bow to his command,
   And fall beneath his feet:
f Lift up your heart, etc.

217
E. Perronet ‡

f 1 ALL hail the power of Jesus' name!
  Let angels prostrate fall;
  Bring forth the royal diadem
  And crown him Lord of all.

mf 2 Crown him, ye morning stars of light,
  Who fixed this floating ball;
  Now hail the Strength of Israel's might,
f   And crown him Lord of all.

mf 3 Crown him, ye martyrs of your God,
  Who from his altar call;
  Extol the Stem-of-Jesse's Rod,
f   And crown him Lord of all.

mf 4 Ye seed of Israel's chosen race,
  Ye ransomed of the fall,
  Hail him who saves you by his grace,
f   And crown him Lord of all.

p   5 Sinners, whose love can ne'er forget
          The wormwood and the gall,
mf   Go spread your trophies at his feet,
f   And crown him Lord of all.

      6 Let every tribe and every tongue
          Before him prostrate fall,
        And shout in universal song
          The crownèd Lord of all.

218
                                    T. Kelly

f   1 THE head that once was crowned with
          Is crowned with glory now: [thorns
        A royal diadem adorns
          The mighty Victor's brow.

      2 The highest place that heaven affords
          Is his, is his by right,
        The King of Kings, and Lord of Lords,
          And heaven's eternal Light;

mf 3 The joy of all who dwell above,
          The joy of all below,
        To whom he manifests his love,
          And grants his name to know.

p   4 To them the Cross, with all its shame,
          With all its grace, is given:
f   Their name an everlasting name,
          Their joy the joy of heaven.

p   5 They suffer with their Lord below,
f   They reign with him above;
        Their profit and their joy to know
          The mystery of his love.

mf 6 The Cross he bore is life and health,
          Though shame and death to him;
f   His people's hope, his people's wealth,
          Their everlasting theme.

219 *J. Montgomery*

f 1 HAIL to the Lord's Anointed,
 Great David's greater Son!
Hail, in the time appointed,
 His reign on earth begun!
He comes to break oppression,
 To set the captive free,
To take away transgression,
 And rule in equity.

2*He comes with succour speedy
 To those who suffer wrong;
To help the poor and needy,
 And bid the weak be strong;
To give them songs for sighing,
 Their darkness turn to light,
Whose souls, condemned and dying,
 Were precious in his sight.

mf 3 He shall come down like showers
 Upon the fruitful earth,
And love, joy, hope, like flowers,
 Spring in his path to birth:
Before him on the mountains
 Shall peace, the herald, go;
And righteousness in fountains
 From hill to valley flow.

4*Arabia's desert-ranger
 To him shall bow the knee;
The Ethiopian stranger
 His glory come to see;
With offerings of devotion
 Ships from the isles shall meet,
To pour the wealth of ocean
 In tribute at his feet.

5 Kings shall bow down before him,
    And gold and incense bring;
All nations shall adore him,
    His praise all people sing:
To him shall prayer unceasing
    And daily vows ascend;
His kingdom still increasing,
    A kingdom without end.

f 6 O'er every foe victorious,
    He on his throne shall rest;
From age to age more glorious,
    All-blessing and all-blest:
The tide of time shall never
    His covenant remove;
His name shall stand for ever,
    His changeless name of Love.

220   *I. Watts*†

1 JESUS shall reign where'er the sun
    Does his successive journeys run;
His kingdom stretch from shore to shore,
Till moons shall wax and wane no more.

2 People and realms of every tongue
    Dwell on his love with sweetest song,
And infant voices shall proclaim
    Their early blessings on his name.

3 Blessings abound where'er he reigns:
    The prisoner leaps to lose his chains;
The weary find eternal rest,
And all the sons of want are blest.

4*To him shall endless prayer be made,
    And praises throng to crown his head;
His name like incense shall arise
With every morning sacrifice.

5 Let every creature rise and bring
  Peculiar honours to our King;
Angels descend with songs again,
  And earth repeat the loud Amen.

221   *I. Watts†*

f   1 COME, let us join our cheerful songs
    With angels round the throne;
Ten thousand thousand are their tongues,
    But all their joys are one.

2 'Worthy the Lamb that died,' they cry,
    'To be exalted thus;'
'Worthy the Lamb,' our lips reply,
    'For he was slain for us.'

mf 3 Jesus is worthy to receive
    Honour and power divine;
And blessings, more than we can give,
    Be, Lord, for ever thine.

f   4 Let all creation join in one
  To bless the sacred name
Of him that sits upon the throne,
    And to adore the Lamb.

222   *J. Hupton and J. M. Neale†*

f   1 COME, ye faithful, raise the anthem,
    Cleave the skies with shouts of praise;
Sing to him who found the ransom,
    Ancient of eternal Days,
God of God, the Word incarnate,
    Whom the heaven of heaven obeys.

mf 2 Ere he raised the lofty mountains,
    Formed the seas, or built the sky,
Love eternal, free, and boundless,
    Moved the Lord of Life to die,
Fore-ordained the Prince of Princes
    For the throne of Calvary.

p   3*There, for us and our redemption,
       See him all his life-blood pour!
mf   There he wins our full salvation,
       Dies that we may die no more;
f   Then, arising, lives for ever,
       Reigning where he was before.

4 High on yon celestial mountains
    Stands his sapphire throne, all bright,
Midst unending Alleluias
    Bursting from the sons of light;
Sion's people tell his praises,
    Victor after hard-won fight.

mf 5 Bring your harps, and bring your incense,
      Sweep the string and pour the lay;
f   Let the earth proclaim his wonders,
      King of that celestial day;
He the Lamb once slain is worthy,
    Who was dead, and lives for ay.

6 Laud and honour to the Father,
    Laud and honour to the Son,
Laud and honour to the Spirit,
    Ever Three and ever One,
Consubstantial, co-eternal,
    While unending ages run.

223   *19th cent. Tr. E. Caswall*

Beim frühen Morgenlicht

1 WHEN morning gilds the skies,
My heart awaking cries,
    May Jesus Christ be praised:
Alike at work and prayer
To Jesus I repair;
    May Jesus Christ be praised.

2 Whene'er the sweet church bell
  Peals over hill and dell,
          May Jesus Christ be praised:
  O hark to what it sings,
  As joyously it rings,
          May Jesus Christ be praised.

3 My tongue shall never tire
  Of chanting with the choir,
          May Jesus Christ be praised:
  This song of sacred joy,
  It never seems to cloy,
          May Jesus Christ be praised.

4 Does sadness fill my mind?
  A solace here I find,
          May Jesus Christ be praised:
  Or fades my earthly bliss?
  My comfort still is this,
          May Jesus Christ be praised.

5*The night becomes as day,
  When from the heart we say,
          May Jesus Christ be praised:
  The powers of darkness fear,
  When this sweet chant they hear,
          May Jesus Christ be praised.

6 Be this, while life is mine,
  My canticle divine,
          May Jesus Christ be praised:
  Be this the eternal song
  Through ages all along,
          May Jesus Christ be praised.

224   *M. Bridges* ‡

f 1   CROWN him with many crowns,
          The Lamb upon his throne;
    Hark! how the heavenly anthem drowns
          All music but its own:
          Awake, my soul, and sing
          Of him who died for thee,
    And hail him as thy matchless King
          Through all eternity.

mf 2   Crown him the Virgin's Son,
          The God incarnate born,
p   Whose arm those crimson trophies won
          Which now his brow adorn:
          Fruit of the mystic Rose,
          As of that Rose the Stem;
    The Root whence mercy ever flows,
          The Babe of Bethlehem.

mf 3   Crown him the Lord of love;
p   Behold his hands and side,
    Those wounds yet visible above
          In beauty glorified:
          No angel in the sky
          Can fully bear that sight,
    But downward bends his burning eye
          At mysteries so bright.

mf 4   Crown him the Lord of peace,
f   Whose power a sceptre sways
    From pole to pole, that wars may cease,
          And all be prayer and praise:
          His reign shall know no end,
mf   And round his piercèd feet
    Fair flowers of Paradise extend
          Their fragrance ever sweet.

f 5 Crown him the Lord of years,
    The Potentate of time,
 Creator of the rolling spheres,
    Ineffably sublime:
    All hail, Redeemer, hail!
    For thou hast died for me;
 Thy praise shall never, never fail
    Throughout eternity.

*Note.—The expression 'mystic Rose' in verse 2,
line 5, is a medieval title for the Blessed Virgin, and
is combined here with a reference to Isaiah II. 1.*

225

       Caroline M. Noel

mf 1 AT the name of Jesus
    Every knee shall bow,
   Every tongue confess him
    King of glory now:
   'Tis the Father's pleasure
    We should call him Lord,
   Who from the beginning
    Was the mighty Word.

f 2*At his voice creation
    Sprang at once to sight,
   All the angel faces,
    All the hosts of light,
   Thrones and Dominations,
    Stars upon their way,
   All the heavenly orders,
    In their great array.

p 3 Humbled for a season,
    To receive a name
   From the lips of sinners
    Unto whom he came,
mf Faithfully he bore it
    Spotless to the last,
   Brought it back victorious,
    When from death he passed:

f   4 Bore it up triumphant
      With its human light,
  Through all ranks of creatures,
      To the central height,
  To the throne of Godhead,
      To the Father's breast;
  Filled it with the glory
      Of that perfect rest.

f   5 Name him, brothers, name him,
      With love as strong as death,
p   But with awe and wonder
      And with bated breath:
mf   He is God the Saviour,
      He is Christ the Lord,
  Ever to be worshipped,
      Trusted, and adored.

    6*In your hearts enthrone him;
      There let him subdue
  All that is not holy,
      All that is not true:
  Crown him as your Captain
      In temptation's hour;
  Let his will enfold you
      In its light and power.

f   7 Brothers, this Lord Jesus
      Shall return again,
  With his Father's glory,
      With his angel train;
  For all wreaths of empire
      Meet upon his brow,
  And our hearts confess him
      King of glory now.

226   *C. Wesley*

1 YE servants of God, your Master proclaim,
   And publish abroad his wonderful name;
   The name all-victorious of Jesus extol:
   His Kingdom is glorious, and rules over all.

2 God ruleth on high, almighty to save;
   And still he is nigh: his presence we have.
   The great congregation his triumph shall sing,
   Ascribing salvation to Jesus our King.

3 Salvation to God who sits on the throne!
   Let all cry aloud, and honour the Son.
   The praises of Jesus the angels proclaim,
   Fall down on their faces, and worship the
       Lamb.

4 Then let us adore, and give him his right:
   All glory and power, all wisdom and might,
   And honour and blessing, with angels above,
   And thanks never-ceasing, and infinite love.

227   *L. Tuttiett*

1 O QUICKLY come, dread Judge of all;
       For, aweful though thine advent be,
   All shadows from the truth will fall,
       And falsehood die, in sight of thee:
   O quickly come! for doubt and fear
   Like clouds dissolve when thou art near.

2 O quickly come, great King of all;
       Reign all around us, and within;
   Let sin no more our souls enthral,
       Let pain and sorrow die with sin:
   O quickly come! for thou alone
   Canst make thy scattered people one.

3 O quickly come, true Life of all;
  For death is mighty all around;
On every home his shadows fall,
  On every heart his mark is found:
O quickly come! for grief and pain⏝
Can never cloud thy glorious reign.

4 O quickly come, sure Light of all,
  For gloomy night broods o'er our way;
And weakly souls begin to fall
  With weary watching for the day:
O quickly come! for round thy throne⏝
No eye is blind, no night is known.

228   *Sir Walter Scott. Based on* Dies irae

mf 1 THAT day of wrath, that dreadful day,
  When heaven and earth shall pass away,
  What power shall be the sinner's stay?
  How shall he meet that dreadful day?

f 2 When, shrivelling like a parchèd scroll,
  The flaming heavens together roll;
  When louder yet, and yet more dread,
  Swells the high trump that wakes the dead:

p 3 O on that day, that wrathful day,
  When man to judgement wakes from clay,
  Be thou, O Christ, the sinner's stay,
  Though heaven and earth shall pass away.

229   *P. Doddridge†*

1   YE servants of the Lord,
        Each in his office wait,
      Observant of his heavenly word,
        And watchful at his gate.

2   Let all your lamps be bright,
        And trim the golden flame;
      Gird up your loins as in his sight,
        For aweful is his name.

3 Watch! 'tis your Lord's command,
　And while we speak, he's near;
Mark the first signal of his hand,
　And ready all appear.

4 O happy servant he
　In such a posture found!
He shall his Lord with rapture see,
　And be with honour crowned.

5 Christ shall the banquet spread
　With his own royal hand,
And raise that faithful servant's head
　Amid the angelic band.

230　　　　　　　　　　　　　　*Harriet Auber*

p 1 OUR blest Redeemer, ere he breathed‿
　His tender last farewell,
A guide, a Comforter, bequeathed
　With us to dwell.

mf 2 He came sweet influence to impart,
　A gracious willing guest,
While he can find one humble heart
　Wherein to rest.

p 3 And his that gentle voice we hear,
　Soft as the breath of even,
That checks each fault, that calms each
　And speaks of heaven.　　　　　[fear,

mf 4 And every virtue we possess,
　And every conquest won,
And every thought of holiness,
　Are his alone.

5 Spirit of purity and grace,
　Our weakness, pitying, see:
O make our hearts thy dwelling-place,
　And worthier thee.

231
C. Coffin. Tr. J. Chandler ‡

O fons amoris, Spiritus

mf 1 O HOLY Spirit, Lord of grace,
Eternal fount of love,
Inflame, we pray, our inmost hearts
With fire from heaven above.

2 As thou in bond of love dost join
The Father and the Son,
So fill us all with mutual love,
And knit our hearts in one.

f 3 All glory to the Father be,
All glory to the Son,
All glory, Holy Ghost, to thee,
While endless ages run.

232
S. Browne and others

1 COME, gracious Spirit, heavenly Dove,
With light and comfort from above;
Be thou our guardian, thou our guide,
O'er every thought and step preside.

2 The light of truth to us display,
And make us know and choose thy way;
Plant holy fear in every heart,
That we from God may ne'er depart.

3 Lead us to Christ, the living Way,
Nor let us from his pastures stray;
Lead us to holiness, the road
That we must take to dwell with God.

4 Lead us to heaven, that we may share
Fulness of joy for ever there;
Lead us to God, our final rest,
To be with him for ever blest.

233
Bishop Chr. Wordsworth

mf 1 GRACIOUS Spirit, Holy Ghost,
Taught by thee, we covet most
Of thy gifts at Pentecost,
　　Holy, heavenly love.

2 Love is kind, and suffers long,
Love is meek, and thinks no wrong,
Love than death itself more strong;
　　Therefore give us love.

3 Prophecy will fade away,
Melting in the light of day;
Love will ever with us stay;
　　Therefore give us love.

4 Faith will vanish into sight;
Hope be emptied in delight;
Love in heaven will shine more bright;
　　Therefore give us love.

5 Faith and hope and love we see
Joining hand in hand agree;
But the greatest of the three,
　　And the best, is love.

p 6 From the overshadowing
Of thy gold and silver wing
Shed on us, who to thee sing,
　　Holy, heavenly love.

234
Sir H. W. Baker

mf 1 O HOLY Ghost, thy people bless
Who long to feel thy might,
And fain would grow in holiness
As children of the light.

2 To thee we bring, who art the Lord,
    Our selves to be thy throne;
Let every thought and deed and word
    Thy pure dominion own.

3 Life-giving Spirit, o'er us move,
    As on the formless deep;
Give life and order, light and love,
    Where now is death or sleep.

f   4 Great gift of our ascended King,
    His saving truth reveal;
Our tongues inspire his praise to sing,
    Our hearts his love to feel.

mf 5 True wind of heaven, from south or north,
    For joy or chastening, blow;
The garden-spices shall spring forth
    If thou wilt bid them flow.

f   6 O Holy Ghost, of sevenfold might,
    All graces come from thee;
Grant us to know and serve aright
    One God in Persons Three.

235   *Bianco da Siena. Tr. R. F. Littledale*
        Discendi, Amor santo

mf 1 COME down, O Love divine,
    Seek thou this soul of mine,
And visit it with thine own ardour glowing;
    O Comforter, draw near,
    Within my heart appear,
And kindle it, thy holy flame bestowing.

2 O let it freely burn,
    Till earthly passions turn⌣
To dust and ashes in its heat consuming;
f   And let thy glorious light
    Shine ever on my sight,   [illuming.
And clothe me round, the while my path

mf 3   Let holy charity
      Mine outward vesture be,
And lowliness become mine inner clothing :
     True lowliness of heart,
     Which takes the humbler part,
And o'er its own shortcomings weeps with
      loathing.

f   4   And so the yearning strong,
     With which the soul will long,
Shall far outpass the power of human telling ;
     For none can guess its grace,
     Till he become the place
Wherein the Holy Spirit makes his dwelling.

236
E. Hatch

mf 1 BREATHE on me, Breath of God,
     Fill me with life anew,
  That I may love what thou dost love,
    And do what thou wouldst do.

    2 Breathe on me, Breath of God,
      Until my heart is pure ;
   Until with thee I will one will,
     To do and to endure.

    3 Breathe on me, Breath of God,
      Till I am wholly thine ;
   Until this earthly part of me
     Glows with thy fire divine.

    4 Breathe on me, Breath of God :
f   So shall I never die,
   But live with thee the perfect life
     Of thine eternity.

237

Pentecostarion, c. 8th cent.
Tr. J. Brownlie

βασιλεῦ οὐράνιε, Παράκλητε

1 O KING enthroned on high,
 Thou Comforter divine,
Blest Spirit of all truth, be nigh
 And make us thine.

2 Thou art the source of life,
 Thou art our treasure-store;
Give us thy peace, and end our strife
 For evermore.

3 Descend, O heavenly Dove,
 Abide with us alway;
And in the fulness of thy love
 Cleanse us, we pray.

238

Yattendon Hymnal. Based on Amor
Patris et Filii, 12th cent.

1 LOVE of the Father, Love of God the Son,
From whom all came, in whom was all begun;
Who formest heavenly beauty out of strife,
Creation's whole desire and breath of life:

2 Thou the all-holy, thou supreme in might,
Thou dost give peace, thy presence maketh right;
Thou with thy favour all things dost enfold,
With thine all-kindness free from harm wilt hold.

3*Hope of all comfort, splendour of all aid,
That dost not fail nor leave the heart afraid:
To all that cry thou dost all help accord,
The angels' armour, and the saints' reward.

4 Purest and highest, wisest and most just,
  There is no truth save only in thy trust;
  Thou dost the mind from earthly dreams recall,
  And bring, through Christ, to him for whom are
      all.

5 Eternal glory, all men thee adore,
  Who art and shalt be worshipped evermore:
  Us whom thou madest, comfort with thy might,
  And lead us to enjoy thy heavenly light.

239   *A. Reed*

1 SPIRIT divine, attend our prayers,
    And make this house thy home;
  Descend with all thy gracious powers;
    O come, great Spirit, come!

2 Come as the light: to us reveal
    Our emptiness and woe;
  And lead us in those paths of life
    Where all the righteous go.

3 Come as the fire: and purge our hearts
    Like sacrificial flame;
  Let our whole soul an offering be
    To our Redeemer's name.

4 Come as the dew: and sweetly bless
    This consecrated hour;
  May barrenness rejoice to own
    Thy fertilizing power.

5 Come as the dove: and spread thy wings,
    The wings of peaceful love;
  And let thy Church on earth become
    Blest as the Church above.

6 Come as the wind, with rushing sound
    And Pentecostal grace,
That all of woman born may see
    The glory of thy face.

7 Spirit divine, attend our prayers;
    Make a lost world thy home;
Descend with all thy gracious powers;
    O come, great Spirit, come!

240 *Ps. 84*   *H. F. Lyte*

mf 1 PLEASANT are thy courts above
    In the land of light and love;
Pleasant are thy courts below
    In this land of sin and woe:
O, my spirit longs and faints
    For the converse of thy saints,
For the brightness of thy face,
    For thy fulness, God of grace.

2 Happy birds that sing and fly
    Round thy altars, O Most High;
Happier souls that find a rest
    In a heavenly Father's breast!
Like the wandering dove that found
    No repose on earth around,
They can to their ark repair,
    And enjoy it ever there.

3 Happy souls, their praises flow
    Even in this vale of woe;
Waters in the desert rise,
    Manna feeds them from the skies;
f On they go from strength to strength,
    Till they reach thy throne at length,
At thy feet adoring fall,
    Who hast led them safe through all.

p   4 Lord, be mine this prize to win,
      Guide me through a world of sin,
      Keep me by thy saving grace,
      Give me at thy side a place.

mf   Sun and Shield alike thou art;
        Guide and guard my erring heart:

f   Grace and glory flow from thee;
        Shower, O shower them, Lord, on me.

241
Bishop R. Heber

1 HOSANNA to the living Lord!
  Hosanna to the incarnate Word!
  To Christ, Creator, Saviour, King,
  Let earth, let heaven Hosanna sing,
  　　　　　Hosanna in the highest!

2 O Saviour, with protecting care
  Abide in this thy house of prayer,
  Where we thy parting promise claim,
  Assembled in thy sacred name:
  　　　　　Hosanna in the highest!

3 But, chiefest, in our cleansèd breast,
  Eternal, bid thy Spirit rest;
  And make our secret soul to be
  A temple pure and worthy thee:
  　　　　　Hosanna in the highest!

4 To God the Father, God the Son,
  And God the Spirit, Three in One,
  Be honour, praise, and glory given
  By all on earth and all in heaven:
  　　　　　Hosanna in the highest!

242
W. Bullock and Sir H. W. Bake

mf 1 WE love the place, O God,
        Wherein thine honour dwells;
        The joy of thine abode
        All earthly joy excels.

2 It is the house of prayer,
    Wherein thy servants meet;
And thou, O Lord, art there
    Thy chosen flock to greet.

3 We love the sacred font;
    For there the holy Dove
To pour is ever wont‿
    His blessing from above.

4 We love thine altar, Lord;
    O what on earth so dear?
For there, in faith adored,
    We find thy presence near.

5 We love the word of life,
    The word that tells of peace,
Of comfort in the strife,
    And joys that never cease.

f 6 We love to sing below
    For mercies freely given;
But O, we long to know‿
    The triumph-song of heaven.

mf 7 Lord Jesus, give us grace
    On earth to love thee more,
f   In heaven to see thy face,
    And with thy saints adore.

243 *Tr. J. Chandler*†

Angularis fundamentum

mf 1 CHRIST is our Corner-stone,
    On him alone we build;
With his true saints alone
    The courts of heaven are filled:
      On his great love
      Our hopes we place
      Of present grace
    And joys above.

f 2 O then with hymns of praise
    These hallowed courts shall ring;
Our voices we will raise
    The Three in One to sing;
      And thus proclaim
        In joyful song,
        Both loud and long,
      That glorious name.

mf 3 Here, gracious God, do thou
    For evermore draw nigh;
Accept each faithful vow,
    And mark each suppliant sigh;
      In copious shower
        On all who pray
        Each holy day
      Thy blessings pour.

p 4 Here may we gain from heaven
    The grace which we implore;
And may that grace, once given,
    Be with us evermore,
      Until that day
        When all the blest
        To endless rest
      Are called away.

244

C. Coffin. Tr. J. Chandler

O quam juvat fratres, Deus

1 O LORD, how joyful 'tis to see
  The brethren join in love to thee!
On thee alone their heart relies,
  Their only strength thy grace supplies.

2 How sweet within thy holy place
  With one accord to sing thy grace,
Besieging thine attentive ear
  With all the force of fervent prayer!

3 O may we love the house of God,
   Of peace and joy the blest abode;
   O may no angry strife destroy
   That sacred peace, that holy joy.

4 The world without may rage, but we
   Will only cling more close to thee,
   With hearts to thee more wholly given,
   More weaned from earth, more fixed on heaven.

5 Lord, shower upon us from above
   The sacred gift of mutual love;
   Each other's wants may we supply,
   And reign together in the sky.

245   *W. Cowper*

mf 1 JESUS, where'er thy people meet,
        There they behold thy mercy-seat;
        Where'er they seek thee thou art found,
        And every place is hallowed ground.

      2 For thou, within no walls confined,
        Inhabitest the humble mind;
        Such ever bring thee when they come,
        And, going, take thee to their home.

f   3 Dear Shepherd of thy chosen few,
        Thy former mercies here renew;
        Here to our waiting hearts proclaim
        The sweetness of thy saving name.

mf 4 Here may we prove the power of prayer
        To strengthen faith and sweeten care,
        To teach our faint desires to rise,
        And bring all heaven before our eyes.

      5 Lord, we are few, but thou art near;
        Nor short thine arm, nor deaf thine ear:
f   O rend the heavens, come quickly down,
        And make a thousand hearts thine own.

246

F. Pott ‡

mf 1 ANGEL-VOICES ever singing
    Round thy throne of light,
Angel-harps for ever ringing,
    Rest not day nor night;
f   Thousands only live to bless thee
      And confess thee
      Lord of might.

mf 2 Thou who art beyond the farthest⌣
    Mortal eye can scan,
Can it be that thou regardest⌣
    Songs of sinful man?
Can we know that thou art near us,
    And wilt hear us?
f   Yea, we can.

mf 3 Yea, we know that thou rejoicest⌣
    O'er each work of thine;
Thou didst ears and hands and voices
    For thy praise design;
Craftsman's art and music's measure
    For thy pleasure
    All combine.

4 In thy house, great God, we offer⌣
    Of thine own to thee;
And for thine acceptance proffer
    All unworthily
Hearts and minds and hands and voices
    In our choicest
    Psalmody.

f 5 Honour, glory, might, and merit
    Thine shall ever be,
Father, Son, and Holy Spirit,
    Blessèd Trinity!
Of the best that thou hast given
    Earth and heaven
    Render thee.

247

J. Newton†

f 1 GREAT Shepherd of thy people, hear,
　　　Thy presence now display;
　　As thou hast given a place for prayer,
　　　So give us hearts to pray.

mf 2 Within these walls let holy peace
　　　And love and concord dwell;
　　Here give the troubled conscience ease,
　　　The wounded spirit heal.

3 May we in faith receive thy word,
　　In faith present our prayers,
　And in the presence of our Lord
　　Unbosom all our cares.

4 The hearing ear, the seeing eye,
　　The contrite heart, bestow;
f　And shine upon us from on high,
　　That we in grace may grow.

248　*Ps. 84*

I. Watts

1 LORD of the worlds above,
　　How pleasant and how fair
　The dwellings of thy love,
　　Thy earthly temples, are!
　　　To thine abode
　　　My heart aspires,
　　　With warm desires
　　To see my God.

2 O happy souls that pray
　　Where God appoints to hear!
　O happy men that pay
　　Their constant service there!
　　　They praise thee still;
　　　And happy they
　　　That love the way
　　To Zion's hill.

3 They go from strength to strength
   Through this dark vale of tears,
Till each arrives at length,
   Till each in heaven appears:
     O glorious seat!
       When God our King
       Shall thither bring
     Our willing feet.

249

G. Tersteegen. Tr. J. Wesley†

Gott ist gegenwärtig!

mf 1 LO, God is here! let us adore,
   And own how dreadful is this place!
Let all within us feel his power,
   And silent bow before his face;
Who know his power, his grace who prove,
p Serve him with awe, with reverence love.

mf 2 Lo, God is here! him day and night
   Rejoicing choirs of angels sing;
To him, enthroned above all height,
   The hosts of heaven their praises bring:
p Disdain not, Lord, our meaner song,
Who praise thee with a faltering tongue.

f 3 Being of beings! may our praise
   Thy courts with grateful fragrance fill;
Still may we stand before thy face,
   Still hear and do thy sovereign will;
To thee may all our thoughts arise
A true and ceaseless sacrifice.

250

Sir H. W. Baker

1 LORD, thy word abideth,
   And our footsteps guideth;
Who its truth believeth
   Light and joy receiveth.

2 When our foes are near us,
 Then thy word doth cheer us,
 Word of consolation,
 Message of salvation.

3 When the storms are o'er us,
 And dark clouds before us,
 Then its light directeth,
 And our way protecteth.

4 Who can tell the pleasure,
 Who recount the treasure,
 By thy word imparted
 To the simple-hearted?

5 Word of mercy, giving
 Succour to the living;
 Word of life, supplying
 Comfort to the dying!

6 O that we discerning
 Its most holy learning,
 Lord, may love and fear thee,
 Evermore be near thee.

251   *Anne Steele*

1 FATHER of mercies, in thy word
 What endless glory shines!
 For ever be thy name adored
 For these celestial lines.

2 Here may the blind and hungry come,
 And light and food receive;
 Here shall the lowliest guest have room,
 And taste and see and live.

3 Here springs of consolation rise
 To cheer the fainting mind,
 And thirsting souls receive supplies,
 And sweet refreshment find.

4 Here the Redeemer's welcome voice
    Spreads heavenly peace around,
And life and everlasting joys
    Attend the blissful sound.

5 O may these heavenly pages be
    My ever dear delight,
And still new beauties may I see,
    And still increasing light.

6 Divine instructor, gracious Lord,
    Be thou for ever near;
Teach me to love thy sacred word,
    And view my Saviour here.

252 *Ps.* 19   *I. Watts*

1 THE heavens declare thy glory, Lord;
    In every star thy wisdom shines;
But when our eyes behold thy word,
    We read thy name in fairer lines.

2 Sun, moon, and stars convey thy praise
    Round the whole earth, and never stand;
So, when thy truth began its race,
    It touched and glanced on every land.

3 Nor shall thy spreading Gospel rest
    Till through the world thy truth has run;
Till Christ has all the nations blest
    That see the light or feel the sun.

4 Great Sun of Righteousness, arise;
    Bless the dark world with heavenly light;
Thy Gospel makes the simple wise,
    Thy laws are pure, thy judgements right.

5 Thy noblest wonders here we view,
    In souls renewed and sins forgiven:
Lord, cleanse my sins, my soul renew,
    And make thy word my guide to heaven.

253 *P. Pusey†. Based on* Christe du Beistand, *M. von Löwenstern*

mf 1 LORD of our life, and God of our salvation,
Star of our night, and hope of every nation,
Hear and receive thy Church's supplication,
　　f　Lord God Almighty.

mf 2 See round thine ark the hungry billows curling;
See how thy foes their banners are unfurling;
Lord, while their darts envenomed they are hurling,
　　f　Thou canst preserve us.

f 3 Lord, thou canst help when earthly armour faileth,
Lord, thou canst save when deadly sin assaileth;
Lord, o'er thy Church nor death nor hell prevaileth:
　　p　Grant us thy peace, Lord.

mf 4 Grant us thy help till foes are backward driven,
Grant them thy truth, that they may be forgiven,
Grant peace on earth, and, after we have striven,
　　p　　Peace in thy heaven.

254 *L. B. C. L. Muirhead*

f 1 THE Church of God a kingdom is,
Where Christ in power doth reign;
mf Where spirits yearn till, seen in bliss,
Their Lord shall come again.

f   2 Glad companies of saints possess
    This Church below, above;
And God's perpetual calm doth bless
    Their paradise of love.

3 An altar stands within the shrine
    Whereon, once sacrificed,
Is set, immaculate, divine,
    The Lamb of God, the Christ.

4 There rich and poor, from countless lands,
    Praise Christ on mystic Rood;
There nations reach forth holy hands
    To take God's holy food.

mf 5 There pure life-giving streams o'erflow
    The sower's garden-ground;
And faith and hope fair blossoms show,
    And fruits of love abound.

6 O King, O Christ, this endless grace
    To us and all men bring,
f   To see the vision of thy face
    In joy, O Christ, our King.

255
S. J. Stone

mf 1 THE Church's one foundation
    Is Jesus Christ her Lord;
She is his new creation
    By water and the word:
From heaven he came and sought her
    To be his holy Bride;
With his own Blood he bought her,
    And for her life he died.

2 Elect from every nation,
    Yet one o'er all the earth,
Her charter of salvation
    One Lord, one faith, one birth;
One holy name she blesses,
    Partakes one holy food,
And to one hope she presses
    With every grace endued.

p 3 *Though with a scornful wonder
    Men see her sore opprest,
By schisms rent asunder,
    By heresies distrest,
mf Yet saints their watch are keeping,
    Their cry goes up,'How long?'
f And soon the night of weeping
    Shall be the morn of song.

mf 4 Mid toil and tribulation,
    And tumult of her war,
She waits the consummation
    Of peace for evermore;
Till with the vision glorious
    Her longing eyes are blest,
f And the great Church victorious
    Shall be the Church at rest.

mf 5 Yet she on earth hath union
    With God the Three in One,
And mystic sweet communion
    With those whose rest is won:
O happy ones and holy!
    Lord, give us grace that we,
Like them the meek and lowly,
    On high may dwell with thee.

256　　　　　　　　　　　　　*E. H. Plumptre*

f　1 THY hand, O God, has guided
　　　　Thy flock, from age to age;
　　The wondrous tale is written,
　　　　Full clear, on every page;
　　Our fathers owned thy goodness,
　　　　And we their deeds record;
　　And both of this bear witness:
　　　　One Church, one faith, one Lord.

　　　2 Thy heralds brought glad tidings
　　　　To greatest, as to least;
　　They bade men rise, and hasten
　　　　To share the great King's feast;
　　And this was all their teaching,
　　　　In every deed and word,
　　To all alike proclaiming
　　　　One Church, one faith, one Lord.

mf　3*When shadows thick were falling,
　　　　And all seemed sunk in night,
　　Thou, Lord, didst send thy servants,
　　　　Thy chosen sons of light.
　　On them and on thy people
　　　　Thy plenteous grace was poured,
f　　And this was still their message:
　　　　One Church, one faith, one Lord.

　　　4 Through many a day of darkness,
　　　　Through many a scene of strife,
　　The faithful few fought bravely,
　　　　To guard the nation's life.
　　Their Gospel of redemption,
　　　　Sin pardoned, man restored,
　　Was all in this enfolded:
　　　　One Church, one faith, one Lord.

mf 5*And we, shall we be faithless?
  Shall hearts fail, hands hang down?
 Shall we evade the conflict,
  And cast away our crown?
 Not so: in God's deep counsels
  Some better thing is stored;
f We will maintain, unflinching,
  One Church, one faith, one Lord.

6 Thy mercy will not fail us,
  Nor leave thy work undone;
 With thy right hand to help us,
  The victory shall be won;
 And then, by men and angels.
  Thy name shall be adored,
 And this shall be their anthem:
  One Church, one faith, one Lord.

257

J. Newton ‡

1 GLORIOUS things of thee are spoken,
  Zion, city of our God;
 He whose word cannot be broken
  Formed thee for his own abode.
 On the Rock of ages founded,
  What can shake thy sure repose?
 With salvation's walls surrounded,
  Thou may'st smile at all thy foes.

2 See, the streams of living waters,
  Springing from eternal love,
 Well supply thy sons and daughters,
  And all fear of want remove.
 Who can faint while such a river
  Ever flows their thirst to assuage:
 Grace which, like the Lord the giver,
  Never fails from age to age?

3*Round each habitation hovering,
   See the cloud and fire appear
For a glory and a covering,
   Showing that the Lord is near.
Thus they march, the pillar leading,
   Light by night and shade by day;
Daily on the manna feeding
   Which he gives them when they pray.

4 Saviour, since of Zion's city
   I through grace a member am,
Let the world deride or pity,
   I will glory in thy name.
Fading is the worldling's pleasure,
   All his boasted pomp and show;
Solid joys and lasting treasure
   None but Zion's children know.

258
                                S. Johnson

1 CITY of God, how broad and far
   Outspread thy walls sublime!
The true thy chartered freemen are
   Of every age and clime:

2 One holy Church, one army strong,
   One steadfast, high intent;
One working band, one harvest-song,
   One King omnipotent.

3 How purely hath thy speech come down
   From man's primeval youth!
How grandly hath thine empire grown
   Of freedom, love, and truth!

4 How gleam thy watch-fires through the
   With never-fainting ray!   [night
How rise thy towers, serene and bright,
   To meet the dawning day!

5 In vain the surge's angry shock,
    In vain the drifting sands:
Unharmed upon the eternal Rock
    The eternal city stands.

259
             F. T. Palgrave

1 O THOU not made with hands,
    Not throned above the skies,
Nor walled with shining walls,
    Nor framed with stones of price,
More bright than gold or gem,
God's own Jerusalem!

2 Where'er the gentle heart
    Finds courage from above;
Where'er the heart forsook
    Warms with the breath of love;
Where faith bids fear depart,
City of God, thou art.

3 Thou art where'er the proud
    In humbleness melts down;
Where self itself yields up;
    Where martyrs win their crown;
Where faithful souls possess
    Themselves in perfect peace;

4 Where in life's common ways
    With cheerful feet we go;
Where in his steps we tread,
    Who trod the way of woe;
Where he is in the heart,
City of God, thou art.

5 Not throned above the skies,
    Nor golden-walled afar,
But where Christ's two or three
    In his name gathered are,
Be in the midst of them,
God's own Jerusalem!

260   *C. A. Alington*

1 YE that know the Lord is gracious,
    Ye for whom a Corner stone
Stands, of God elect and precious,
    Laid that ye may build thereon,
See that on that sure foundation
    Ye a living temple raise,
Towers that may tell forth salvation,
    Walls that may re-echo praise.

2 Living stones, by God appointed
    Each to his allotted place,
Kings and priests, by God anointed,
    Shall ye not declare his grace?
Ye, a royal generation,
    Tell the tidings of your birth,
Tidings of a new creation
    To an old and weary earth.

3 Tell the praise of him who called you
    Out of darkness into light,
Broke the fetters that enthralled you,
    Gave you freedom, peace and sight:
Tell the tale of sins forgiven,
    Strength renewed and hope restored,
Till the earth, in tune with heaven,
    Praise and magnify the Lord!

261   *Yattendon Hymnal. Based on* O quam
                          juvat, *C. Coffin*

1 HAPPY are they, they that love God,
    Whose hearts have Christ confest,
Who by his Cross have found their life,
    And 'neath his yoke their rest.

2 Glad is the praise, sweet are the songs,
    When they together sing;
And strong the prayers that bow the ear
    Of heaven's eternal King.

3 Christ to their homes giveth his peace,
    And makes their loves his own:
    But ah, what tares the evil one
        Hath in his garden sown!

4 Sad were our lot, evil this earth,
    Did not its sorrows prove‿
    The path whereby the sheep may find
        The fold of Jesus' love.

5 Then shall they know, they that love him,
    How all their pain is good;
    And death itself cannot unbind
        Their happy brotherhood.

262

L. Hensley

mf 1 THY Kingdom come, O God,
    Thy rule, O Christ, begin;
    Break with thine iron rod
        The tyrannies of sin.

p 2 Where is thy reign of peace
    And purity and love?
    When shall all hatred cease,
        As in the realms above?

   3 When comes the promised time
    That war shall be no more,
    And lust, oppression, crime
        Shall flee thy face before?

mf 4 We pray thee, Lord, arise,
    And come in thy great might;
    Revive our longing eyes,
        Which languish for thy sight.

p 5 Men scorn thy sacred name,
    And wolves devour thy fold;
    By many deeds of shame
        We learn that love grows cold.

6 O'er heathen lands afar
   Thick darkness broodeth yet:
f   Arise, O morning star,
   Arise, and never set!

263   *F. L. Hosmer*

1 THY Kingdom come! on bended knee
   The passing ages pray;
And faithful souls have yearned to see
   On earth that Kingdom's day:

2 But the slow watches of the night
   Not less to God belong;
And for the everlasting right
   The silent stars are strong.

3 And lo, already on the hills
   The flags of dawn appear;
Gird up your loins, ye prophet souls,
   Proclaim the day is near:

4 The day in whose clear-shining light
   All wrong shall stand revealed,
When justice shall be throned in might,
   And every hurt be healed;

5 When knowledge, hand in hand with peace,
   Shall walk the earth abroad:
The day of perfect righteousness,
   The promised day of God.

264 *Ps. 67*   *H. F. Lyte*

mf 1 GOD of mercy, God of grace,
   Show the brightness of thy face;
   Shine upon us, Saviour, shine,
   Fill thy Church with light divine;
   And thy saving health extend
   Unto earth's remotest end.

f 2 Let the people praise thee, Lord!
    Be by all that live adored;
    Let the nations shout and sing
      Glory to their Saviour King;
mf   At thy feet their tribute pay,
    And thy holy will obey.

f 3 Let the people praise thee, Lord!
    Earth shall then her fruits afford;
    God to man his blessing give,
      Man to God devoted live;
    All below, and all above,
    One in joy and light and love.

265
Bishop R. Heber

mf 1 FROM Greenland's icy mountains,
    From India's coral strand,
    Where Afric's sunny fountains
      Roll down their golden sand,
    From many an ancient river,
    From many a palmy plain,
    They call us to deliver
      Their land from error's chain.

2 What though the spicy breezes
    Blow soft o'er Java's isle,
  Though every prospect pleases
    And only man is vile:
  In vain with lavish kindness
    The gifts of God are strown;
  The heathen in his blindness
    Bows down to wood and stone.

3 Can we, whose souls are lighted
    With wisdom from on high,
  Can we to men benighted
    The lamp of life deny?
f Salvation! O salvation!
    The joyful sound proclaim,
  Till each remotest nation
    Has learned Messiah's name.

4 Waft, waft, ye winds, his story,
   And you, ye waters, roll,
Till, like a sea of glory,
   It spreads from pole to pole;
Till o'er our ransomed nature
   The Lamb for sinners slain,
Redeemer, King, Creator,
   In bliss returns to reign.

266   *J. Marriott*†

f   1 THOU, whose almighty word
    Chaos and darkness heard,
      And took their flight;
mf   Hear us, we humbly pray,
    And where the Gospel-day
    Sheds not its glorious ray,
f   Let there be light!

mf   2 Thou, who didst come to bring
    On thy redeeming wing
      Healing and sight,
Health to the sick in mind,
Sight to the inly blind,
O now to all mankind
f   Let there be light!

mf   3 Spirit of truth and love,
    Life-giving, holy Dove,
      Speed forth thy flight;
Move on the water's face,
Bearing the lamp of grace,
And in earth's darkest place
f   Let there be light!

4 Holy and blessèd Three,
    Glorious Trinity,
      Wisdom, Love, Might;
Boundless as ocean's tide
Rolling in fullest pride,
Through the earth far and wide
      Let there be light!

267   *H. Downton*

mf 1 LORD, her watch thy Church is keeping;
          When shall earth thy rule obey?
          When shall end the night of weeping?
          When shall break the promised day?
p   See the whitening harvest languish,
          Waiting still the labourers' toil;
mf   Was it vain, thy Son's deep anguish?
          Shall the strong retain the spoil?

p   2 Tidings, sent to every creature,
          Millions yet have never heard;
          Can they hear without a preacher?
mf   Lord almighty, give the word:
f   Give the word; in every nation
          Let the Gospel-trumpet sound,
          Witnessing a world's salvation
          To the earth's remotest bound.

      3 Then the end: thy Church completed,
          All thy chosen gathered in,
          With their King in glory seated,
          Satan bound, and banished sin;
          Gone for ever parting, weeping,
          Hunger, sorrow, death, and pain:
          Lo, her watch thy Church is keeping;
          Come, Lord Jesus, come to reign!

268   *Bishop G. W. Doane*

      1 FLING out the banner! let it float
          Skyward and seaward, high and wide:
          Our glory only in the Cross,
          Our only hope the Crucified.

2 Fling out the banner! angels bend
   In anxious silence o'er the sign,
And vainly seek to comprehend
   The wonders of the love divine.

3 Fling out the banner! heathen lands
   Shall see from far the glorious sight,
And nations, crowding to be born,
   Baptize their spirits in its light.

4 Fling out the banner! wide and high,
   Seaward and skyward let it shine;
Nor skill nor might nor merit ours:
   We conquer only in that sign.

269　　　　　　　　　　　　*C. E. Oakley*

1　HILLS of the north, rejoice;
   River and mountain-spring,
Hark to the advent voice;
   Valley and lowland, sing:
Though absent long, your Lord is nigh;
He judgement brings and victory.

2　Isles of the southern seas,
   Deep in your coral caves
Pent be each warring breeze,
   Lulled be your restless waves:
He comes to reign with boundless sway,
And makes your wastes his great highway.

3　Lands of the east, awake,
   Soon shall your sons be free;
The sleep of ages break,
   And rise to liberty.
On your far hills, long cold and grey,
Has dawned the everlasting day.

4   Shores of the utmost west,
           Ye that have waited long,
       Unvisited, unblest,
           Break forth to swelling song;
       High raise the note, that Jesus died,
       Yet lives and reigns, the Crucified.

5   Shout, while ye journey home;
           Songs be in every mouth;
       Lo, from the north we come,
           From east and west and south.
       City of God, the bond are free,
       We come to live and reign in thee!

270   *A. Brooks*

1 TRUMPET of God, sound high,
       Till the hearts of the heathen shake,
   And the souls that in slumber lie
       At the voice of the Lord awake.
           Till the fencèd cities fall
           At the blast of the Gospel call,
       Trumpet of God, sound high!

2 Hosts of the Lord, go forth:
       Go, strong in the power of his rest,
   Till the south be at one with the north,
       And peace upon east and west;
           Till the far-off lands shall thrill
           With the gladness of God's good will,
       Hosts of the Lord, go forth!

3 Come, as of old, like fire;
       O force of the Lord, descend,
   Till with love of the world's Desire
       Earth burn to its utmost end;
           Till the ransomed people sing
           To the glory of Christ the King,
       Come, as of old, like fire!

271

A. C. Ainger

mf 1 GOD is working his purpose out as year
    succeeds to year,
    God is working his purpose out and the time
    is drawing near;
    Nearer and nearer draws the time, the time
    that shall surely be,
f   When the earth shall be filled with the glory
    of God as the waters cover the sea.

mf 2 From utmost east to utmost west where'er
    man's foot hath trod,
    By the mouth of many messengers goes forth
    the voice of God,
f   'Give ear to me, ye continents, ye isles, give
    ear to me,
    That the earth may be filled with the glory of
    God as the waters cover the sea.'

p 3 What can we do to work God's work, to
    prosper and increase
    The brotherhood of all mankind, the reign of
    the Prince of Peace?
    What can we do to hasten the time, the time
    that shall surely be,
f   When the earth shall be filled with the glory
    of God as the waters cover the sea?

4 March we forth in the strength of God with
    the banner of Christ unfurled,
    That the light of the glorious Gospel of truth
    may shine throughout the world.
    Fight we the fight with sorrow and sin, to set
    their captives free,
    That the earth may be filled with the glory of
    God as the waters cover the sea.

p 5 All we can do is nothing worth unless God
        blesses the deed;
      Vainly we hope for the harvest-tide till God
        gives life to the seed;
mf   Yet nearer and nearer draws the time, the
        time that shall surely be,
f   When the earth shall be filled with the glory
        of God as the waters cover the sea.

272
                                   C. Wesley and others
mf 1 LET saints on earth in concert sing
        With those whose work is done;
      For all the servants of our King
        In heaven and earth are one.

      2 One family, we dwell in him,
          One Church, above, beneath;
p   Though now divided by the stream,
          The narrow stream of death.

mf 3 One army of the living God,
          To his command we bow:
        Part of the host have crossed the flood,
p   And part are crossing now.

      4 E'en now to their eternal home
          There pass some spirits blest;
        While others to the margin come,
          Waiting their call to rest.

mf 5 Jesu, be thou our constant guide;
f   Then, when the word is given,
        Bid Jordan's narrow stream divide,
          And bring us safe to heaven.

273
                                   J. M. Neale and Compilers
p   1 THEY whose course on earth is o'er,
        Think they of their brethren more?
        They before the throne who bow,
        Feel they for their brethren now?

2 We by enemies distrest,
   They in Paradise at rest;
   We the captives, they the freed—
   We and they are one indeed.

3 Those whom many a land divides,
   Many mountains, many tides,
   Have they with each other part,
   Fellowship of heart with heart?

4 Each to each may be unknown,
   Wide apart their lots be thrown;
   Differing tongues their lips may speak,
   One be strong, and one be weak:

mf 5 Yet in Sacrament and prayer
      Each with other hath a share;
      Hath a share in tear and sigh,
      Watch and fast and litany.

6 Saints departed even thus
   Hold communion still with us;
   Still with us, beyond the veil
   Praising, pleading, without fail.

f 7 With them still our hearts we raise,
     Share their work and join their praise,
     Rendering worship, thanks, and love
     To the Trinity above.

274

R. Baxter†

1 HE wants not friends that hath thy love,
   And may converse and walk with thee,
   And with thy saints here and above,
   With whom for ever I must be.

2 In the blest fellowship of saints
   Is wisdom, safety, and delight;
   And when my heart declines and faints,
   It's raisèd by their heat and light.

3 As for my friends, they are not lost;
    The several vessels of thy fleet,
Though parted now, by tempests tost,
    Shall safely in the haven meet.

4 Still we are centred all in thee,
    Members, though distant, of one Head;
In the same family we be,
    By the same faith and spirit led.

5 Before thy throne we daily meet
    As joint-petitioners there;
In spirit we each other greet,
    And shall again each other see.

6 The heavenly hosts, world without end,
    Shall be my company above;
And thou, my best and surest Friend,
    Who shall divide me from thy love?

275   *Bernard of Cluny. Tr. J. M. Neale*†

                Hic breve vivitur

p   1 BRIEF life is here our portion,
      Brief sorrow, short-lived care:
mf   The life that knows no ending,
      The tearless life, is there.
    O happy retribution:
      Short toil, eternal rest;
    For mortals and for sinners
      A mansion with the blest!

    2 And now we fight the battle,
f   But then shall wear the crown
    Of full and everlasting‿
      And passionless renown.
mf   And now we watch and struggle,
      And now we live in hope,
    And Sion in her anguish
      With Babylon must cope.

f 3 But he whom now we trust in
    Shall then be seen and known,
And they that know and see him
    Shall have him for their own.
The morning shall awaken,
    The shadows shall decay,
And each true-hearted servant
    Shall shine as doth the day.

4 There God, our King and portion,
    In fulness of his grace,
Shall we behold for ever,
    And worship face to face.
Then all the halls of Sion
    For ay shall be complete,
And in the Land of Beauty
    All things of beauty meet.

276   *Bernard of Cluny. Tr. J. M. Neale†*
        Hora novissima

mf 1 THE world is very evil,
    The times are waxing late;
Be sober and keep vigil,
    The Judge is at the gate:
The Judge who comes in mercy,
    The Judge who comes with might,
Who comes to end the evil,
    Who comes to crown the right.

2 Arise, arise, good Christian,
    Let right to wrong succeed;
Let penitential sorrow
    To heavenly gladness lead,
To light that has no evening,
    That knows no moon nor sun,
The light so new and golden,
    The light that is but one.

3 O home of fadeless splendour,
   Of flowers that bear no thorn,
Where they shall dwell as children
p   Who here as exiles mourn!
mf 'Midst power that knows no limit,
   Where wisdom has no bound,
The beatific vision
   Shall glad the saints around.

4 O happy, holy portion,
   Refection for the blest,
True vision of true beauty,
   True cure of the distrest!
f Strive, man, to win that glory;
   Toil, man, to gain that light;
Send hope before to grasp it,
   Till hope be lost in sight.

277   *Bernard of Cluny. Tr. J. M. Neale†*

O bona patria

mf 1 FOR thee, O dear, dear country,
   Mine eyes their vigils keep;
For very love, beholding
   Thy happy name, they weep.
The mention of thy glory
   Is unction to the breast,
And medicine in sickness,
   And love and life and rest.

2 O one, O only mansion!
   O Paradise of joy!
Where tears are ever banished,
   And smiles have no alloy;
The Lamb is all thy splendour,
   The Crucified thy praise;
His laud and benediction
   Thy ransomed people raise.

3 With jasper glow thy bulwarks,
    Thy streets with emeralds blaze;
The sardius and the topaz
    Unite in thee their rays;
Thine ageless walls are bonded
    With amethyst unpriced;
The saints build up thy fabric,
    Thy Corner-stone is Christ.

4 Thou hast no shore, fair ocean!
    Thou hast no time, bright day!
Dear fountain of refreshment
    To pilgrims far away!
f Upon the Rock of ages
    They raise thy holy tower;
Thine is the victor's laurel,
    And thine the golden dower.

278   *Bernard of Cluny*
                Tr. J. M. Neale and Compilers
            Urbs Sion aurea
mf 1 JERUSALEM the golden,
        With milk and honey blest,
    Beneath thy contemplation
        Sink heart and voice opprest.
    I know not, O, I know not
        What joys await us there,
    What radiancy of glory,
        What bliss beyond compare.

f 2 They stand, those halls of Sion,
        All jubilant with song,
    And bright with many an angel,
        And all the martyr throng;
    The Prince is ever with them,
        The daylight is serene,
    The pastures of the blessèd
        Are decked in glorious sheen.

mf 3 There is the throne of David;
  And there, from care released,
  The shout of them that triumph,
  The song of them that feast;
f   And they, who with their Leader
  Have conquered in the fight,
  For ever and for ever
  Are clad in robes of white.

mf 4 O sweet and blessèd country,
  The home of God's elect!
  O sweet and blessèd country
  That eager hearts expect!
p   Jesu, in mercy bring us
  To that dear land of rest;
mf   Who art, with God the Father
  And Spirit, ever blest.

279   *Ascribed to Thomas à Kempis*
       Tr. J. M. Neale†
   Jerusalem luminosa

1 LIGHT'S abode, celestial Salem,
  Vision whence true peace doth spring,
 Brighter than the heart can fancy,
  Mansion of the highest King;
 O how glorious are the praises
  Which of thee the prophets sing!

2 There for ever and for ever
  Alleluia is outpoured;
 For unending, for unbroken
  Is the feast-day of the Lord;
 All is pure and all is holy
  That within thy walls is stored.

3 There no cloud or passing vapour
  Dims the brightness of the air;
 Endless noon-day, glorious noon-day,
  From the Sun of suns is there;
 There no night brings rest from labour,
  For unknown are toil and care.

4*O how glorious and resplendent,
    Fragile body, shalt thou be,
When endued with so much beauty,
    Full of health and strong and free,
Full of vigour, full of pleasure
    That shall last eternally!

5*Now with gladness, now with courage,
    Bear the burden on thee laid,
That hereafter these thy labours
    May with endless gifts be paid;
And in everlasting glory
    Thou with brightness be arrayed.

6 Laud and honour to the Father,
    Laud and honour to the Son,
Laud and honour to the Spirit,
    Ever Three and ever One,
Consubstantial, co-eternal,
    While unending ages run.

280   *S. Crossman*

mf 1 JERUSALEM on high
    My song and city is,
    My home whene'er I die,
    The centre of my bliss:
f   O happy place!
        When shall I be,
        My God, with thee,
    To see thy face?

mf 2 There dwells my Lord, my King,
    Judged here unfit to live;
    There angels to him sing,
    And lowly homage give:
f   O happy, etc.

mf 3 The patriarchs of old
    There from their travels cease;
The prophets there behold
    Their longed-for Prince of Peace:
f   O happy, etc.

mf 4 The Lamb's apostles there
    I might with joy behold,
The harpers I might hear
    Harping on harps of gold:
f   O happy, etc.

mf 5 The bleeding martyrs, they
    Within those courts are found,
Clothèd in pure array,
    Their scars with glory crowned:
f   O happy, etc.

p 6 Ah me! ah me! that I
    In Kedar's tents here stay:
No place like that on high;
    Lord, thither guide my way;
f   O happy, etc.

281
Peter Abelard. Tr. J. M. Neale ‡

O quanta qualia sunt illa sabbata

mf 1 O WHAT their joy and their glory must be,
Those endless sabbaths the blessèd ones see!
Crown for the valiant, to weary ones rest;
God shall be all, and in all ever blest.

2 *What are the Monarch, his court, and his
    throne?
What are the peace and the joy that they own?
O that the blest ones, who in it have share,
All that they feel could as fully declare!

3 Truly Jerusalem name we that shore,
'Vision of peace,' that brings joy evermore!
Wish and fulfilment can severed be ne'er,
Nor the thing prayed for come short of the
   prayer.

4 There, where no troubles distraction can
   bring,
We the sweet anthems of Sion shall sing,
While for thy grace, Lord, their voices of
   praise
Thy blessèd people eternally raise.

5*There dawns no sabbath, no sabbath is o'er,
Those sabbath-keepers have one evermore;
f   One and unending is that triumph-song
Which to the angels and us shall belong.

p 6 Now in the meanwhile, with hearts raised on
   high,
We for that country must yearn and must
   sigh;
Seeking Jerusalem, dear native land,
Through our long exile on Babylon's strand.

mf 7 Low before him with our praises we fall,
Of whom, and in whom, and through whom
   are all:
f   Of whom, the Father; and in whom, the Son;
Through whom, the Spirit, with them ever
   One.

282   *'F. B. P.' (c.* 1600) *and Compilers*

mf 1 JERUSALEM, my happy home,
   Name ever dear to me,
When shall my labours have an end?
   Thy joys when shall I see?

2 When shall these eyes thy heaven-built walls
  And pearly gates behold?
 Thy bulwarks with salvation strong,
  And streets of shining gold?

f 3 Apostles, martyrs, prophets, there‿
  Around my Saviour stand;
 And all I love in Christ below
  Will join the glorious band.

mf 4 Jerusalem, my happy home,
  When shall I come to thee?
 When shall my labours have an end?
  Thy joys when shall I see?

 5 O Christ, do thou my soul prepare
  For that bright home of love;
 That I may see thee and adore,
  With all thy saints above.

*Note.—The poem on which this hymn is based
will be found (abbreviated) in the 'Processional'
section (623).*

283 *Mozarabic (5th–8th cent.) Tr. J. Ellerton*

   Alleluia piis edite laudibus

1 SING Alleluia forth in duteous praise,
 Ye citizens of heaven; O sweetly raise‿
   An endless Alleluia.

2 Ye powers who stand before the eternal Light,
 In hymning choirs re-echo to the height
   An endless Alleluia.

3 The holy city shall take up your strain,
 And with glad songs resounding wake again
   An endless Alleluia.

4 In blissful antiphons ye thus rejoice
  To render to the Lord with thankful voice
              An endless Alleluia.

5 Ye who have gained at length your palms in
      bliss,
  Victorious ones, your chant shall still be this:
              An endless Alleluia.

6 There, in one grand acclaim, for ever ring
  The strains which tell the honour of your King:
              An endless Alleluia.

7 This is sweet rest for weary ones brought back,
  This is glad food and drink which ne'er shall
      lack:
              An endless Alleluia.

8 While thee, by whom were all things made, we
      praise
  For ever, and tell out in sweetest lays
              An endless Alleluia.

9 Almighty Christ, to thee our voices sing
  Glory for evermore; to thee we bring
              An endless Alleluia.

284   H. Alford

  f   1 TEN thousand times ten thousand,
              In sparkling raiment bright,
          The armies of the ransomed saints
              Throng up the steeps of light:
  mf   'Tis finished! all is finished,
              Their fight with death and sin;
  f   Fling open wide the golden gates,
              And let the victors in.

2 What rush of Alleluias
   Fills all the earth and sky!
What ringing of a thousand harps
   Bespeaks the triumph nigh!
O day, for which creation
   And all its tribes were made!
O joy, for all its former woes
   A thousand-fold repaid!

mf 3 O then what raptured greetings
   On Canaan's happy shore,
What knitting severed friendships up,
   Where partings are no more!
Then eyes with joy shall sparkle
   That brimmed with tears of late:
Orphans no longer fatherless,
   Nor widows desolate.

4 Bring near thy great salvation,
   Thou Lamb for sinners slain,
f Fill up the roll of thine elect,
   Then take thy power and reign:
mf Appear, Desire of Nations;
   Thine exiles long for home;
f Show in the heavens thy promised sign;
   Thou Prince and Saviour, come.

285
I. Watts

f 1 THERE is a land of pure delight,
   Where saints immortal reign;
Infinite day excludes the night,
   And pleasures banish pain.

2 There everlasting spring abides,
   And never-withering flowers;
p Death, like a narrow sea, divides
   That heavenly land from ours.

mf 3 Sweet fields beyond the swelling flood
    Stand dressed in living green;
So to the Jews old Canaan stood,
    While Jordan rolled between.

p 4 But timorous mortals start and shrink
    To cross the narrow sea,
And linger shivering on the brink,
    And fear to launch away.

mf 5 O could we make our doubts remove,
    Those gloomy doubts that rise,
And see the Canaan that we love
    With unbeclouded eyes;

f 6 Could we but climb where Moses stood,
    And view the landscape o'er;
Not Jordan's stream, nor death's cold flood,
    Should fright us from the shore.

286

Henry Vaughan

1 MY soul, there is a country
    Far beyond the stars,
Where stands a wingèd sentry
    All skilful in the wars:

2 There above noise, and danger,
    Sweet peace sits crowned with smiles,
And One born in a manger
    Commands the beauteous files.

3 He is thy gracious Friend,
    And—O my soul, awake!—
Did in pure love descend,
    To die here for thy sake.

4 If thou canst get but thither,
    There grows the flower of peace,
The Rose that cannot wither,
    Thy fortress and thy ease.

5 Leave then thy foolish ranges,
   For none can thee secure
But one who never changes,
   Thy God, thy life, thy cure.

287   *R. Campbell and others*

mf 1 THEY come, God's messengers of love,
They come from realms of peace above,
From homes of never-fading light,
From blissful mansions ever bright.

2 They come to watch around us here,
To soothe our sorrow, calm our fear:
Ye heavenly guides, speed not away;
God willeth you with us to stay.

p 3 But chiefly at its journey's end
'Tis yours the spirit to befriend,
And whisper to the faithful heart,
'O Christian soul, in peace depart.'

4 Blest Jesu, thou whose groans and tears
Have sanctified frail nature's fears,
To earth in bitter sorrow weighed,
Thou didst not scorn thine angel's aid:

mf 5 An angel guard to us supply,
When on the bed of death we lie;
And by thine own almighty power
p O shield us in the last dread hour.

f 6 To God the Father, God the Son,
And God the Spirit, Three in One,
From all above and all below
Let joyful praise unceasing flow.

288 *J. M. Neale†. Based on φωστῆρες τῆς ἀΰλου,*
St. Joseph the Hymnographer

f   1 STARS of the morning, so gloriously bright,
Filled with celestial virtue and light,
These that, where night never followeth day,
Praise the Thrice-Holy for ever and ay:

mf 2 These are thy ministers, these dost thou own,
Lord God of Sabaoth, nearest thy throne;
These are thy messengers, these dost thou
send,
Help of the helpless ones, man to defend.

3 These keep the guard amidst Salem's dear
bowers,
Thrones, Principalities, Virtues, and Powers,
Where, with the Living Ones, mystical four,
Cherubim, Seraphim, bow and adore.

4 Then, when the earth was first poised in mid
space,
Then, when the planets first sped on their
race,
Then, when was ended the six days' employ,
f   Then all the sons of God shouted for joy.

mf 5 Still let them succour us; still let them fight,
Lord of angelic hosts, battling for right;
f   Till, where their anthems they ceaselessly
pour,
We with the angels may bow and adore.

289
J. M. Neale

mf 1 O HAPPY band of pilgrims,
If onward ye will tread
With Jesus as your fellow
To Jesus as your Head!

2 O happy if ye labour
　　As Jesus did for men!
　O happy if ye hunger
　　As Jesus hungered then!

p 3 The Cross that Jesus carried
　　He carried as your due:
f The Crown that Jesus weareth
　　He weareth it for you.

mf 4 The faith by which ye see him,
　　The hope in which ye yearn,
　The love that through all troubles
　　To him alone will turn,

p 5 The trials that beset you,
　　The sorrows ye endure,
　The manifold temptations
　　That death alone can cure,

mf 6 What are they but his jewels
　　Of right celestial worth?
　What are they but the ladder
　　Set up to heaven on earth?

f 7 O happy band of pilgrims,
　　Look upward to the skies,
　Where such a light affliction
　　Shall win so great a prize.

290 *Ps. 34.*　　　　　　*N. Tate and N. Brady*
　　　　　　　　　　　　　　　　(New Version)

mf 1 THROUGH all the changing scenes of life,
　　In trouble and in joy,
　The praises of my God shall still
　　My heart and tongue employ.

2 O magnify the Lord with me,
   With me exalt his name;
When in distress to him I called,
   He to my rescue came.

3 The hosts of God encamp around
   The dwellings of the just;
Deliverance he affords to all
   Who on his succour trust.

4 O make but trial of his love:
   Experience will decide
How blest are they, and only they,
   Who in his truth confide.

5 Fear him, ye saints, and you will then
   Have nothing else to fear;
Make you his service your delight,
   Your wants shall be his care.

f 6 To Father, Son, and Holy Ghost,
   The God whom we adore,
Be glory, as it was, is now,
   And shall be evermore.

291
H. Kirke White and others

mf 1 OFT in danger, oft in woe,
   Onward, Christians, onward go;
Bear the toil, maintain the strife,
   Strengthened with the Bread of Life.

2 Onward, Christians, onward go,
   Join the war, and face the foe;
Will ye flee in danger's hour?
   Know ye not your Captain's power?

3 Let not sorrow dim your eye;
   Soon shall every tear be dry:
Let not fears your course impede;
f   Great your strength, if great your need.

mf 4 Let your drooping hearts be glad;
    March in heavenly armour clad;
    Fight, nor think the battle long:
f   Soon shall victory wake your song.

   5 Onward then in battle move;
    More than conquerors ye shall prove:
    Though opposed by many a foe,
    Christian soldiers, onward go.

292   *B. S. Ingemann. Tr. S. Baring-Gould*
          Igjennem Nat og Trængsel

mf 1 THROUGH the night of doubt and sorrow
    Onward goes the pilgrim band,
    Singing songs of expectation,
    Marching to the Promised Land.
    Clear before us through the darkness
    Gleams and burns the guiding light;
    Brother clasps the hand of brother,
    Stepping fearless through the night.

   2 One the light of God's own presence
    O'er his ransomed people shed,
    Chasing far the gloom and terror,
    Brightening all the path we tread:
    One the object of our journey,
    One the faith which never tires,
    One the earnest looking forward,
    One the hope our God inspires:

f 3*One the strain that lips of thousands
    Lift as from the heart of one:
    One the conflict, one the peril,
    One the march in God begun:
    One the gladness of rejoicing
    On the far eternal shore,
    Where the one almighty Father
    Reigns in love for evermore.

mf 4 Onward, therefore, pilgrim brothers,
      Onward with the Cross our aid;
Bear its shame, and fight its battle,
      Till we rest beneath its shade.
f   Soon shall come the great awaking,
      Soon the rending of the tomb;
Then the scattering of all shadows,
      And the end of toil and gloom.

293

John Bunyan†

1 WHO would true valour see,
    Let him come hither;
One here will constant be,
    Come wind, come weather;
There's no discouragement
Shall make him once relent
His first avowed intent
    To be a pilgrim.

2 Whoso beset him round
    With dismal stories,
Do but themselves confound;
    His strength the more is.
No lion can him fright;
He'll with a giant fight,
But he will have the right
    To be a pilgrim.

3 No goblin nor foul fiend
    Can daunt his spirit;
He knows he at the end
    Shall life inherit.
Then, fancies, fly away;
He'll not fear what men say;
He'll labour night and day
    To be a pilgrim.

294

J. A. Warner

1 BROTHERS, joining hand to hand
　　In one bond united,
Pressing onward to that land
　　Where all wrongs are righted:
Let your words and actions be
　　Worthy your vocation;
Chosen of the Lord, and free,
　　Heirs of Christ's salvation.

2 Christ, the Way, the Truth, the Life,
　　Who hath gone before you
Through the turmoil and the strife,
　　Holds his banner o'er you:
All who see the sacred sign
　　Press towards heaven's portal,
Fired by hope that is divine,
　　Love that is immortal.

3 They who follow fear no foe,
　　Care not who assail them;
Where the Master leads they go,
　　He will never fail them.
Courage, brothers! we are one,
　　In the love that sought us;
Soon the warfare shall be done,
　　Through the grace he brought us.

295

J. Cennick†

mf 1 CHILDREN of the heavenly King,
　　As ye journey, sweetly sing;
Sing your Saviour's worthy praise,
Glorious in his works and ways.

2 We are travelling home to God
　　In the way the fathers trod;
They are happy now, and we
Soon their happiness shall see.

f   3 Lift your eyes, ye sons of light!
        Sion's city is in sight;
        There our endless home shall be,
        There our Lord we soon shall see.

       4 Fear not, brethren! joyful stand
        On the borders of your land;
        Jesus Christ, your Father's Son,
        Bids you undismayed go on.

p   5 Lord, obedient we would go,
        Gladly leaving all below;
mf   Only thou our leader be,
f   And we still will follow thee.

296   *W. Williams. Tr. P. and W. Williams*‡
        Arglwydd arwain trwy'r anialwch

mf   1 GUIDE me, O thou great Redeemer,
        Pilgrim through this barren land;
        I am weak, but thou art mighty;
        Hold me with thy powerful hand:
            Bread of heaven,
        Feed me now and evermore.

       2 Open now the crystal fountain
            Whence the healing stream doth flow;
        Let the fiery cloudy pillar
            Lead me all my journey through:
                Strong deliverer,
f   Be thou still my strength and shield.

p   3 When I tread the verge of Jordan,
            Bid my anxious fears subside;
f   Death of death, and hell's destruction,
            Land me safe on Canaan's side:
                Songs and praises
        I will ever give to thee.

297 *P. H. B. Lyon*

f 1 LIFT up your voice, ye Christian folk,
  To praise the Holy One,
  Who ransoms us from Satan's yoke
  Through Christ, his blessed Son.
mf Lo, we who were in grievous state
  By reason of our sin,
f Our heads look up, our fears abate,
  Our triumphs now begin.

p 2 The mists hung cold, the night was black,
  About the way we trod;
  Our feet were stumbling from the track
  Which leads the soul to God.
mf But Christ, who broke from death's dark
  shroud,
  Hath sent his quickening ray:
f The sun breaks through the drifting cloud,
  And now 'tis glorious day.

  3 Lift up your voice! with shout and song
  Extol his majesty,
  Whose power hath made the feeble strong
  And caused the blind to see.
  And when the sound of praise grows dim
  Still may our lives forth tell,
  In all we do, our love of him
  Who doeth all things well.

298 *Cardinal J. H. Newman*

mf 1 LEAD, kindly Light, amid the encircling
  gloom,
  Lead thou me on;
p The night is dark, and I am far from home;
  Lead thou me on.
mf Keep thou my feet; I do not ask to see
  The distant scene; one step enough for me.

2 I was not ever thus, nor prayed that thou
         Shouldst lead me on;
I loved to choose and see my path; but now
         Lead thou me on.
I loved the garish day, and, spite of fears,
Pride ruled my will: remember not past
     years.

3 So long thy power hath blest me, sure it still
         Will lead me on,
O'er moor and fen, o'er crag and torrent, till
         The night is gone,
And with the morn those angel faces smile,
Which I have loved long since, and lost a
     while.

299
P. Doddridge

mf   1 O GOD of Bethel, by whose hand
         Thy people still are fed,
Who through this weary pilgrimage
         Hast all our fathers led;

2 Our vows, our prayers, we now present
         Before thy throne of grace;
God of our fathers, be the God
         Of their succeeding race.

p   3 Through each perplexing path of life
         Our wandering footsteps guide;
Give us each day our daily bread,
         And raiment fit provide.

mf   4 O spread thy covering wings around,
         Till all our wanderings cease,
And at our Father's loved abode
         Our souls arrive in peace.

300   *I. Williams*

mf 1 BE thou my guardian and my guide,
          And hear me when I call;
          Let not my slippery footsteps slide,
          And hold me lest I fall.

p   2 The world, the flesh, and Satan dwell
          Around the path I tread;
          O save me from the snares of hell,
          Thou quickener of the dead.

      3 And if I tempted am to sin,
          And outward things are strong,
          Do thou, O Lord, keep watch within,
          And save my soul from wrong.

mf 4 Still let me ever watch and pray,
          And feel that I am frail;
          That if the tempter cross my way,
          Yet he may not prevail.

301   *John Bunyan*

      1 HE that is down needs fear no fall,
          He that is low no pride;
          He that is humble ever shall
          Have God to be his guide.

      2 I am content with what I have,
          Little be it or much;
          And, Lord, contentment still I crave,
          Because thou savest such.

      3 Fullness to such a burden is
          That go on pilgrimage;
          Here little, and hereafter bliss,
          Is best from age to age.

302
Ada R. Greenaway

1 RISE in the strength of God,
　And face life's uphill way:
　The steps which other feet have trod
　　You tread to-day.

2 Press onward, upward still,
　To win your way at last,
　With better hope and stronger will
　　Than in the past:

3 Life's work more nobly wrought,
　Life's race more bravely run,
　Life's daily conflict faced and fought,
　　Life's duty done.

303
C. Wesley

1 SOLDIERS of Christ, arise,
　And put your armour on,
Strong in the strength which God supplies,
　Through his eternal Son;

2 Strong in the Lord of Hosts,
　And in his mighty power:
Who in the strength of Jesus trusts
　Is more than conqueror.

3 Stand then in his great might,
　With all his strength endued;
And take, to arm you for the fight,
　The panoply of God.

4 From strength to strength go on,
　Wrestle and fight and pray;
Tread all the powers of darkness down,
　And win the well-fought day;

5 That, having all things done,
　And all your conflicts past,
Ye may o'ercome, through Christ alone,
　And stand entire at last.

304 *J. S. B. Monsell†*

f 1 FIGHT the good fight with all thy might!
Christ is thy strength, and Christ thy right;
Lay hold on life, and it shall be
Thy joy and crown eternally.

2 Run the straight race through God's good
grace,
Lift up thine eyes, and seek his face;
Life with its way before us lies;
Christ is the path, and Christ the prize.

mf 3 Cast care aside, lean on thy guide;
His boundless mercy will provide;
Trust, and thy trusting soul shall prove
Christ is its life, and Christ its love.

f 4 Faint not nor fear, his arms are near;
He changeth not, and thou art dear;
Only believe, and thou shalt see
That Christ is all in all to thee.

305 *Bishop W. Walsham How*

f 1 SOLDIERS of the Cross, arise!
Gird you with your armour bright:
Mighty are your enemies,
Hard the battle ye must fight.

mf 2 O'er a faithless fallen world
Raise your banner in the sky;
Let it float there wide unfurled;
Bear it onward, lift it high.

3 'Mid the homes of want and woe,
Strangers to the living word,
f Let the Saviour's herald go,
Let the voice of hope be heard.

mf 4 Where the shadows deepest lie,
     Carry truth's unsullied ray;
   Where are crimes of blackest dye,
     There the saving sign display.

p 5 To the weary and the worn
     Tell of realms where sorrows cease;
   To the outcast and forlorn
     Speak of mercy and of peace.

mf 6 Guard the helpless, seek the strayed;
     Comfort troubles, banish grief;
   In the might of God arrayed,
     Scatter sin and unbelief.

f 7 Be the banner still unfurled,
     Still unsheathed the Spirit's sword,
   Till the kingdoms of the world
     Are the Kingdom of the Lord.

306

J. Montgomery†

f 1 LIFT up your heads, ye gates of brass;
     Ye bars of iron, yield!
  And let the King of Glory pass:
     The Cross is in the field.

2 That banner, brighter than the star
     That leads the train of night,
  Shines on the march, and guides from far
     His servants to the fight.

mf 3 A holy war those servants wage:
     In that mysterious strife
  The powers of heaven and hell engage,
     For more than death or life.

4 Ye armies of the living God,
     Sworn warriors of Christ's host,
  Where hallowed footsteps never trod
     Take your appointed post.

5 Though few and small and weak your bands,
   Strong in your Captain's strength,
Go to the conquest of all lands:
   All must be his at length.

6 The spoils at his victorious feet
   You shall rejoice to lay,
And lay yourselves as trophies meet,
   In his great judgement day.

f 7 Then fear not, faint not, halt not now;
   In Jesus' name be strong!
To him shall all the nations bow,
   And sing the triumph song:

8 Uplifted are the gates of brass,
   The bars of iron yield;
Behold the King of Glory pass:
   The Cross hath won the field!

307   *G. Duffield*

f 1 STAND up, stand up for Jesus,
   Ye soldiers of the Cross!
Lift high his royal banner,
   It must not suffer loss.
From victory unto victory
   His army he shall lead,
Till every foe is vanquished,
   And Christ is Lord indeed.

mf 2*Stand up, stand up for Jesus!
   The solemn watchword hear;
If while ye sleep he suffers,
   Away with shame and fear.
Where'er ye meet with evil,
   Within you or without,
f Charge for the God of battles,
   And put the foe to rout.

mf   3 Stand up, stand up for Jesus!
        The trumpet call obey;
    Forth to the mighty conflict
        In this his glorious day.
    Ye that are men now serve him
        Against unnumbered foes;
    Let courage rise with danger
        And strength to strength oppose.

     4 Stand up, stand up for Jesus!
        Stand in his strength alone;
    The arm of flesh will fail you,
        Ye dare not trust your own.
f   Put on the Gospel armour,
        Each piece put on with prayer;
    When duty calls or danger
        Be never wanting there.

mf   5 Stand up, stand up for Jesus!
        The strife will not be long;
    This day the noise of battle,
        The next the victor's song.
f   To him that overcometh
        A crown of life shall be;
    He with the King of Glory
        Shall reign eternally.

308

Charlotte Elliott

mf   1 'CHRISTIAN, seek not yet repose,'
      Hear thy guardian angel say;
    'Thou art in the midst of foes:
      Watch and pray!'

     2 Principalities and powers,
      Mustering their unseen array,
    Wait for thine unguarded hours:
      Watch and pray!

f 3 Gird thy heavenly armour on,
     Wear it ever night and day;
   Ambushed lurks the evil one:
     Watch and pray!

   4 Hear the victors who o'ercame;
     Still they mark each warrior's way;
   All with one sweet voice exclaim:
     'Watch and pray!'

mf 5 Hear, above all, hear thy Lord,
     Him thou lovest to obey;
   Hide within thy heart his word:
     'Watch and pray!'

   6 Watch, as if on that alone
     Hung the issue of the day;
   Pray, that help may be sent down:
     Watch and pray!

309
T. Hughes

mf 1 O GOD of truth, whose living word
   Upholds whate'er hath breath,
   Look down on thy creation, Lord,
   Enslaved by sin and death.

f 2 Set up thy standard, Lord, that we
   Who claim a heavenly birth
   May march with thee to smite the lies
   That vex thy ransomed earth.

mf 3 Ah, would we join that blest array,
   And follow in the might
   Of him, the Faithful and the True,
   In raiment clean and white?

   4 We fight for truth? we fight for God?
   Poor slaves of lies and sin!
   He who would fight for thee on earth
   Must first be true within.

f   5 Then, God of truth, for whom we long,
     Thou who wilt hear our prayer,
   Do thine own battle in our hearts,
     And slay the falsehood there.

    6 Yea, come! Then, tried as in the fire,
     From every lie set free,
   Thy perfect truth shall dwell in us,
     And we shall live in thee.

310

J. Wesley and others. Cento from
Befiehl du deine Wege, P. Gerhardt

f   1 PUT thou thy trust in God,
     In duty's path go on;
   Walk in his strength with faith and hope,
     So shall thy work be done.

mf   2 Commit thy ways to him,
     Thy works into his hands,
   And rest on his unchanging word,
     Who heaven and earth commands.

    3 Though years on years roll on,
     His covenant shall endure;
f   Though clouds and darkness hide his path,
     The promised grace is sure.

mf   4 Give to the winds thy fears;
     Hope, and be undismayed:
   God hears thy sighs and counts thy tears;
f   God shall lift up thy head.

mf   5 Through waves and clouds and storms
     His power will clear thy way:
f   Wait thou his time; the darkest night
     Shall end in brightest day.

mf 6 Leave to his sovereign sway
To choose and to command;
So shalt thou, wondering, own his way,
How wise, how strong his hand.

311
J. Edmeston

mf 1 LEAD us, heavenly Father, lead us
O'er the world's tempestuous sea;
Guard us, guide us, keep us, feed us,
For we have no help but thee;
Yet possessing every blessing,
If our God our Father be.

p 2 Saviour, breathe forgiveness o'er us:
All our weakness thou dost know;
Thou didst tread this earth before us,
Thou didst feel its keenest woe;
Lone and dreary, faint and weary,
Through the desert thou didst go.

mf 3 Spirit of our God, descending,
Fill our hearts with heavenly joy,
Love with every passion blending,
Pleasure that can never cloy:
Thus provided, pardoned, guided,
Nothing can our peace destroy.

312
St. Anatolius. Tr. J. M. Neale†

ζοφερᾶς τρικυμίας

f 1 FIERCE was the wild billow,
Dark was the night;
Oars laboured heavily,
Foam glimmered white;
Trembled the mariners,
Peril was nigh:
Then said the God of God,
p 'Peace! It is I.'

f   2 Ridge of the mountain-wave,
      Lower thy crest!
   Wail of the hurricane,
      Be thou at rest!
   Sorrow can never be,
      Darkness must fly,
   Where saith the Light of Light,
p   'Peace! It is I.'

mf   3 Jesus, deliverer,
      Nigh to us be;
   Soothe thou my voyaging
      Over life's sea:
f   Thou, when the storm of death
      Roars, sweeping by,
p   Whisper, O Truth of Truth,
      'Peace! It is I.'

313
G. Thring

mf   1 FIERCE raged the tempest o'er the deep,
     Watch did thine anxious servants keep,
p   But thou wast wrapped in guileless sleep,
         Calm and still.

mf   2 'Save, Lord, we perish,' was their cry,
     'O save us in our agony!'
     Thy word above the storm rose high,
         'Peace, be still.'

   3 The wild winds hushed; the angry deep
     Sank, like a little child, to sleep;
     The sullen billows ceased to leap,
         At thy will.

   4 So, when our life is clouded o'er,
     And storm-winds drift us from the shore,
     Say, lest we sink to rise no more,
      p   'Peace, be still.'

314 *Ps. 42.* *N. Tate and N. Brady*
(New Version)

mf 1 AS pants the hart for cooling streams
    When heated in the chase,
So longs my soul, O God, for thee,
    And thy refreshing grace.

2 For thee, my God, the living God,
    My thirsty soul doth pine:
O when shall I behold thy face,
    Thou majesty divine?

p
f 3 Why restless, why cast down, my soul?
    Hope still, and thou shalt sing
The praise of him who is thy God,
    Thy health's eternal spring.

4 To Father, Son, and Holy Ghost,
    The God whom we adore,
Be glory, as it was, is now,
    And shall be evermore.

315 *E. H. Blakeney*

f 1 UP to the throne on high,
    In loyal love and trust,
We, children of an hour,
    Lift voices from the dust.

mf 2 Suffer us not to stray
    From thee, our God, our guide,
Whatever trials come,
    Whatever ills betide.

3 Grant us in mercy, Lord,
    The gifts thou deemest best,
Help for the daily task,
    And for our spirits rest.

f 4 Strong in the power of faith,
    From doubt and care set free,
We tread the appointed path
    That brings us home to thee.

5 Bid empty terror cease,
    Neath thy o'ershadowing might
    Uphold our hearts in hope,
    And lead us into light.

316   *C. Coffin. Tr. I. William*
Supreme motor cordium

1 GREAT mover of all hearts, whose hand
    Doth all the secret springs command
        Of human thought and will,
    Thou, since the world was made, dost bless
    Thy saints with fruits of holiness,
        Their order to fulfil.

2 Faith, hope, and love here weave one chain;
    But love alone shall then remain
        When this short day is gone:
f O Love, O Truth, O endless Light,
    When shall we see thy sabbath bright
        With all our labours done?

p 3 We sow 'mid perils here and tears;
    There the glad hand the harvest bears,
        Which here in grief hath sown:
mf Great Three in One, the increase give;
    Thy gifts of grace, by which we live,
        With heavenly glory crown.

317   *J. Montgomery*

1 LORD, teach us how to pray aright
        With reverence and with fear;
    Though dust and ashes in thy sight,
        We may, we must, draw near.

2 We perish if we cease from prayer:
        O grant us power to pray;
    And, when to meet thee we prepare,
        Lord, meet us by the way.

3 God of all grace, we bring to thee
  A broken, contrite heart;
Give what thine eye delights to see,
  Truth in the inward part;

4 Faith in the only Sacrifice
  That can for sin atone,
To cast our hopes, to fix our eyes,
  On Christ, on Christ alone;

5 Patience to watch and wait and weep,
  Though mercy long delay;
Courage our fainting souls to keep,
  And trust thee though thou slay.

6 Give these, and then thy will be done;
  Thus, strengthened with all might,
We, through thy Spirit and thy Son,
  Shall pray, and pray aright.

318   C. Wesley†

mf 1 SHEPHERD divine, our wants relieve
    In this our evil day;
  To all thy tempted followers give
    The power to watch and pray.

2 Long as our fiery trials last,
    Long as the cross we bear,
  O let our souls on thee be cast
    In never-ceasing prayer.

3 The Spirit's interceding grace
    Give us in faith to claim;
  To wrestle till we see thy face,
    And know thy hidden Name.

4 Till thou thy perfect love impart,
    Till thou thyself bestow,
  Be this the cry of every heart,
    'I will not let thee go.'

5 I will not let thee go, unless
  Thou tell thy Name to me;
With all thy great salvation bless,
  And make me all like thee.

f 6 Then let me on the mountain-top
  Behold thy open face;
Where faith in sight is swallowed up,
  And prayer in endless praise.

*Note.—The latter part of this hymn makes referenc
to Jacob's encounter with the angel (Gen. 32. 24–30*

319   *J. Newton*

mf 1 COME, my soul, thy suit prepare:
  Jesus loves to answer prayer;
He himself has bid thee pray,
  Therefore will not say thee nay.

2 Thou art coming to a King:
  Large petitions with thee bring;
For his grace and power are such
  None can ever ask too much.

p 3 With my burden I begin:
  Lord, remove this load of sin;
Let thy Blood, for sinners spilt,
  Set my conscience free from guilt.

4 Lord, I come to thee for rest;
  Take possession of my breast;
There thy blood-bought right maintain,
  And without a rival reign.

mf 5 While I am a pilgrim here,
  Let thy love my spirit cheer;
Be my guide, my guard, my friend,
  Lead me to my journey's end.

320   *H. H. Milman*

1 O HELP us, Lord! each hour of need
   Thy heavenly succour give;
Help us in thought and word and deed
   Each hour on earth we live.

2 O help us, when our spirits bleed
   With contrite anguish sore;
And when our hearts are cold and dead,
   O help us, Lord, the more.

3 O help us, through the prayer of faith
   More firmly to believe;
For still the more the servant hath,
   The more shall he receive.

4 O help us, Jesu, from on high;
   We know no help but thee:
O help us so to live and die
   As thine in heaven to be.

321   *J. J. Cummins†*

mf 1 JESUS, Lord of life and glory,
   Bend from heaven thy gracious ear;
While our waiting souls adore thee,
   Friend of helpless sinners, hear:
p   By thy mercy,
     O deliver us, good Lord.

mf 2 From the depths of nature's blindness,
   From the hardening power of sin,
From all malice and unkindness,
   From the pride that lurks within:
p   By thy mercy, etc.

3 When temptation sorely presses,
 In the day of Satan's power,
In our times of deep distresses,
 In each dark and trying hour:
  By thy mercy, etc.

mf 4 When the world around is smiling,
 In the time of wealth and ease,
Earthly joys our hearts beguiling,
 In the day of health and peace:
p   By thy mercy, etc.

5 In the weary hours of sickness,
 In the times of grief and pain,
When we feel our mortal weakness,
 When all human help is vain:
  By thy mercy, etc.

6 In the solemn hour of dying,
 In the aweful judgement day,
mf May our souls, on thee relying,
 Find thee still our Rock and stay:
p   By thy mercy, etc.

322 *Ps. 130*   *Sir H. W. Baker*

p 1 OUT of the deep I call
  To thee, O Lord, to thee;
 Before thy throne of grace I fall:
  Be merciful to me.

2 Out of the deep I cry,
  The woeful deep of sin,
 Of evil done in days gone by,
  Of evil now within.

3 Out of the deep of fear,
  And dread of coming shame,
 From morning watch till night is near
  I plead the precious name.

mf 4   Lord, there is mercy now,
      As ever was, with thee;
    Before thy throne of grace I bow:
p   Be merciful to me.

323   *Mrs. C. F. Alexander*

1 FORSAKEN once, and thrice denied,
    The risen Lord gave pardon free,
    Stood once again at Peter's side,
      And asked him, 'Lov'st thou me?'

2 How many times with faithless word
    Have we denied his holy name,
    How oft forsaken our dear Lord,
      And shrunk when trial came!

3 Saint Peter, when the cock crew clear,
    Went out, and wept his broken faith:
    Strong as a rock through strife and fear,
      He served his Lord till death.

4 How oft his cowardice of heart
    We have without his love sincere,
    The sin without the sorrow's smart,
      The shame without the tear!

5 O oft forsaken, oft denied,
    Forgive our shame, wash out our sin;
    Look on us from thy Father's side
      And let that sweet look win.

6 Hear when we call thee from the deep,
    Still walk beside us on the shore,
    Give hands to work, and eyes to weep,
      And hearts to love thee more.

324　　　　　　　　　　　　　　　*H. Twell*

p 1 NOT for our sins alone
　　　Thy mercy, Lord, we sue;
　Let fall thy pitying glance
　　　On our devotions too,
　What we have done for thee,
　　　And what we think to do.

mf 2 The holiest hours we spend
　　　In prayer upon our knees,
　The times when most we deem
　　　Our songs of praise will please,
　Thou searcher of all hearts,
p　　Forgiveness pour on these.

mf 3 And all the gifts we bring,
　　　And all the vows we make,
　And all the acts of love
　　　We plan for thy dear sake,
p　Into thy pardoning thought,
　　　O God of mercy, take.

mf 4 And most, when we, thy flock,
　　　Before thine altar bend,
　And strange, bewildering thoughts
　　　With those sweet moments blend,
p　By him whose Death we plead,
　　　Good Lord, thy help extend.

mf 5 Bow down thine ear and hear!
　　　Open thine eyes and see!
　Our very love is shame,
　　　And we must come to thee
　To make it of thy grace
　　　What thou wouldst have it be.

325　　　　　　　　　　　　　　*C. Wesley*

1 O FOR a heart to praise my God,
　　A heart from sin set free;
　A heart that's sprinkled with the Blood
　　So freely shed for me:

2 A heart resigned, submissive, meek,
　　My great Redeemer's throne;
　Where only Christ is heard to speak,
　　Where Jesus reigns alone:

3 A humble, lowly, contrite heart,
　　Believing, true, and clean,
　Which neither life nor death can part
　　From him that dwells within:

4 A heart in every thought renewed,
　　And full of love divine;
　Perfect and right and pure and good—
　　A copy, Lord, of thine!

5 Thy nature, gracious Lord, impart,
　　Come quickly from above;
　Write thy new name upon my heart,
　　Thy new best name of Love.

326　　　　　　　　　　　　　*W. Cowper*

1 O FOR a closer walk with God,
　　A calm and heavenly frame;
　A light to shine upon the road
　　That leads me to the Lamb!

2 What peaceful hours I once enjoyed!
　　How sweet their memory still!
　But they have left an aching void
　　The world can never fill.

3 Return, O holy Dove, return,
　　Sweet messenger of rest:
　I hate the sins that made thee mourn,
　　And drove thee from my breast.

4 The dearest idol I have known,
　　Whate'er that idol be,
　Help me to tear it from thy throne,
　　And worship only thee.

5 So shall my walk be close with God,
  Calm and serene my frame;
So purer light shall mark the road
  That leads me to the Lamb.

327 *Bishop Chr. Wordsworth*

1 LORD, be thy word my rule,
  In it may I rejoice;
Thy glory be my aim,
  Thy holy will my choice;

2 Thy promises my hope,
  Thy providence my guard,
Thine arm my strong support,
  Thyself my great reward.

328 *C. Wesley*

1 A CHARGE to keep I have,
  A God to glorify,
A never-dying soul to save,
  And fit it for the sky.

2 To serve the present age,
  My calling to fulfil,
O may it all my powers engage
  To do my Master's will.

3 Arm me with jealous care,
  As in thy sight to live;
And O, thy servant, Lord, prepare
  A good account to give.

4 Help me to watch and pray,
  And on thyself rely;
And let me ne'er my trust betray,
  But press to realms on high.

329

C. Wesley†

1 O THOU who camest from above
    The fire celestial to impart,
  Kindle a flame of sacred love
    On the mean altar of my heart.

2 There let it for thy glory burn
    With inextinguishable blaze,
  And trembling to its source return
    In humble prayer and fervent praise.

3 Jesus, confirm my heart's desire
    To work and speak and think for thee;
  Still let me guard the holy fire
    And still stir up the gift in me.

4 Still let me prove thy perfect will,
    My acts of faith and love repeat;
  Till death thy endless mercies seal,
    And make the sacrifice complete.

330

Mrs. M. F. Maude

1 THINE for ever! God of love,
  Hear us from thy throne above;
  Thine for ever may we be
  Here and in eternity.

2 Thine for ever! Lord of life,
  Shield us through our earthly strife;
  Thou the Life, the Truth, the Way,
  Guide us to the realms of day.

3 Thine for ever! O how blest
  They who find in thee their rest!
  Saviour, guardian, heavenly friend,
  O defend us to the end.

4*Thine for ever! Shepherd, keep
　　Us thy frail and trembling sheep;
　　Safe alone beneath thy care,
　　Let us all thy goodness share.

5 Thine for ever! thou our guide,
　　All our wants by thee supplied,
　　All our sins by thee forgiven,
　　Lead us, Lord, from earth to heaven.

331

J. E. Bode

1 O JESUS, I have promised
　　　　To serve thee to the end;
　　Be thou for ever near me,
　　　　My Master and my Friend:
　　I shall not fear the battle
　　　　If thou art by my side,
　　Nor wander from the pathway
　　　　If thou wilt be my guide.

2*O let me feel thee near me:
　　　　The world is ever near;
　　I see the sights that dazzle,
　　　　The tempting sounds I hear;
　　My foes are ever near me,
　　　　Around me and within;
　　But, Jesus, draw thou nearer,
　　　　And shield my soul from sin.

3 O let me hear thee speaking
　　　　In accents clear and still,
　　Above the storms of passion,
　　　　The murmurs of self-will;
　　O speak to reassure me,
　　　　To hasten or control;
　　O speak, and make me listen,
　　　　Thou guardian of my soul.

4 O Jesus, thou hast promised
   To all who follow thee,
That where thou art in glory
   There shall thy servant be;
And, Jesus, I have promised
   To serve thee to the end:
O give me grace to follow,
   My Master and my Friend.

5 O let me see thy foot-marks,
   And in them plant mine own;
My hope to follow duly
   Is in thy strength alone:
O guide me, call me, draw me,
   Uphold me to the end;
And then in heaven receive me,
   My Saviour and my Friend.

332   *Pynson's Horae* (1514)

1 GOD be in my head,
   And in my understanding;

2 God be in my eyes,
   And in my looking;

3 God be in my mouth,
   And in my speaking;

4 God be in my heart,
   And in my thinking;

5 God be at my end,
   And at my departing.

333   *C. W. Everest* ‡

1 TAKE up thy cross, the Saviour said,
   If thou wouldst my disciple be;
Deny thyself, the world forsake,
   And humbly follow after me.

2 Take up thy cross! let not its weight
    Fill thy weak spirit with alarm:
His strength shall bear thy spirit up,
    And brace thy heart, and nerve thine arm.

3 Take up thy cross, nor heed the shame,
    Nor let thy foolish pride rebel:
Thy Lord for thee the Cross endured,
    To save thy soul from death and hell.

4 Take up thy cross then in his strength,
    And calmly every danger brave;
'Twill guide thee to a better home,
    And lead to victory o'er the grave.

5 Take up thy cross, and follow Christ,
    Nor think till death to lay it down;
For only he who bears the cross
    May hope to wear the glorious crown.

6 To thee, great Lord, the One in Three,
    All praise for evermore ascend:
O grant us in our home to see
    The heavenly life that knows no end.

334

J. H. Gurney

1 LORD, as to thy dear Cross we flee,
    And plead to be forgiven,
So let thy life our pattern be,
    And form our souls for heaven.

2 Help us, through good report and ill,
    Our daily cross to bear;
Like thee, to do our Father's will,
    Our brethren's griefs to share.

3 Let grace our selfishness expel,
    Our earthliness refine,
And kindness in our bosoms dwell
    As free and true as thine.

4 If joy shall at thy bidding fly,
    And grief's dark day come on,
We in our turn would meekly cry,
    'Father, thy will be done.'

5 Kept peaceful in the midst of strife,
    Forgiving and forgiven,
O may we lead the pilgrim's life,
    And follow thee to heaven.

335   *J. Keble and others*

1   BLEST are the pure in heart,
    For they shall see our God;
The secret of the Lord is theirs,
    Their soul is Christ's abode.

2   The Lord, who left the heavens
    Our life and peace to bring,
To dwell in lowliness with men,
    Their pattern and their King;

3   Still to the lowly soul
    He doth himself impart,
And for his dwelling and his throne
    Chooseth the pure in heart.

4   Lord, we thy presence seek;
    May ours this blessing be;
Give us a pure and lowly heart,
    A temple meet for thee.

336   *C. Wesley†*

1 FORTH in thy name, O Lord, I go,
    My daily labour to pursue;
Thee, only thee, resolved to know,
    In all I think or speak or do.

2   The task thy wisdom hath assigned
     O let me cheerfully fulfil;
   In all my works thy presence find,
     And prove thy good and perfect will.

3   Thee may I set at my right hand,
     Whose eyes my inmost substance see,
   And labour on at thy command,
     And offer all my works to thee.

4   Give me to bear thy easy yoke,
     And every moment watch and pray,
   And still to things eternal look,
     And hasten to thy glorious day;

5   For thee delightfully employ
     Whate'er thy bounteous grace hath given,
   And run my course with even joy,
     And closely walk with thee to heaven.

337

George Herbert

1   TEACH me, my God and King,
     In all things thee to see;
  And what I do in anything
     To do it as for thee.

2   A man that looks on glass,
     On it may stay his eye;
  Or, if he pleaseth, through it pass,
     And then the heaven espy.

3   All may of thee partake;
     Nothing can be so mean
  Which, with this tincture, *For thy sake*,
     Will not grow bright and clean.

4   A servant with this clause
     Makes drudgery divine;
  Who sweeps a room, as for thy laws,
     Makes that and the action fine.

5   This is the famous stone
     That turneth all to gold;
For that which God doth touch and own
     Cannot for less be told.

338   *J. H. Gurney*

mf 1   FAIR waved the golden corn
          In Canaan's pleasant land,
     When full of joy, some shining morn,
          Went forth the reaper-band.

f   2   To God so good and great
          Their cheerful thanks they pour;
     Then carry to his Temple-gate
          The choicest of their store.

mf 3   Like Israel, Lord, we give
          Our earliest fruits to thee,
     And pray that, long as we shall live,
          We may thy children be.

      4   Thine is our youthful prime,
          And life and all its powers:
     Be with us in our morning time,
          And bless our evening hours.

      5   In wisdom let us grow,
          As years and strength are given,
f That we may serve thy Church below,
          And join thy saints in heaven.

339   *Jane L. Borthwick*

1   COME, labour on!
Who dares stand idle on the harvest plain,
While all around him waves the golden grain?
And to each servant does the Master say,
     'Go, work to-day!'

2   Come, labour on!
Away with gloomy doubts and faithless fear!
No arm so weak but may do service here;
By feeblest agents can our God fulfil
   His righteous will.

3   Come, labour on!
No time for rest, till glows the western sky,
Till the long shadows o'er our pathway lie,
And a glad sound comes with the setting sun,
   'Servants, well done!'

4   Come, labour on!
The toil is pleasant, the reward is sure;
Blessèd are those who to the end endure:
How full their joy, how deep their rest, shall be,
   O Lord, with thee!

340
P. H. B. Lyon

1 O GOD, before whose altar
   The stars like tapers burn,
At whose inscrutable decree
   The planets wheel and turn,
Though earth and sea and heaven
   Unite thy praise to sing,
Man in his weakness yet may give
   A worthier offering.

2 Those who give up life's bounty
   To serve a race to be,
Whose bones lie white along the trail
   Which leads the world to thee;
Those who when fears beset them
   Stand fast and fight and die,
Their unconsidered lives go up
   Like incense to the sky.

3 All those oppressed or lonely
    Or long at strife with pain,
Who face the darkness undismayed
    And turn their loss to gain,
Those who with love and meekness
    Outlast the years of wrong,
Their silent courage pleads to heaven
    More eloquent than song.

4 O Lord, be ours the glory
    Beyond all earthly fame,
Like those to conquer for thy sake
    Despair and doubt and shame;
Till through a world made noble,
    Through lands from sin set free,
The armies of the living God
    Shall march to victory.

341
H. Montagu Butler

1 'LIFT up your hearts!' We lift them, Lord, to
    thee;
Here at thy feet none other may we see:
'Lift up your hearts!' E'en so, with one accord,
We lift them up, we lift them to the Lord.

2 Above the level of the former years,
The mire of sin, the slough of guilty fears,
The mist of doubt, the blight of love's decay,
O Lord of Light, lift all our hearts to-day!

3*Above the swamps of subterfuge and shame,
The deeds, the thoughts, that honour may not
    name,
The halting tongue that dares not tell the whole,
O Lord of Truth, lift every Christian soul!

4 Lift every gift that thou thyself hast given:
　　Low lies the best till lifted up to heaven;
　　Low lie the bounding heart, the teeming brain,
　　Till, sent from God, they mount to God again.

5 Then, as the trumpet-call in after years,
　　'Lift up your hearts!' rings pealing in our ears,
　　Still shall those hearts respond with full accord,
　　'We lift them up, we lift them to the Lord!'

────────────

HYMNS OF PERSONAL DEVOTION

342　　　　　　　　　　　　　　　　　*R. Baxter*†

1 LORD, it belongs not to my care
　　　Whether I die or live:
　　To love and serve thee is my share,
　　　And this thy grace must give.

2 Christ leads me through no darker rooms
　　　Than he went through before;
　　He that unto God's Kingdom comes
　　　Must enter by this door.

3 Come, Lord, when grace hath made me meet
　　　Thy blessèd face to see;
　　For if thy work on earth be sweet,
　　　What will thy glory be!

4 Then I shall end my sad complaints
　　　And weary, sinful days,
　　And join with the triumphant saints
　　　That sing my Saviour's praise.

5 My knowledge of that life is small,
　　　The eye of faith is dim;
　　But 'tis enough that Christ knows all,
　　　And I shall be with him.

343

C. Wesley†

mf 1 COME, O thou Traveller unknown,
   Whom still I hold, but cannot see;
   My company before is gone,
   And I am left alone with thee;
   With thee all night I mean to stay,
   And wrestle till the break of day.

p 2 I need not tell thee who I am,
   My misery or sin declare;
   Thyself hast called me by my name;
   Look on thy hands, and read it there!
   But who, I ask thee, who art thou?
   Tell me thy Name, and tell me now.

mf 3 In vain thou strugglest to get free;
   I never will unloose my hold.
   Art thou the Man that died for me?
   The secret of thy love unfold:
   Wrestling, I will not let thee go,
   Till I thy Name, thy nature know.

4 Yield to me now, for I am weak,
   But confident in self-despair;
   Speak to my heart, in blessings speak,
   Be conquered by my instant prayer.
   Speak, or thou never hence shalt move,
   And tell me if thy Name is Love?

f 5 'Tis Love! 'tis Love! thou diedst for me!
   I hear thy whisper in my heart!
   The morning breaks, the shadows flee;
   Pure universal Love thou art:
   To me, to all, thy mercies move;
   Thy nature and thy Name is Love.

Note.—*This hymn is based on the story of Jacob's
encounter with the angel in Gen.* **32.** *24–30.*

344   *W. Cowper*

mf 1 HARK, my soul! it is the Lord;
  'Tis thy Saviour, hear his word;
  Jesus speaks, and speaks to thee,
p   'Say, poor sinner, lov'st thou me?

mf 2 'I delivered thee when bound,
  And, when wounded, healed thy wound;
  Sought thee wandering, set thee right,
  Turned thy darkness into light.

 3 'Can a woman's tender care
  Cease towards the child she bare?
  Yes, she may forgetful be,
  Yet will I remember thee.

f 4 'Mine is an unchanging love,
  Higher than the heights above,
  Deeper than the depths beneath,
  Free and faithful, strong as death.

 5 'Thou shalt see my glory soon,
  When the work of grace is done;
  Partner of my throne shalt be:
p   Say, poor sinner, lov'st thou me?'

mf 6 Lord, it is my chief complaint
  That my love is weak and faint;
f   Yet I love thee, and adore;
  O for grace to love thee more!

345   *J. Newton*

mf 1 APPROACH, my soul, the mercy-seat,
  Where Jesus answers prayer;
  There humbly fall before his feet,
  For none can perish there.

p 2 Thy promise is my only plea,
   With this I venture nigh:
   Thou callest burdened souls to thee,
   And such, O Lord, am I.

3 Bowed down beneath a load of sin,
   By Satan sorely pressed,
   By war without and fears within,
   I come to thee for rest.

4 Be thou my shield and hiding-place,
   That, sheltered near thy side,
   I may my fierce accuser face,
   And tell him thou hast died.

mf 5 O wondrous love, to bleed and die,
   To bear the Cross and shame,
   That guilty sinners, such as I,
   Might plead thy gracious name!

346   *J. Montgomery*

1 'FOR ever with the Lord!'
   Amen; so let it be:
   Life from the dead is in that word,
   'Tis immortality.
   Here in the body pent,
   Absent from him I roam,
   Yet nightly pitch my moving tent
   A day's march nearer home.

2 My Father's house on high,
   Home of my soul, how near
   At times to faith's foreseeing eye
   Thy golden gates appear!
   Ah, then my spirit faints
   To reach the land I love,
   The bright inheritance of saints,
   Jerusalem above.

3 'For ever with the Lord!'
    Father, if 'tis thy will,
The promise of that faithful word
    Even here to me fulfil.
Be thou at my right hand,
    Then can I never fail;
Uphold thou me, and I shall stand,
    Fight, and I must prevail.

4 So when my latest breath
    Shall rend the veil in twain,
By death I shall escape from death,
    And life eternal gain.
Knowing as I am known,
    How shall I love that word,
And oft repeat before the throne,
    'For ever with the Lord!'

347   R. Palmer

1 JESUS, these eyes have never seen
    That radiant form of thine;
The veil of sense hangs dark between
    Thy blessèd face and mine.

2 I see thee not, I hear thee not,
    Yet art thou oft with me;
And earth hath ne'er so dear a spot
    As where I meet with thee.

3 Yet, though I have not seen, and still
    Must rest in faith alone,
I love thee, dearest Lord, and will,
    Unseen, but not unknown.

4 When death these mortal eyes shall seal
    And still this throbbing heart,
The rending veil shall thee reveal
    All glorious as thou art.

348

J. M. Neale†

p   1 ART thou weary, art thou languid,
   Art thou sore distrest?
mf   'Come to me,' saith One, 'and coming
    p   Be at rest!'

2 Hath he marks to lead me to him,
   If he be my guide?
p   'In his feet and hands are wound-prints,
   And his side.'

mf   3 Hath he diadem as Monarch
   That his brow adorns?
p   'Yea, a crown, in very surety,
   But of thorns.'

r:f   4 If I find him, if I follow,
   What his guerdon here?
p   'Many a sorrow, many a labour,
   Many a tear.'

mf   5 If I still hold closely to him,
   What hath he at last?
f   'Sorrow vanquished, labour ended,
   Jordan past.'

mf   6 If I ask him to receive me,
   Will he say me nay?
f   'Not till earth, and not till heaven,
   Pass away.'

mf   7 Finding, following, keeping, struggling,
   Is he sure to bless?
f   'Angels, martyrs, prophets, virgins,
   Answer, Yes!'

349

Charlotte Elliott

p   1 JUST as I am, without one plea
  But that thy Blood was shed for me,
  And that thou bidst me come to thee,
   O Lamb of God, I come.

2 Just as I am, though tossed about
   With many a conflict, many a doubt,
   Fightings and fears within, without,
      O Lamb of God, I come.

3 Just as I am, poor, wretched, blind;
   Sight, riches, healing of the mind,
   Yea, all I need, in thee to find,
      O Lamb of God, I come.

mf 4 Just as I am, thou wilt receive,
   Wilt welcome, pardon, cleanse, relieve:
   Because thy promise I believe,
      O Lamb of God, I come.

5 Just as I am (thy love unknown
   Has broken every barrier down),
f   Now to be thine, yea, thine alone,
      O Lamb of God, I come.

mf 6 Just as I am, of that free love
   The breadth, length, depth, and height to
      prove,
f   Here for a season, then above,
      O Lamb of God, I come.

350

W. Chatterton Dix

mf 1 'COME unto me, ye weary,
    And I will give you rest.'
   O blessèd voice of Jesus,
    Which comes to hearts opprest!
   It tells of benediction,
    Of pardon, grace, and peace,
   Of joy that hath no ending,
    Of love which cannot cease.

2 'Come unto me, ye wanderers,
    And I will give you light.'
O loving voice of Jesus,
    Which comes to cheer the night!

p   Our hearts were filled with sadness,
    And we had lost our way;
f   But he has brought us gladness
    And songs at break of day.

mf 3 'Come unto me, ye fainting,
    And I will give you life.'
O cheering voice of Jesus,
    Which comes to aid our strife!
The foe is stern and eager,
    The fight is fierce and long;
f   But he has made us mighty,
    And stronger than the strong.

mf 4 'And whosoever cometh,
    I will not cast him out.'
f   O welcome voice of Jesus,
    Which drives away our doubt!
Which call us very sinners,
    Unworthy though we be
Of love so free and boundless,
    To come, dear Lord, to thee.

351
H. Bonar

mf 1 I HEARD the voice of Jesus say,
    'Come unto me and rest;
Lay down, thou weary one, lay down
    Thy head upon my breast:'
f   I came to Jesus as I was,
    Weary and worn and sad;
I found in him a resting-place,
    And he has made me glad.

mf 2 I heard the voice of Jesus say,
  'Behold, I freely give
  The living water, thirsty one;
   Stoop down and drink and live:'
f I came to Jesus, and I drank
   Of that life-giving stream;
  My thirst was quenched, my soul revived,
  And now I live in him.

mf 3 I heard the voice of Jesus say,
  'I am this dark world's Light;
  Look unto me, thy morn shall rise,
   And all thy day be bright:'
f I looked to Jesus, and I found
   In him my Star, my Sun;
  And in that Light of life I'll walk
  Till travelling days are done.

352
        Mrs. S. F. Adams†

mf 1 NEARER, my God, to thee,
  Nearer to thee!
 E'en though it be a cross
  That raiseth me;
 Still all my song shall be,
 'Nearer, my God, to thee,
  Nearer to thee!'

p 2 Though, like the wanderer,
  The sun gone down,
 Darkness comes over me,
  My rest a stone;
 Yet in my dreams I'd be
 Nearer, my God, to thee,
  Nearer to thee.

mf 3 There let my way appear
          Steps unto heaven,
      All that thou sendest me
          In mercy given;
      Angels to beckon me
      Nearer, my God, to thee,
          Nearer to thee.

f 4 Then, with my waking thoughts
          Bright with thy praise,
      Out of my stony griefs
          Beth-el I'll raise;
      So by my woes to be
      Nearer, my God, to thee,
          Nearer to thee.

Note.—*This hymn is based on the story of Jacob's
dream in Gen.* 28. 11–19.

353   *Frances R. Havergal*

  1 I COULD not do without thee,
        O Saviour of the lost,
    Whose precious Blood redeemed me
        At such tremendous cost:
    Thy righteousness, thy pardon,
        Thy precious Blood, must be
    My only hope and comfort,
        My glory and my plea.

  2 I could not do without thee,
        I cannot stand alone,
    I have no strength or goodness,
        No wisdom of my own;
    But thou, belovèd Saviour,
        Art all in all to me,
    And weakness will be power
        If leaning hard on thee.

3 I could not do without thee,
    O Jesus, Saviour dear;
E'en when my eyes are holden,
    I know that thou art near:
How dreary and how lonely
    This changeful life would be
Without the sweet communion,
    The secret rest, with thee!

4 I could not do without thee,
    For years are fleeting fast,
And soon in solemn loneness
    The river must be passed;
But thou wilt never leave me,
    And, though the waves roll high,
I know thou wilt be near me,
    And whisper, 'It is I.'

354

F. W. Faber†

mf 1 HARK! hark, my soul! angelic songs are
    swelling
    O'er earth's green fields and ocean's wave-
    beat shore:
    How sweet the truth those blessèd strains are
    telling
    Of that new life when sin shall be no more!
p   Angels of Jesus, angels of light,
    Singing to welcome the pilgrims of the night!

mf 2 Onward we go, for still we hear them sing-
    ing,
p   'Come, weary souls, for Jesus bids you
    come,'
mf   And through the dark, its echoes sweetly
    ringing,
    The music of the Gospel leads us home.
p   Angels of Jesus, etc.

3*Far, far away, like bells at evening pealing,
 The voice of Jesus sounds o'er land and
  sea,
And laden souls, by thousands meekly stealing,
 Kind Shepherd, turn their weary steps to
  thee.
p Angels of Jesus, etc.

mf 4 Rest comes at length: though life be long and
 dreary,
 The day must dawn, and darksome night
  be past;
Faith's journey ends in welcome to the weary,
 And heaven, the heart's true home, will
  come at last.
p Angels of Jesus, etc.

f 5 Angels, sing on, your faithful watches keeping,
 Sing us sweet fragments of the songs above;
Till morning's joy shall end the night of
 weeping,
 And life's long shadows break in cloudless
  love.
p Angels of Jesus, etc.

355   *Bishop W. Walsham How*

p 1 O JESU, thou art standing
  Outside the fast-closed door,
 In lowly patience waiting
  To pass the threshold o'er:
mf Shame on us, Christian brethren,
  His name and sign who bear,
 O shame, thrice shame upon us
p To keep him standing there!

2 O Jesu, thou art knocking;
    And lo, that hand is scarred,
And thorns thy brow encircle,
    And tears thy face have marred:
mf   O love that passeth knowledge,
    So patiently to wait!
O sin that hath no equal
    So fast to bar the gate!

p 3 O Jesu, thou art pleading
    In accents meek and low,
'I died for you, my children,
    And will ye treat me so?'
mf   O Lord, with shame and sorrow
    We open now the door:
Dear Saviour, enter, enter,
    And leave us nevermore.

356   H. Bonar

mf 1 THY way, not mine, O Lord,
    However dark it be;
Lead me by thine own hand,
    Choose out the path for me.

2 Smooth let it be or rough,
    It will be still the best;
Winding or straight, it leads
    Right onward to thy rest.

3 I dare not choose my lot;
    I would not if I might:
Choose thou for me, my God,
    So shall I walk aright.

4 The Kingdom that I seek
    Is thine; so let the way
That leads to it be thine,
    Else I must surely stray

p 5 Take thou my cup, and it
  With joy or sorrow fill,
 As best to thee may seem;
  Choose thou my good and ill.

6 Choose thou for me my friends,
  My sickness or my health;
 Choose thou my cares for me,
  My poverty or wealth.

mf 7 Not mine, not mine, the choice
  In things or great or small;
 Be thou my guide, my strength,
  My wisdom, and my all.

357
Charlotte Elliott

1 MY God, my Father, while I stray,
 Far from my home, on life's rough way,
 O teach me from my heart to say,
    'Thy will be done!'

2 Though dark my path, and sad my lot,
 Let me be still and murmur not,
 Or breathe the prayer divinely taught,
    'Thy will be done!'

3 What though in lonely grief I sigh
 For friends beloved no longer nigh,
 Submissive would I still reply,
    'Thy will be done!'

4 If thou shouldst call me to resign
 What most I prize, it ne'er was mine;
 I only yield thee what is thine:
    Thy will be done!

5 Let but my fainting heart be blest
 With thy sweet Spirit for its guest,
 My God, to thee I leave the rest:
    Thy will be done!

6 Renew my will from day to day,
　Blend it with thine, and take away⌣
　All that now makes it hard to say,
　　　　　'Thy will be done!'

358　　　　　　　　*Bishop E. H. Bickersteth*

mf 1 PEACE, perfect peace, in this dark world of
　　　sin?
p　The Blood of Jesus whispers peace within.

mf 2 Peace, perfect peace, by thronging duties
　　　pressed?
p　To do the will of Jesus, this is rest.

mf 3 Peace, perfect peace, with sorrows surging
　　　round?
p　On Jesus' bosom naught but calm is found.

mf 4 Peace, perfect peace, with loved ones far away?
p　In Jesus' keeping we are safe and they.

mf 5 Peace, perfect peace, our future all unknown?
f　Jesus we know, and he is on the throne.

p 6 Peace, perfect peace, death shadowing us and
　　　ours?
f　Jesus has vanquished death and all its powers.

mf 7 It is enough: earth's struggles soon shall cease,
　　And Jesus call us to heaven's perfect peace.

359　　　　　　　　*G. Matheson*

mf 1 O LOVE that wilt not let me go,
　　I rest my weary soul in thee:
　　I give thee back the life I owe,
　　That in thine ocean depths its flow⌣
　　　May richer, fuller, be.

p 2 O Light that followest all my way,
  I yield my flickering torch to thee:
mf My heart restores its borrowed ray,
  That in thy sunshine's blaze its day⌣
   May brighter, fairer be.

p 3 O Joy that seekest me through pain,
  I cannot close my heart to thee:
mf I trace the rainbow through the rain,
  And feel the promise is not vain
   That morn shall tearless be.

  4 O Cross that liftest up my head,
  I dare not ask to fly from thee:
  I lay in dust life's glory dead,
f And from the ground there blossoms red
   Life that shall endless be.

360

Bishop W. Walsham How

p 1 O MY Saviour, lifted⌣
  From the earth for me,
  Draw me, in thy mercy,
  Nearer unto thee.

  2 Lift my earth-bound longings,
  Fix them, Lord, above;
  Draw me with the magnet⌣
  Of thy mighty love.

mf 3 Lord, thine arms are stretching
  Ever far and wide,
  To enfold thy children
  To thy loving side.

  4 And I come, O Jesus:
  Dare I turn away?
f No, thy love hath conquered,
  And I come to-day;

mf 5 Bringing all my burdens,
  Sorrow, sin, and care,
  At thy feet I lay them,
  And I leave them there.

361   *Frances R. Haverga*

1 TAKE my life, and let it be
Consecrated, Lord, to thee;
Take my moments and my days,
Let them flow in ceaseless praise.
Take my hands, and let them move
At the impulse of thy love.
Take my feet, and let them be
Swift and beautiful for thee.

2 Take my voice, and let me sing
Always, only, for my King;
Take my lips, and let them be
Filled with messages from thee.
Take my silver and my gold;
Not a mite would I withhold.
Take my intellect, and use
Every power as thou shalt choose.

3 Take my will, and make it thine:
It shall be no longer mine.
Take my heart: it is thine own;
It shall be thy royal throne.
Take my love; my Lord, I pour
At thy feet its treasure-store.
Take myself, and I will be
Ever, only, all for thee.

362   *A. Midlan*

1 REVIVE thy work, O Lord!
Thy mighty arm make bare;
Speak with the voice that wakes the dead,
And make thy people hear.

2 Revive thy work, O Lord!
Disturb this sleep of death;
Quicken the smouldering embers now
By thine almighty breath.

3 Revive thy work, O Lord!
   Create soul-thirst for thee:
And hungering for the Bread of Life
   O may our spirits be.

4 Revive thy work, O Lord!
   Exalt thy precious name;
And by the Holy Ghost our love
   For thee and thine inflame.

5 Revive thy work, O Lord!
   Give Pentecostal showers;
The glory shall be all thine own,
   The blessing, Lord, be ours.

363   *Emily E. S. Elliott*

mf 1 THOU didst leave thy throne and thy kingly
        crown,
   When thou camest to earth for me;
But in Bethlehem's home was there found no
        room
   For thy holy Nativity:
      O come to my heart, Lord Jesus;
      There is room in my heart for thee.

2 Heaven's arches rang when the angels sang,
   Proclaiming thy royal degree;
But in lowly birth didst thou come to earth,
   And in great humility:
      O come to my heart, etc.

mf 3 The foxes found rest, and the bird had its
        nest
   In the shade of the cedar tree;
But thy couch was the sod, O thou Son of
        God,
   In the desert of Galilee:
      O come to my heart, etc.

mf 4 Thou camest, O Lord, with the living word
  That should set thy people free;
p But with mocking scorn and with crown of
   thorn
   They bore thee to Calvary:
    O come to my heart, etc.

f 5 When the heavens shall ring, and the angels
   sing,
   At thy coming to victory,
  Let thy voice call me home, saying, 'Yes
   there is room,
   There is room at my side for thee:'
    O come to my heart, etc.

364
F. W. Faber

1 SOULS of men! why will ye scatter
  Like a crowd of frightened sheep?
Foolish hearts! why will ye wander
  From a love so true and deep?

2 Was there ever kindest shepherd
  Half so gentle, half so sweet,
As the Saviour who would have us
  Come and gather round his feet?

3 There's a wideness in God's mercy
  Like the wideness of the sea;
There's a kindness in his justice
  Which is more than liberty.

4 There is no place where earth's sorrows
  Are more felt than up in heaven;
There is no place where earth's failings
  Have such kindly judgement given.

5 There is plentiful redemption
  In the Blood that has been shed;
There is joy for all the members
  In the sorrows of the Head.

6 For the love of God is broader
　　Than the measures of man's mind;
　And the heart of the Eternal
　　Is most wonderfully kind.

7 Pining souls! come nearer Jesus,
　　And oh, come not doubting thus,
　But with faith that trusts more bravely
　　His huge tenderness for us.

8 If our love were but more simple,
　　We should take him at his word;
　And our lives would be all sunshine
　　In the sweetness of our Lord.

---

365 *Ps.* 103.   *H. F. Lyte*†

f 1 PRAISE, my soul, the King of heaven,
　　To his feet thy tribute bring;
　Ransomed, healed, restored, forgiven,
　　Who like me his praise should sing?
　　　Alleluia! Alleluia!
　　Praise the everlasting King.

mf 2 Praise him for his grace and favour
　　To our fathers in distress;
　Praise him still the same as ever,
　　Slow to chide, and swift to bless:
f　　　Alleluia! Alleluia!
　　Glorious in his faithfulness.

p 3 Father-like, he tends and spares us,
　　Well our feeble frame he knows;
　In his hands he gently bears us,
　　Rescues us from all our foes:
f　　　Alleluia! Alleluia!
　　Widely as his mercy flows.

4 Angels, help us to adore him;
   Ye behold him face to face;
Sun and moon, bow down before him,
   Dwellers all in time and space:
     Alleluia! Alleluia!
   Praise with us the God of grace.

366   *J. J. Schütz. Tr. Frances E. Cox*

Sei Lob und Ehr' dem höchsten Gut

1 SING praise to God who reigns above,
   The God of all creation,
The God of power, the God of love,
   The God of our salvation;
With healing balm my soul he fills,
And every faithless murmur stills:
   To God all praise and glory.

2 The Lord is never far away,
   But, through all grief distressing,
An ever-present help and stay,
   Our peace and joy and blessing;
As with a mother's tender hand,
He leads his own, his chosen band:
   To God all praise and glory.

3 Thus all my gladsome way along
   I sing aloud thy praises,
That men may hear the grateful song
   My voice unwearied raises.
Be joyful in the Lord, my heart;
Both soul and body bear your part:
   To God all praise and glory.

367   *George Herbert*

f   1   KING of glory, King of peace,
          I will love thee;
      And, that love may never cease,
          I will move thee.
      Thou hast granted my request,
          Thou hast heard me;
      Thou didst note my working breast,
          Thou hast spared me. Alleluia!

      2   Wherefore with my utmost art
          I will sing thee,
      And the cream of all my heart
          I will bring thee.
mf Though my sins against me cried,
          Thou didst clear me,
      And alone, when they replied,
          Thou didst hear me. Alleluia!

f   3   Seven whole days, not one in seven,
          I will praise thee;
      In my heart, though not in heaven,
          I can raise thee.
mf Small it is, in this poor sort
          To enrol thee:
f   E'en eternity's too short
          To extol thee. Alleluia!

368   *Ps. 148. Foundling Hospital Collection, 1796*

      1   PRAISE the Lord! ye heavens, adore him;
          Praise him, angels, in the height;
      Sun and moon, rejoice before him,
          Praise him, all ye stars and light.
      Praise the Lord! for he hath spoken;
          Worlds his mighty voice obeyed:
      Laws, which never shall be broken,
          For their guidance he hath made.

2 Praise the Lord! for he is glorious;
   Never shall his promise fail:
God hath made his saints victorious;
   Sin and death shall not prevail.
Praise the God of our salvation;
   Hosts on high, his power proclaim;
Heaven and earth and all creation,
   Laud and magnify his name!

369   *J. Montgomery and Compilers*

mf 1 SONGS of praise the angels sang,
Heaven with Alleluias rang,
When creation was begun,
When God spake and it was done.

2 Songs of praise awoke the morn
When the Prince of Peace was born;
f Songs of praise arose when he
Captive led captivity.

p 3 Heaven and earth must pass away;
Songs of praise shall crown that day:
f God will make new heavens and earth;
Songs of praise shall hail their birth.

p 4 And will man alone be dumb
Till that glorious Kingdom come?
f No, the Church delights to raise
Psalms and hymns and songs of praise.

mf 5 Saints below, with heart and voice,
Still in songs of praise rejoice;
Learning here, by faith and love,
Songs of praise to sing above.

f 6 Hymns of glory, songs of praise,
Father, unto thee we raise,
Jesu, glory unto thee,
With the Spirit, ever be.

370 *Ps.* 100. *I. Watts* ‡

mf 1 BEFORE Jehovah's awful throne,
  Ye nations, bow with sacred joy;
  Know that the Lord is God alone:
  He can create, and he destroy.

2 His sovereign power, without our aid,
  Made us of clay, and formed us men;
  And, when like wandering sheep we strayed,
  He brought us to his fold again.

f 3 We'll crowd thy gates with thankful songs,
  High as the heavens our voices raise;
  And earth, with her ten thousand tongues,
  Shall fill thy courts with sounding praise.

4 Wide as the world is thy command,
  Vast as eternity thy love;
  Firm as a rock thy truth shall stand,
  When rolling years shall cease to move.

371 *R. Baxter and J. H. Gurney*

f 1 YE holy angels bright,
    Who wait at God's right hand,
  Or through the realms of light
    Fly at your Lord's command,
      Assist our song,
        For else the theme
      Too high doth seem
    For mortal tongue.

mf 2 Ye blessèd souls at rest,
    Who ran this earthly race,
  And now, from sin released,
    Behold the Saviour's face,
      His praises sound,
        As in his light
      With sweet delight
    Ye do abound.

3 Ye saints who toil below,
   Adore your heavenly King,
And onward as ye go
   Some joyful anthem sing;
   Take what he gives
     And praise him still,
     Through good and ill,
   Who ever lives.

f   4 My soul, bear thou thy part,
    Triumph in God above,
And with a well-tuned heart
    Sing thou the songs of love.
    Let all thy days
     Till life shall end,
     Whate'er he send,
    Be filled with praise.

372
W. Chalmers Smith

1 IMMORTAL, invisible, God only wise,
In light inaccessible hid from our eyes,
Most blessèd, most glorious, the Ancient of Days
Almighty, victorious, thy great name we praise.

2 Unresting, unhasting, and silent as light,
Nor wanting, nor wasting, thou rulest in might;
Thy justice like mountains high soaring above
Thy clouds which are fountains of goodness and
   love.

3 To all life thou givest, to both great and small;
In all life thou livest, the true life of all;
We blossom and flourish as leaves on the tree,
And wither and perish; but naught changeth thee

4 Great Father of glory, pure Father of light,
Thine angels adore thee, all veiling their sight;
All laud we would render: O help us to see
'Tis only the splendour of light hideth thee.

373

H. Bonar†

1 FILL thou my life, O Lord my God,
  In every part with praise,
That my whole being may proclaim
  Thy being and thy ways.

2 Not for the lip of praise alone,
  Nor e'en the praising heart,
I ask, but for a life made up
  Of praise in every part:

3 Praise in the common things of life,
  Its goings out and in;
Praise in each duty and each deed,
  However small and mean.

4 Fill every part of me with praise:
  Let all my being speak
Of thee and of thy love, O Lord,
  Poor though I be and weak.

5*So shalt thou, Lord, receive from me
  The praise and glory due;
And so shall I begin on earth
  The song for ever new.

6*So shall each fear, each fret, each care,
  Be turnèd into song;
And every winding of the way
  The echo shall prolong.

7 So shall no part of day or night
  Unblest or common be;
But all my life, in every step,
  Be fellowship with thee.

374

J. Montgomery

1   STAND up, and bless the Lord,
    Ye people of his choice;
Stand up, and bless the Lord your God
    With heart and soul and voice,

2   Though high above all praise,
        Above all blessing high,
    Who would not fear his holy name,
        And laud and magnify?

3   O for the living flame
        From his own altar brought,
    To touch our lips, our mind inspire,
        And wing to heaven our thought!

4   God is our strength and song,
        And his salvation ours;
    Then be his love in Christ proclaimed
        With all our ransomed powers.

5   Stand up, and bless the Lord,
        The Lord your God adore;
    Stand up, and bless his glorious name
        Henceforth for evermore.

375   *George Herbert*

1   LET all the world in every corner sing,
            My God and King!
        The heavens are not too high,
        His praise may thither fly:
        The earth is not too low,
        His praises there may grow.
    Let all the world in every corner sing,
            My God and King!

2   Let all the world in every corner sing,
            My God and King!
        The Church with psalms must shout,
        No door can keep them out;
        But above all the heart
        Must bear the longest part.
    Let all the world in every corner sing,
            My God and King!

376   *Based on Ps. 150.*   *Sir H. W. Baker*

f   1 O PRAISE ye the Lord! praise him in the
           height;
          Rejoice in his word, ye angels of light;
          Ye heavens adore him by whom ye were
           made,
          And worship before him, in brightness
           arrayed.

mf 2 O praise ye the Lord! praise him upon earth,
          In tuneful accord, ye sons of new birth;
f   Praise him who hath brought you his grace
           from above,
          Praise him who hath taught you to sing of
           his love.

   3 O praise ye the Lord, all things that give
           sound;
          Each jubilant chord re-echo around;
          Loud organs, his glory forth tell in deep tone,
mf   And, sweet harp, the story of what he hath
           done.

f   4 O praise ye the Lord! thanksgiving and song
          To him be outpoured all ages along:
          For love in creation, for heaven restored,
          For grace of salvation, O praise ye the Lord!

377   *Ps. 136*   *John Milton ‡*

f   1 LET us, with a gladsome mind,
          Praise the Lord, for he is kind:
            For his mercies ay endure,
            Ever faithful, ever sure.

   2 Let us blaze his name abroad,
          For of gods he is the God:
            For his mercies, etc.

3 He with all-commanding might
  Filled the new-made world with light:
      For his mercies, etc.

mf 4 He the golden-tressèd sun
    Caused all day his course to run:
f   For his mercies, etc.

p 5 And the hornèd moon at night
   'Mid her spangled sisters bright:
f   For his mercies, etc.

mf 6 All things living he doth feed,
    His full hand supplies their need:
f   For his mercies, etc.

7 Let us, with a gladsome mind,
  Praise the Lord, for he is kind:
      For his mercies, etc.

378   *Thanksgiving for the Church's work overseas*
                               S. J. Stone

mf 1 LORD of the Harvest, it is right and meet
  That we should lay our first-fruits at thy feet
      With joyful Alleluia.

2 Sweet is the soul's thanksgiving after prayer;
  Sweet is the worship that with heaven we
    share,
      Who sing the Alleluia.

3 Lowly we prayed, and thou didst hear on high,
  Didst lift our hearts and change our sup-
    pliant cry
      To festal Alleluia.

4 So sing we now in tune with that great song,
That all the age of ages shall prolong,
         The endless Alleluia.

5*To thee, O Lord of Harvest, who hast heard,
And to thy white-robed reapers given the
    word,
         We sing our Alleluia.

6*O Christ, who in the wide world's ghostly sea
Hast bid the net be cast anew, to thee‿
         We sing our Alleluia.

7*To thee, eternal Spirit, who again
Hast moved with life upon the slumbrous
    main,
         We sing our Alleluia.

8 Yea, for sweet hope new-born, blest work
    begun,
Sing Alleluia to the Three in One,
         Adoring Alleluia.

f   9 'Glory to God!' the Church in patience cries;
'Glory to God!' the Church at rest replies,
         With endless Alleluia.

379   *M. Rinkart. Tr. Catherine Winkworth*
              Nun danket alle Gott

f   1   NOW thank we all our God,
With heart and hands and voices,
Who wondrous things hath done,
In whom his world rejoices;
Who from our mother's arms
Hath blessed us on our way
With countless gifts of love,
And still is ours to-day.

mf 2   O may this bounteous God
      Through all our life be near us,
      With ever joyful hearts
      And blessèd peace to cheer us;
        And keep us in his grace,
          And guide us when perplexed,
        And free us from all ills
        In this world and the next.

f 3   All praise and thanks to God
      The Father now be given,
      The Son, and him who reigns
      With them in highest heaven,
        The one eternal God,
          Whom earth and heaven adore,
        For thus it was, is now,
        And shall be evermore.

380   *Ps.* 145   *Nichol Grieve*

1 WE would extol thee, ever-blessèd Lord;
    Thy holy name for ever be adored;
    Each day we live to thee our psalm we raise:
    Thou, God and King, art worthy of our praise,
    Great and unsearchable in all thy ways.

2 Age shall to age pass on the endless song,
    Telling the wonders which to thee belong,
    Thy mighty acts with joy and fear relate;
    Laud we thy glory while on thee we wait,
    Glad in the knowledge of thy love so great.

3 Thou, Lord, art gracious, merciful to all,
    Nigh to thy children when on thee they call;
    Slow unto anger, pitiful and kind,
    Thou to compassion ever art inclined:
    We love thee with our heart and strength and
      mind.

      Verse 1 *may be repeated at the end*

381 *Ps. 148*   *T. B. Browne*

1 PRAISE the Lord of heaven, praise him in the
    height;
  Praise him, all ye angels, praise him, stars and
    light;
  Praise him, skies and waters, which above the
    skies,
  When his word commanded, stablished did
    arise.

2 Praise the Lord, ye fountains of the deeps and
    seas,
  Rocks and hills and mountains, cedars and all
    trees;
  Praise him, clouds and vapours, snow and hail
    and fire,
  Stormy wind fulfilling only his desire.

3 Praise him, fowls and cattle, princes and all
    kings;
  Praise him, men and maidens, all created things;
  For the name of God is excellent alone:
  On the earth his footstool, over heaven his
    throne.

382   *J. Neander. Tr. Catherine Winkworth* ‡
                  Lobe den Herrn

f 1 PRAISE to the Lord, the Almighty, the King
      of creation;
   O my soul, praise him, for he is thy health
      and salvation:
          All ye who hear,
          Now to his temple draw near,
   Joining in glad adoration.

2 Praise to the Lord, who o'er all things so
  wondrously reigneth,
mf Shieldeth thee gently from harm, or when
  fainting sustaineth:
    Hast thou not seen
    How thy heart's wishes have been
  Granted in what he ordaineth?

f 3 Praise to the Lord, who doth prosper thy
  work and defend thee;
  Surely his goodness and mercy shall daily
  attend thee:
    Ponder anew
    What the Almighty can do,
  If to the end he befriend thee.

4 Praise to the Lord! O let all that is in me
  adore him!
  All that hath life and breath, come now with
  praises before him!
    Let the Amen
    Sound from his people again:
  Gladly for ay we adore him.

HOLY COMMUNION

383   *St. Thomas Aquinas*
    Tr. E. Caswall, J. M. Neale, and others

Pange, lingua, gloriosi Corporis mysterium

mf 1 NOW, my tongue, the mystery telling
   Of the glorious Body sing,
  And the Blood, all price excelling,
   Which the Gentiles' Lord and King,
p In a Virgin's womb once dwelling,
   Shed for this world's ransoming.

mf 2 Given for us, and condescending
    To be born for us below,
He, with men in converse blending,
    Dwelt the seed of truth to sow,
p   Till he closed with wondrous ending
      His most patient life of woe.

mf 3 That last night, at supper lying,
    'Mid the Twelve, his chosen band,
Jesus, with the law complying,
    Keeps the feast its rites demand;
Then, more precious food supplying,
    Gives himself with his own hand.

p 4 Word made flesh, true bread he maketh
    By his word his Flesh to be,
Wine his Blood; which whoso taketh
    Must from carnal thoughts be free:
mf   Faith alone, though sight forsaketh,
      Shows true hearts the mystery.

PART 2

Tantum ergo

p 5 Therefore we, before him bending,
    This great Sacrament revere:
Types and shadows have their ending,
    For the newer rite is here;
mf   Faith, our outward sense befriending,
      Makes our inward vision clear.

f 6 Glory let us give and blessing
    To the Father and the Son,
Honour, might, and praise addressing,
    While eternal ages run;
Ever too his love confessing,
    Who, from Both, with Both is One.

384

St. Thomas Aquinas
Tr. J. M. Neale, E. Caswall, and others

Verbum supernum prodiens

mf 1 THE heavenly Word, proceeding forth
    Yet leaving not the Father's side,
    Accomplishing his work on earth
p   Had reached at length life's eventide.

mf 2 By false disciple to be given
    To foemen for his life athirst,
    Himself, the very Bread of heaven,
    He gave to his disciples first.

  3 He gave himself in either kind,
    His precious Flesh, his precious Blood;
    In love's own fulness thus designed
    Of the whole man to be the food.

p 4 By birth their fellow-man was he,
    Their meat, when sitting at the board;
    He died, their ransomer to be;
f   He ever reigns, their great reward.

PART 2

O salutaris

p 5 O saving Victim, opening wide
    The gate of heaven to man below,
    Our foes press on from every side;
    Thine aid supply, thy strength bestow.

f 6 All praise and thanks to thee ascend
    For evermore, blest One in Three;
    O grant us life that shall not end
    In our true native land with thee.

385
St. Thomas Aquinas
Tr. Bishop J. R. Woodford†

Adoro te devote, latens Deitas

1 THEE we adore, O hidden Saviour, thee,
Who in thy Sacrament dost deign to be;
Both flesh and spirit at thy Presence fail,
Yet here thy Presence we devoutly hail.

2 O blest memorial of our dying Lord,
Who living Bread to men doth here afford!
O may our souls for ever feed on thee,
And thou, O Christ, for ever precious be.

3 Fountain of goodness, Jesu, Lord and God,
Cleanse us, unclean, with thy most cleansing
Blood;
Increase our faith and love, that we may know
The hope and peace which from thy Presence
flow.

4 O Christ, whom now beneath a veil we see,
May what we thirst for soon our portion be:
To gaze on thee unveiled, and see thy face,
The vision of thy glory and thy grace.

386 *7th cent. Tr. J. M. Neale and Compilers* (1904)

Sancti, venite, Christi Corpus sumite

p 1 DRAW nigh and take the Body of the Lord,
And drink the holy Blood for you outpoured.

2 Saved by that Body and that holy Blood,
With souls refreshed, we render thanks to
God.

3 Salvation's giver, Christ the only Son,
By his dear Cross and Blood the victory won.

4 Offered was he for greatest and for least,
Himself the Victim, and himself the Priest.

5*Victims were offered by the law of old,
Which in a type this heavenly mystery told.

mf 6*He, Lord of life, and Saviour of our race,
Hath given to his saints a wondrous grace.

p 7 Approach ye then with faithful hearts sincere,
And take the safeguard of salvation here.

mf 8 He that his saints in this world rules and
shields
To all believers life eternal yields;

9 He feeds the hungry with the Bread of heaven,
And living streams to those who thirst are
given.

p 10*Alpha and Omega, to whom shall bow
All nations at the Doom, is with us now.

Note.—Alpha and Omega, *the first and last letters
of the Greek alphabet, are used in the book of Revela-
tion as a title of Jesus Christ, who, as the Word of
God, is the beginning and the end of all creation.*

387   *Cento from* Jesu dulcis memoria
Tr. R. Palmer

Jesu, dulcedo cordium

1 JESU, thou joy of loving hearts!
Thou fount of life, thou Light of men!
From the best bliss that earth imparts
We turn unfilled to thee again.

2 Thy truth unchanged hath ever stood;
Thou savest those that on thee call;
To them that seek thee thou art good,
To them that find thee all in all.

3 We taste thee, O thou living Bread,
　　And long to feast upon thee still;
　We drink of thee, the fountain-head,
　　And thirst our souls from thee to fill.

4 Our restless spirits yearn for thee,
　　Where'er our changeful lot is cast,
　Glad when thy gracious smile we see,
　　Blest when our faith can hold thee fast.

5 O Jesu, ever with us stay;
　　Make all our moments calm and bright;
　Chase the dark night of sin away;
　　Shed o'er the world thy holy light.

388　　　　　*John Mauburn. Tr. J. M. C. Crum*
　　　　　　　Eia, Jesu adorande

1 O LORD Jesus, I adore thee
　　For the bread of worth untold
　Freely given in thy Communion,
　　Wonderful a thousandfold,
　Given to-day in loving bounty
　　More than my poor heart can hold.

2 Make thou of my soul an orchard
　　Quickened into fruitfulness;
　Come, O come, life-giving Manna,
　　Making glad my wilderness:
　Sweeter far than any sweetness
　　Tongue can taste, or words express.

PART 2

3 Ah, Lord Jesus, go not from me,
　　Stay, ah, stay with me, my Lord;
　Make me shrink from whatsoever
　　Will not with thy name accord;
　Act through me in every action,
　　Speak through me in every word.

4 Would that I could keep thee always
    In mine inmost heart to be,
Thou and only thou suggesting
    Every thought and wish in me;
All my soul, with singing, offered
    For a sacrifice to thee.

389   *17th cent. Tr. Compilers*
         O esca viatorum

1 O FOOD that weary pilgrims love,
O Bread of angel-hosts above,
    O Manna of the saints,
The hungry soul would feed on thee;
Ne'er may the heart unsolaced be
    Which for thy sweetness faints.

2 O fount of love, O cleansing tide,
Which from the Saviour's piercèd side
    And sacred heart dost flow,
Be ours to drink of thy pure rill,
Which only can our spirits fill,
    And all our need bestow.

3 Lord Jesu, whom, by power divine
Now hidden 'neath the outward sign,
    We worship and adore,
Grant, when the veil away is rolled,
With open face we may behold
    Thyself for evermore.

390   *Liturgy of St. James. Tr. G. Moultrie*
       σιγησάτω πᾶσα σάρξ

p   1 LET all mortal flesh keep silence
    And with fear and trembling stand;
Ponder nothing earthly-minded,
    For with blessing in his hand
mf   Christ our God to earth descendeth,
    Our full homage to demand.

2 King of Kings, yet born of Mary,
   As of old on earth he stood,
Lord of Lords, in human vesture—
   In the Body and the Blood—
He will give to all the faithful
   His own self for heavenly food.

f 3 Rank on rank the host of heaven
      Spreads its vanguard on the way,
   As the Light of Light descendeth
      From the realms of endless day,
   That the powers of hell may vanish
      As the darkness clears away.

mf 4 At his feet the six-winged seraphs,
      Cherubim with sleepless eye,
   Veil their faces to the Presence,
      As with ceaseless voice they cry,
f   Alleluia, Alleluia,
      Alleluia! Lord most high.

391 *The Cherubic Hymn*

6th cent. Tr. C. S. Phillips

οἱ τὰ χερουβὶμ μυστικῶς εἰκονίζοντες

1 HERE, while the cherubim within the veil
   Adore the blest, life-giving Trinity,
We, in earth's worship echoing their part,
   Hymn the Thrice-Holy in their company.

2 So let all earthly cares be cast aside,
   That we may welcome him who draweth nigh,
The King of Glory entering his courts,
   Girt by the hidden armies of the sky.

   Alleluia! Alleluia! Alleluia!

392   *Liturgy of St. James. Tr. A. J. Mason*
σιγησάτω πᾶσα σάρξ

mf 1 NOT a thought of earthly things!
    Every head in awe be bended:
f   Christ our God, the King of Kings,
        Comes by angel troops attended.

mf 2 Forth he comes, a Victim he
    For the wide world's need availing,
And his people's food to be,
    With himself their souls regaling.

    3 Cherubim with watchful eyes,
    Seraphim their brows concealing,
f Powers and Principalities,
    Cry aloud, like thunder pealing,
        Alleluia!

393   *J. Franck. Tr. Catherine Winkworth*
Schmücke dich

f 1 DECK thyself, my soul, with gladness,
Leave the gloomy haunts of sadness;
Come into the daylight's splendour,
There with joy thy praises render
Unto him whose grace unbounded
Hath this wondrous banquet founded:
High o'er all the heavens he reigneth,
Yet to dwell with thee he deigneth.

p 2 Now I sink before thee lowly,
Filled with joy most deep and holy,
As with trembling awe and wonder
On thy mighty works I ponder:
How, by mystery surrounded,
Depth no man hath ever sounded,
None may dare to pierce unbidden
Secrets that with thee are hidden.

PART 2

mf 3 Sun, who all my life dost brighten,
    Light, who dost my soul enlighten,
    Joy, the sweetest man e'er knoweth,
    Fount, whence all my being floweth,
    At thy feet I cry, my Maker,
    Let me be a fit partaker
    Of this blessèd food from heaven,
    For our good, thy glory, given.

    4 Jesus, Bread of Life, I pray thee,
    Let me gladly here obey thee;
    Never to my hurt invited,
    Be thy love with love requited:
    From this banquet let me measure,
    Lord, how vast and deep its treasure;
    Through the gifts thou here dost give me,
    As thy guest in heaven receive me.

394
J. Wesley

p 1 AUTHOR of life divine,
    Who hast a table spread,
    Furnished with mystic Wine
    And everlasting Bread,
mf Preserve the life thyself hast given,
    And feed and train us up for heaven.

p 2 Our needy souls sustain
    With fresh supplies of love,
    Till all thy life we gain,
    And all thy fulness prove,
mf And, strengthened by thy perfect grace,
    Behold without a veil thy face.

395　　　　　　　　　　　　　　　　*C. Wesley and others*

1 O THOU, before the world began
　　Ordained a Sacrifice for man,
　And by the eternal Spirit made
　　An Offering in the sinner's stead;
　Our everlasting Priest art thou,
　Pleading thy Death for sinners now.

2 Thy Offering still continues new
　　Before the righteous Father's view;
　Thyself the Lamb for ever slain,
　　Thy Priesthood doth unchanged remain;
　Thy years, O God, can never fail,
　Nor thy blest work within the veil.

3 O that our faith may never move,
　　But stand unshaken as thy love!
　Sure evidence of things unseen,
　　Now let it pass the years between,
　And view thee bleeding on the Tree,
　My Lord, my God, who dies for me.

396　　　　　　　　　　　　　　　　*P. Doddridge†*

mf 1 MY God, and is thy table spread,
　　And doth thy cup with love o'erflow?
　Thither be all thy children led,
　　And let them all thy sweetness know.

2 Hail, sacred feast which Jesus makes,
　　Rich banquet of his Flesh and Blood!
　Thrice happy he who here partakes
　　That sacred stream, that heavenly food.

p 3 Why are its bounties all in vain
　　Before unwilling hearts displayed?
　Was not for them the Victim slain?
　　Are they forbid the children's Bread?

mf 4 O let thy table honoured be,
　　And furnished well with joyful guests;
　And may each soul salvation see,
　　That here its sacred pledges tastes.

397   *W. Bright*

p 1 AND now, O Father, mindful of the love
        That bought us, once for all, on Calvary's
            Tree,
    And having with us him that pleads above,
        We here present, we here spread forth to
            thee
mf   That only Offering perfect in thine eyes,
      The one true, pure, immortal Sacrifice.

p 2 Look, Father, look on his anointed face,
        And only look on us as found in him;
    Look not on our misusings of thy grace,
        Our prayer so languid, and our faith so
            dim:
mf   For lo, between our sins and their reward
      We set the Passion of thy Son our Lord.

p 3 And then for those, our dearest and our
            best,
        By this prevailing Presence we appeal:
mf   O fold them closer to thy mercy's breast,
        O do thine utmost for their souls' true
            weal;
    From tainting mischief keep them white and
            clear,
    And crown thy gifts with strength to
            persevere.

p 4 And so we come: O draw us to thy feet,
        Most patient Saviour, who canst love us
            still;
mf   And by this food, so aweful and so sweet,
      Deliver us from every touch of ill:
f   In thine own service make us glad and free,
      And grant us never more to part with thee.

398   *W. Bright*

mf 1 ONCE, only once, and once for all,
        His precious life he gave;
      Before the Cross our spirits fall,
        And own it strong to save.

      2 'One Offering, single and complete,
        With lips and heart we say;
      But what he never can repeat
        He shows forth day by day.

      3 For, as the priest of Aaron's line
        Within the Holiest stood,
      And sprinkled all the mercy-shrine
        With sacrificial blood;

p   4 So he who once atonement wrought,
        Our Priest of endless power,
      Presents himself for those he bought
        In that dark noontide hour.

mf 5 His Manhood pleads where now it lives
        On heaven's eternal throne,
      And where in mystic rite he gives
        Its Presence to his own.

      6 And so we show thy Death, O Lord,
        Till thou again appear;
      And feel, when we approach thy board,
        We have an altar here.

f   7 All glory to the Father be,
        All glory to the Son,
      All glory, Holy Ghost, to thee,
        While endless ages run.

399   *W. Chatterton Dix*

f 1 ALLELUIA! sing to Jesus!
        His the sceptre, his the throne;
    Alleluia! his the triumph,
        His the victory alone:
    Hark! the songs of peaceful Sion
        Thunder like a mighty flood;
    Jesus out of every nation
        Hath redeemed us by his Blood.

mf 2 Alleluia! not as orphans⌣
        Are we left in sorrow now;
    Alleluia! he is near us,
        Faith believes, nor questions how:
    Though the cloud from sight received him,
        When the forty days were o'er,
    Shall our hearts forget his promise,
        'I am with you evermore'?

    3 Alleluia! Bread of angels,
        Thou on earth our food, our stay;
    Alleluia! here the sinful⌣
        Flee to thee from day to day:
    Intercessor, Friend of sinners,
        Earth's Redeemer, plead for me,
    Where the songs of all the sinless
        Sweep across the crystal sea.

    4 Alleluia! King eternal,
        Thee the Lord of Lords we own;
    Alleluia! born of Mary,
        Earth thy footstool, heaven thy throne:
    Thou within the veil hast entered,
        Robed in flesh, our great High Priest;
    Thou on earth both Priest and Victim
        In the Eucharistic feast.

The first verse may be repeated at the end

400

G. H. Bourne

f 1 LORD, enthroned in heavenly splendour,
    First-begotten from the dead,
  Thou alone, our strong defender,
    Liftest up thy people's head.
        Alleluia!
    Jesu, true and living Bread.

mf 2 Here our humblest homage pay we,
    Here in loving reverence bow;
  Here for faith's discernment pray we,
    Lest we fail to know thee now.
f   Alleluia!
    Thou art here, we ask not how.

p 3 Though the lowliest form doth veil thee
    As of old in Bethlehem,
  Here as there thine angels hail thee,
    Branch and Flower of Jesse's Stem.
f   Alleluia!
    We in worship join with them.

mf 4 Paschal Lamb, thine Offering, finished
    Once for all when thou wast slain,
  In its fulness undiminished
    Shall for evermore remain,
f   Alleluia!
    Cleansing souls from every stain.

  5 Life-imparting heavenly Manna,
    Stricken Rock with streaming side,
  Heaven and earth with loud Hosanna
    Worship thee, the Lamb who died,
        Alleluia!
    Risen, ascended, glorified!

401

V. S. S. Coles

1 WE pray thee, heavenly Father,
　　To hear us in thy love,
And pour upon thy children
　　The unction from above;
That so in love abiding,
　　From all defilement free,
We may in pureness offer
　　Our Eucharist to thee.

2 Be thou our guide and helper,
　　O Jesus Christ, we pray;
So may we well approach thee,
　　If thou wilt be the Way:
Thou, very Truth, hast promised
　　To help us in our strife,
Food of the weary pilgrim,
　　Eternal source of Life.

3 And thou, Creator Spirit,
　　Look on us, we are thine;
Renew in us thy graces,
　　Upon our darkness shine;
That, with thy benediction
　　Upon our souls outpoured,
We may receive in gladness
　　The Body of the Lord.

4 O Trinity of Persons!
　　O Unity most high!
On thee alone relying
　　Thy servants would draw nigh:
Unworthy in our weakness,
　　On thee our hope is stayed,
And blessed by thy forgiveness
　　We will not be afraid.

402

W. H. Turton

mf 1 O THOU, who at thy Eucharist didst pray
      That all thy Church might be for ever
         one,
p   Grant us at every Eucharist to say
      With longing heart and soul, 'Thy will be
         done:'
      O may we all one Bread, one Body be,
      Through this blest Sacrament of unity.

mf 2 For all thy Church, O Lord, we intercede;
      Make thou our sad divisions soon to cease;
      Draw us the nearer each to each, we plead,
      By drawing all to thee, O Prince of Peace:
      Thus may we all one Bread, one Body be,
p   Through this blest Sacrament of unity.

   3 We pray thee too for wanderers from thy
         fold;
      O bring them back, Good Shepherd of the
         sheep,
      Back to the faith which saints believed of
         old,
      Back to the Church which still that faith
         doth keep:
      Soon may we all one Bread, one Body be,
      Through this blest Sacrament of unity.

mf 4 So, Lord, at length when sacraments shall
         cease,
      May we be one with all thy Church above,
      One with thy saints in one unbroken peace,
      One with thy saints in one unbounded
         love:
      More blessèd still, in peace and love to be
p   One with the Trinity in Unity.

403

Bishop R. G. Parsons

f 1 WE hail thy Presence glorious,
       O Christ our great High Priest,
   O'er sin and death victorious,
       At thy thanksgiving feast:
   As thou art interceding
       For us in heaven above,
   Thy Church on earth is pleading
       Thy perfect work of love.

mf 2 Through thee in every nation
       Thine own their hearts upraise,
   Offering one pure Oblation,
       One Sacrifice of praise:
   With thee in blest communion
       The living and the dead
   Are joined in closest union,
       One Body with one Head.

    3 O Living Bread from heaven,
       Jesu, our Saviour good,
   Who thine own self hast given
       To be our souls' true food;
   For us thy body broken
       Hung on the Cross of shame:
   This Bread its hallowed token
       We break in thy dear name.

    4 O stream of love unending,
       Poured from the one true Vine,
   With our weak nature blending
       The strength of life divine;
   Our thankful faith confessing
       In thy life-blood outpoured,
   We drink this Cup of blessing
       And praise thy name, O Lord.

5 May we thy word believing
      Thee through thy gifts receive,
That, thou within us living,
      We all to God may live;
Draw us from earth to heaven
      Till sin and sorrow cease,
Forgiving and forgiven,
      In love and joy and peace.

404   *Bishop C. H. Boutflower*

1 O JOY of God, that comest in the morning,
      For thee, unsunned, we wait and eastward gaze,
Lift on our dark the splendours of thy dawning,
      Flood all our being in the feast of praise.

2 O life of God, for whom our spirits hunger,
      Except we eat and drink indeed of thee,
With love and faith renewed and hope grown
      younger
   Send us out hence thy saving health to see.

3 O peace of God, that passest understanding,
      Guard thou our heart through every fretting
         day:
   In him who is our Peace, our wills commanding,
      Direct our path and perfect all our way.

405   *At the Offertory*   *V. S. S. Coles*

f   1 ALMIGHTY Father, Lord most high,
               Who madest all, who fillest all,
          Thy name we praise and magnify,
               For all our needs on thee we call.

mf   2 We offer to thee of thine own
               Ourselves and all that we can bring,
          In Bread and Cup before thee shown,
               Our universal offering.

3 All that we have we bring to thee,
    Yet all is naught when all is done,
Save that in it thy love can see⌣
    The Sacrifice of thy dear Son.

4 By his command in Bread and Cup
    His Body and his Blood we plead:
p What on the Cross he offered up
    Is here our Sacrifice indeed.

mf 5 For all thy gifts of life and grace,
    Here we thy servants humbly pray
That thou would'st look upon the face⌣
    Of thine anointed Son to-day.

406   *At the Offertory*   S. N. Sedgwick

1 LORD, accept the alms we offer,
    Tokens of our love to thee;
Out of grateful hearts we render
    This our act of charity;
Even though full well we know
All we have to thee we owe.

2 Use them, Father, to thy glory,
    Teach us fully how to give,
For his sake who leaving heaven
    Gave us all that we might live:
All we have could not suffice
To repay his Sacrifice.

3 Now the priest upon the altar
    Doth present the bread and wine,
To become, in wondrous manner,
    For our souls the food divine:
Soul and body by thee fed,
Praise we give for daily bread.

4 With our alms and our oblations
　　Take, O Lord, our prayers of love;
Make thy Church in fullest concord
　　Serve as one, below, above;
And in fellowship complete
Reach at last thy mercy-seat.

407 *At the Communion*
　　　　　　　　14th cent. *Tr. H. N. Oxenham* ‡
　　　　Ave verum Corpus natum

1 HAIL, true Body, born of Mary,
　　By a wondrous Virgin-birth!
Thou who on the Cross wast offered
　　To redeem the sons of earth;

2 Thou whose side became a fountain
　　Pouring forth thy precious Blood,
Give us now, and at our dying,
　　Thine own self to be our food.

　　　O sweetest Jesu,
　　　O gracious Jesu,
　　O Jesu, blessèd Mary's Son.

408 *At the Communion*　　　　*T. Clausnitzer*
　　　　　　　　　　　Tr. G. R. Woodward
　　　　Liebster Jesu, wir sind hier

mf 1 DEAREST Jesu, we are here,
　　At thy call, thy Presence owning;
Pleading now in holy fear
　　That great Sacrifice atoning:
p　Word incarnate, much in wonder
On this mystery deep we ponder.

mf 2 Jesu, strong to save—the same⁀
　　Yesterday, to-day, for ever—
Make us fear and love thy name,
　　Serving thee with best endeavour:
f　In this life, O ne'er forsake us,
But to bliss hereafter take us.

409 *At the Communion*   *Bishop R. Heber*

p   1 BREAD of the world in mercy broken,
     Wine of the soul in mercy shed,
mf   By whom the words of life were spoken,
     And in whose Death our sins are dead;

p   2 Look on the heart by sorrow broken,
     Look on the tears by sinners shed;
mf   And be thy feast to us the token
     That by thy grace our souls are fed.

410 *At the Communion*   *Bishop R. Heber*

     O MOST merciful!
     O most bountiful!
     God the Father Almighty,
     By the Redeemer's
     Sweet intercession,
Hear us, help us, when we cry.

411 *At the Communion*   *J. Conder* ‡

mf   1 BREAD of heaven, on thee we feed,
     For thy Flesh is meat indeed;
     Ever may our souls be fed
     With this true and living Bread;
     Day by day with strength supplied
     Through the life of him who died.

     2 Vine of heaven, thy Blood supplies
     This blest Cup of Sacrifice;
p   Lord, thy wounds our healing give,
     To thy Cross we look and live:
mf   Jesus, may we ever be
     Grafted, rooted, built in thee.

412 *At the Communion*　　　E. Osler

p　1 O GOD, unseen yet ever near,
　　　Thy Presence may we feel;
　　　And, thus inspired with holy fear,
　　　Before thine altar kneel.

mf　2 Here may thy faithful people know
　　　The blessings of thy love,
　　　The streams that through the desert flow,
　　　The manna from above.

　3 We come, obedient to thy word,
　　　To feast on heavenly food;
　　　Our meat the Body of the Lord,
　　　Our drink his precious Blood.

　4 Thus may we all thy word obey,
　　　For we, O God, are thine;
f　　And go rejoicing on our way,
　　　Renewed with strength divine.

413 *At the Communion*　　　J. S. B. Monsell

p　1 I HUNGER and I thirst:
　　　Jesu, my manna be;
　　　Ye living waters, burst
　　　Out of the rock for me.

　2 Thou bruised and broken Bread,
　　　My life-long wants supply;
　　　As living souls are fed,
　　　O feed me, or I die.

mf　3 Thou true life-giving Vine,
　　　Let me thy sweetness prove;
　　　Renew my life with thine,
　　　Refresh my soul with love.

p 4 Rough paths my feet have trod
　　Since first their course began:
　　Feed me, thou Bread of God;
　　Help me, thou Son of Man.

　　5 For still the desert lies
　　My thirsting soul before:
mf　O living waters, rise
　　Within me evermore.

414 *At the Communion*　　　*H. Bonar*

mf 1 HERE, O my Lord, I see thee face to face;
　　Here faith would touch and handle things
　　　　unseen;
　　Here grasp with firmer hand the eternal grace,
　　And all my weariness upon thee lean.

　　2 Here would I feed upon the Bread of God;
　　Here drink with thee the royal Wine of
　　　　heaven;
　　Here would I lay aside each earthly load;
　　Here taste afresh the calm of sin forgiven.

p 3 I have no help but thine; nor do I need
　　Another arm save thine to lean upon:
mf　It is enough, my Lord, enough indeed,
　　My strength is in thy might, thy might
　　　　alone.

415 *At the Communion*　　　*T. B. Pollock*

　　1 FAITHFUL Shepherd, feed me
　　In the pastures green;
　　Faithful Shepherd, lead me
　　Where thy steps are seen.

　　2 Hold me fast, and guide me
　　In the narrow way;
　　So, with thee beside me,
　　I shall never stray.

3 Daily bring me nearer‿
    To the heavenly shore;
  Make my faith grow clearer,
    May I love thee more.

4 Hallow every pleasure,
    Every gift and pain;
  Be thyself my treasure,
    Though none else I gain.

5 Day by day prepare me
    As thou seest best,
  Then let angels bear me‿
    To thy promised rest.

416   *At the Communion*   *W. H. H. Jervois*

1 WHEREFORE, O Father, we thy humble ser-
      vants
  Here bring before thee Christ thy well-belovèd,
  All perfect Offering, Sacrifice immortal,
      Spotless Oblation.

2 See now thy children, making intercession
  Through him our Saviour, Son of God incarnate,
  For all thy people, living and departed,
      Pleading before thee.

417   *After Communion*   *Liturgy of St. James*
                                Tr. C. W. Humphreys

ἀπὸ δόξης εἰς δόξαν πορευόμενοι

1 FROM glory to glory advancing, we praise thee,
      O Lord;
  Thy name with the Father and Spirit be ever
  adored.

2 From strength unto strength we go forward on
   Sion's highway,
  To appear before God in the city of infinite day.

3 Thanksgiving, and glory and worship, and
   blessing and love,
  One heart and one song have the saints upon
   earth and above.

4 Evermore, O Lord, to thy servants thy presence
   be nigh;
  Ever fit us by service on earth for thy service on
   high.

418   *After Communion*   *F. W. Faber*

p   1 JESU, gentlest Saviour,
      Thou art in us now:
mf   Fill us with thy goodness,
      Till our hearts o'erflow.

p   2 Multiply our graces,
      Chiefly love and fear,
mf   And, dear Lord, the chiefest,
      Grace to persevere.

    3*Nature cannot hold thee,
      Heaven is all too strait
      For thine endless glory
      And thy royal state.

    4*Yet the hearts of children
      Hold what worlds cannot,
      And the God of wonders
      Loves the lowly spot.

    5 O how can we thank thee
      For a gift like this,
      Gift that truly maketh
      Heaven's eternal bliss?

p   6 Ah, when wilt thou always
          Make our hearts thy home?
mf   We must wait for heaven;
          Then the day will come.

419   *After Communion*   T. *Kingo*
                                          Tr. A. J. *Mason*

O Jesu, sode Jesu, dig

mf   1 O JESU, blessèd Lord, to thee
          My heartfelt thanks for ever be,
          Who hast so lovingly bestowed
          On me thy Body and thy Blood.

f   2 Break forth, my soul, for joy, and say,
          'What wealth is come to me to-day!
mf   My Saviour dwells within me now;
          How blest am I! how good art thou!'

420   C. *Wesley*†

f   1 HOW glorious is the life above
          Which in this ordinance we taste,
          That fulness of celestial love,
          That joy which shall for ever last!

mf   2 That heavenly life in Christ concealed
          These earthen vessels could not bear;
          The part which now we find revealed
          No tongue of angels can declare.

f   3 The light of life eternal darts⏝
          Into our souls a dazzling ray;
          A drop of heaven o'erflows our hearts,
          And floods with joy the house of clay.

     4 Sure pledge of ecstasies unknown
          Shall this divine Communion be:
          The ray shall rise into a sun,
          The drop shall swell into a sea.

421   *C. Wesley*

f   1 HOSANNA in the highest
To our exalted Saviour,
     Who left behind
     For all mankind
These tokens of his favour:
mf   His bleeding love and mercy
His all-redeeming Passion;
f   Who here displays,
       And gives the grace
Which brings us our salvation.

2 Louder than gathered waters,
Or bursting peals of thunder,
     We lift our voice
     And speak our joys,
And shout our loving wonder.
Shout, all our elder brethren,
While we record the story
       Of him that came
       And suffered shame,
To carry us to glory.

mf   3 Angels in fixed amazement
Around our altars hover,
     With eager gaze
     Adore the grace
Of our eternal Lover:
Himself and all his fulness
Who gives to the believer;
f   And by this Bread
       Whoe'er are fed
Shall live with God for ever.

422

Bishop E. R. Morgan

1 THEE, living Christ, our eyes behold
    Amid thy Church appearing,
All girt about thy breast with gold
    And bright apparel wearing;
Thy countenance is burning light,
A sun that shineth in his might:
    Lord Christ, we see thy glory.

2 Thy glorious feet have sought and found
    Thy sons of every nation;
Thine everlasting voice doth sound
    The call of our salvation;
Thine eyes of flame do search and scan
The whole outspreading realm of man:
    Lord Christ, we see thy glory.

3 O risen Christ, who art alive,
    Amid thy Church abiding,
Who dost thy Blood and Body give
    New life and strength providing,
We join in heavenly company
To sing thy praise triumphantly:
    For we have seen thy glory.

Note.—This hymn is based on the vision of the Glorified Christ in Rev. 1. 12–16.

423

Adam Fox

1 LET us employ all notes of joy
    And praise that never endeth
To God above, whose mighty love
    Our hearts and minds defendeth;
Who by his grace, in every place,
To all who need and duly plead
    His power and presence lendeth.

2 For, ere he died, the Crucified
    Wrought things eternal for us
By bread and wine, which Love divine
    Hath given to assure us:
O taste and see; find him to be
Our great reward, our living Lord
    Most willing to restore us.

3 The word he spoke, the bread he broke
    Shall fill our lives with glory,
If we are true and loving too
    And for our sins are sorry:
O do his will, and praise him still,
And still proclaim his glorious name
    And deathless Gospel story.

The following hymns are also suitable:

494 Hands that have been handling.
622 Praise, O Sion, praise thy Master.

HOLY BAPTISM

424   *H. Alford*

mf 1 IN token that thou shalt not fear
        Christ crucified to own,
    We print the cross upon thee here,
        And stamp thee his alone.

2 In token that thou shalt not blush
        To glory in his name,
    We blazon here upon thy front
        His glory and his shame.

3 In token that thou shalt not flinch
        Christ's quarrel to maintain,
    But 'neath his banner manfully
        Firm at thy post remain;

4 In token that thou too shalt tread⌣
   The path he travelled by,
Endure the cross, despise the shame,
   And sit thee down on high;

f   5 Thus outwardly and visibly⌣
   We seal thee for his own;
And may the brow that wears his Cross
   Hereafter share his crown.

425
           H. von Laufenberg
         Tr. Catherine Winkworth ‡

Ach lieber Herre, Jesu Christ

1 LORD Jesu Christ, our Lord most dear,
As thou wast once an infant here,
So give this child of thine, we pray,
Thy grace and blessing day by day:
   O holy Jesu, Lord divine.

2 As in thy heavenly kingdom, Lord,
All things obey thy sacred word,
Do thou thy mighty succour give,
And shield this child by morn and eve:
   O holy Jesu, Lord divine.

3 Their watch let angels round *him* keep
Where'er *he* be, awake, asleep;
Thy holy Cross now let *him* bear,
That *he* thy crown with saints may wear:
   O holy Jesu, Lord divine.

426
           Bishop Gilbert White

1 O FATHER, for this little life
   Entrusted from above,
Ere yet *he* face earth's sin and strife,
   We supplicate thy love.

2 As Hannah to the Temple gate
  Her dearest treasure bore,
So, Lord, to thee we consecrate
  This child for evermore.

3 Thy faithful soldier, may *he* fight
  With falsehood, sin, and shame,
And losing all to win the right
  Confess thy holy name.

4 Thy faithful servant, may *he* learn
  To love and labour still,
And with a flaming spirit burn
  To know and do thy will.

5 O Saviour, all *he* is is thine,
  And all *he* yet may be:
O shelter *him* with love divine,
  And draw *him* near to thee.

6 For thou, O Lord, art all our life,
  In thee all struggles end:
Through all the sorrow and the strife
  Our Maker and our Friend.

427   *C. A. Alington*

1 O LOVING Father, to thy care
  We give again this child of thine,
Baptized and blessed with faithful prayer
  And sealed with Love's victorious sign.

2 As Christ, thy Son, did not refuse
  The homage of the children's cry,
So teach *him* childhood's gifts to use
  Thy name to praise and magnify.

3 Through youth and age, through shine and
    shade,
  Grant *him* to run *his* earthly race,
Forgetting not that man was made
    To show thy glory and thy grace:

4 A loving child, a faithful friend,
    A light in doubt and darkness given
To point the path that knows no end
    Save in the fuller light of heaven;

5 Till, at the last, before thy throne
    He lays *his* earthly armour down,
His task of loving service done,
    And, in thy mercy, takes *his* crown.

428

Ronald, Lord Gorell

1 TO thee, O Father, lamp of all the living,
We offer now this life of thine own giving:
Humbly we pray thee, through this earth's
    endeavour
      Light *his* steps ever.

2 Jesus, thyself a baby once from heaven,
To thee this little pilgrim here is given:
Within the mercy of thy fold befriend *him*;
      Thy love attend *him*.

3 Spirit of Comfort, fountain ever welling,
This infant's heart take now to be thy dwelling;
So may *he* live, grace, pity, truth confessing,
      Thy peace possessing.

4 Gather *him*, Holy Trinity, for ever
Into the wisdom of thy strength, that never
In life's dark shadow-lands thy love may leave
    him:
      Thine own receive *him*.

FOR THE YOUNG

429 *Morning*   *W. Canton*

1 THROUGH the night thy angels kept
Watch beside me while I slept;
Now the dark has passed away,
Thank thee, Lord, for this new day.

2 North and south and east and west
May thy holy name be blest;
Everywhere beneath the sun,
As in heaven, thy will be done.

3 Give me food that I may live;
Every naughtiness forgive;
Keep all evil things away
From thy little child this day.

430 *Morning*   *E. D. Sedding*

1 A WORK hath Christ for thee to do:
He bore the Cross, he laboured too.
He marks thine every deed and word:
Be true this day to Christ thy Lord.

2 A way hath Christ for thee to go,
The royal way he trod below:
Fear not, for he is at thy side,
Thy heart to cheer, thy steps to guide.

3 Then bravely forth his praise to tell,
With song on lip, to serve him well.
Life this new dawn begins anew:
For Jesus' sake be true, be true.

431 *Evening*   *S. Baring-Gould*

p   1 NOW the day is over,
       Night is drawing nigh,
       Shadows of the evening
       Steal across the sky.

    2 Now the darkness gathers,
       Stars begin to peep,
       Birds and beasts and flowers
       Soon will be asleep.

mf 3 Jesu, give the weary
       Calm and sweet repose;
p   With thy tenderest blessing
       May mine eyelids close.

mf 4 Grant to little children
       Visions bright of thee;
       Guard the sailors tossing
       On the deep blue sea.

p   5 Comfort every sufferer
       Watching late in pain;
       Those who plan some evil
       From their sin restrain.

    6 Through the long night watches
       May thine angels spread
       Their white wings above me,
       Watching round my bed.

mf 7 When the morning wakens,
       Then may I arise
       Pure and fresh and sinless
       In thy holy eyes.

f   8 Glory to the Father,
       Glory to the Son,
       And to thee, blest Spirit,
       Whilst all ages run.

432 *Suitable for Christmas*

Mrs. C. F. Alexander

mf 1 ONCE in royal David's city
    Stood a lowly cattle shed,
  Where a mother laid her baby
    In a manger for his bed:
  Mary was that Mother mild,
  Jesus Christ her little Child.

2 He came down to earth from heaven
    Who is God and Lord of all,
p   And his shelter was a stable,
    And his cradle was a stall;
  With the poor and mean and lowly
  Lived on earth our Saviour holy.

mf 3 And through all his wondrous childhood
    He would honour and obey,
  Love and watch the lowly Maiden,
    In whose gentle arms he lay:
  Christian children all must be
  Mild, obedient, good as he.

4 For he is our childhood's pattern,
    Day by day like us he grew,
p   He was little, weak, and helpless,
    Tears and smiles like us he knew;
mf   And he feeleth for our sadness,
  And he shareth in our gladness.

f 5 And our eyes at last shall see him,
    Through his own redeeming love,
  For that Child so dear and gentle
    Is our Lord in heaven above;
  And he leads his children on
  To the place where he is gone.

mf 6 Not in that poor lowly stable,
    With the oxen standing by,
We shall see him; but in heaven,
f   Set at God's right hand on high;
Where like stars his children crowned
All in white shall wait around.

433   *Suitable for Lent*   *Mrs. C. F. Alexander*

mf 1 DO no sinful action,
    Speak no angry word:
Ye belong to Jesus,
    Children of the Lord.

2 Christ is kind and gentle,
    Christ is pure and true;
And his little children
    Must be holy too.

p 3 There's a wicked spirit
    Watching round you still,
And he tries to tempt you
    To all harm and ill.

mf 4 But ye must not hear him,
    Though 'tis hard for you
To resist the evil,
    And the good to do.

5 For ye promised truly,
    In your infant days,
To renounce him wholly,
    And forsake his ways.

6 Ye are new-born Christians,
    Ye must learn to fight
With the bad within you,
    And to do the right.

7 Christ is your own Master,
    He is good and true,
And his little children
    Must be holy too.

434   *Suitable for Lent*   *Margaret Cropper*

1   WE have a King who came to earth
      To win the world for God,
    And we, the children of the King,
      Must follow where he trod.

2   The banner that our King unfurled
      Was love to every man,
    So we must try to show that love
      In all the ways we can.

3   The enemies he came to fight
      Are selfishness and sin:
    Then who would be a traitor now
      And let his foemen in?

4   He bids us keep our bodies pure,
      For 'tis the pure and clean
    Can see the glory of the King,
      And tell what they have seen.

5   We are a little company,
      But we are pledged to bring
    Pure holy lives, kind joyful hearts,
      And bring them to the King.

435   *Suitable for Passiontide*
                    Bishop W. Walsham How

mf 1   IT is a thing most wonderful,
          Almost too wonderful to be,
        That God's own Son should come from
          heaven,
        And die to save a child like me.

2   And yet I know that it is true:
      He chose a poor and humble lot,
p   And wept and toiled and mourned and died
      For love of those who loved him not.

mf 3 I cannot tell how he could love
     A child so weak and full of sin;
     His love must be most wonderful,
     If he could die my love to win.

p 4 I sometimes think about the Cross,
     And shut my eyes, and try to see
     The cruel nails and crown of thorns,
     And Jesus crucified for me.

     5 But even could I see him die,
     I could but see a little part
mf   Of that great love which, like a fire,
     Is always burning in his heart.

     6 It is most wonderful to know
     His love for me so free and sure;
p   But 'tis more wonderful to see
     My love for him so faint and poor.

mf 7 And yet I want to love thee, Lord!
     O light the flame within my heart,
f   And I will love thee more and more,
     Until I see thee as thou art.

436   *Suitable for Passiontide*
         H. E. Hardy (Father Andrew)

     1 O DEAREST Lord, thy sacred head
     With thorns was pierced for me;
     O pour thy blessing on my head
     That I may think for thee.

     2 O dearest Lord, thy sacred hands
     With nails were pierced for me;
     O shed thy blessing on my hands
     That they may work for thee.

     3 O dearest Lord, thy sacred feet
     With nails were pierced for me;
     O pour thy blessing on my feet
     That they may follow thee.

4 O dearest Lord, thy sacred heart
   With spear was pierced for me;
O pour thy Spirit in my heart
   That I may live for thee.

437   *Suitable for Palm Sunday*   J. King

1 WHEN, his salvation bringing,
   To Zion Jesus came,
The children all stood singing
   Hosanna to his name;
Nor did their zeal offend him,
   But, as he rode along,
He let them still attend him,
   And listened to their song:
     Hosanna to Jesus they sang.

2 And since the Lord retaineth
   His love for children still,
Though now as King he reigneth
   On Zion's heavenly hill,
We'll flock around his banner,
   Who sits upon the throne,
And cry aloud 'Hosanna'
   To David's royal Son:
     Hosanna to Jesus we'll sing.

3 For should we fail proclaiming
   Our great Redeemer's praise,
The stones, our silence shaming,
   Would their Hosannas raise.
But shall we only render
   The tribute of our words?
No, while our hearts are tender,
   They, too, shall be the Lord's:
     Hosanna to Jesus, our King!

438 *Easter* *Alda M. Milner-Barry*

1 GOOD Joseph had a garden,
  Close by that sad green hill
 Where Jesus died a bitter death
  To save mankind from ill.

2 One evening in that garden,
  Their faces dark with gloom,
 They laid the Saviour's body
  Within good Joseph's tomb.

3 There came the holy women
  With spices and with tears;
 The angels tried to comfort them,
  But could not calm their fears.

4 Came Mary to that garden
  And sobbed with heart forlorn;
 She thought she heard the gardener ask
  'Whom seekest thou this morn?'

5 She heard her own name spoken,
  And then she lost her care:
 All in his strength and beauty
  The risen Lord stood fair!

6 Good Joseph had a garden;
  Amid its trees so tall
 The Lord Christ stood on Easter Day:
  He lives to save us all.

7 And as he rose at Easter
  He is alive for ay,
 The very same Lord Jesus Christ
  Who hears us sing to-day.

8 Go tell the Lord Christ's message,
  The Easter triumph sing,
 Till all his waiting children know
  That Jesus is their King.

439 *Ascension*   *Mrs. C. F. Alexander*

1 THE golden gates are lifted up,
    The doors are opened wide,
The King of Glory is gone up
    Unto his Father's side.

2 And ever on our earthly path
    A gleam of glory lies,
A light still breaks behind the cloud
    That veils thee from our eyes.

3 Lift up our hearts, lift up our minds,
    And let thy grace be given,
That, while we linger yet below,
    Our treasure be in heaven;

4 That, where thou art at God's right hand,
    Our hope, our love may be:
Dwell in us now, that we may dwell
    For evermore in thee.

440 *Suitable for Whitsuntide*   *J. M. C. Crum*

mf 1 THOU Wind of God, whose coming stirred
    A world as yet unmade,
And things, which were not, woke and heard
    And answered and obeyed;

2 By thee the lives that live and move
    In earth and sea began,
And human thought and human love
    Lit up the heart of man;

p 3 Until thou camest, Holy One,
    In Jesus' heart to dwell,
That man, in him, might be a son
    And please the Father well.

mf 4 O thou, who from the Father art,
    Upon our spirits move,
f Until the children's thankful heart
    Reflects the Father's love.

441   *Suitable for Dedication*   *E. D. Sedding*

1 O FATHER, we thank thee for Jesus thy Son,
   For all that for us by his death he hath won,
   His rising at Easter, his reign on thy throne,
   His gift of the Spirit to make us thine own.

2 All praise to thee, Lord, for evangelists brave,
   The witness by word and by life that they gave,
   The Church of our fathers, the home of us all,
   Her sturdy grey towers and steeples so tall.

3 All praise for the masons who built them so true
   With axe and with chisel, the best that they
      knew;
   All praise for the craftsmen who carved with a
      will,
   The nave and the chancel with glory to fill.

4 How surely they painted, those guildsmen of
      old,
   The screen with its martyrs aglimmer with gold!
   How fair shone their windows which let the sun
      through,
   And flecked the white pillars with crimson and
      blue!

5 Then ring out, ye belfries, from hill and from
      plain,
   And thunder, ye organs, in deep-toned refrain:
   Praise God, priest and people, for blessings out-
      poured
   On Britain, our homeland. Yes, praise ye the
      Lord!

Note.—Most of the above hymns, while being specially suitable for the seasons indicated, may be sung throughout the year.

442
Mrs. C. F. Alexander

f 1 ALL things bright and beautiful,
   All creatures great and small,
   All things wise and wonderful,
   The Lord God made them all.

mf 2 Each little flower that opens,
   Each little bird that sings,
   He made their glowing colours,
   He made their tiny wings,
f   All things bright, etc.

mf 3 The purple-headed mountain,
   The river running by,
   The sunset, and the morning
   That brightens up the sky:
f   All things bright, etc.

mf 4 The cold wind in the winter,
   The pleasant summer sun,
   The ripe fruits in the garden,
   He made them every one.
f   All things bright, etc.

mf 5*The tall trees in the greenwood,
   The meadows where we play,
   The rushes by the water
   We gather every day:
f   All things bright, etc.

mf 6 He gave us eyes to see them,
   And lips that we might tell
   How great is God Almighty,
   Who has made all things well.
f   All things bright, etc.

443
Jane Taylor

1 LORD, I would own thy tender care,
   And all thy love to me;
   The food I eat, the clothes I wear,
   Are all bestowed by thee.

2 'Tis thou preservest me from death
    And dangers every hour;
I cannot draw another breath
    Unless thou give me power.

3 Kind angels guard me every night,
    As round my bed they stay;
Nor am I absent from thy sight
    In darkness or by day.

4 My health and friends and parents dear
    To me by God are given;
I have not any blessings here
    But what is sent from heaven.

5 Such goodness, Lord, and constant care
    I never can repay;
But may it be my daily prayer,
    To love thee and obey.

444   *Jane E. Leeson*

mf 1 LOVING Shepherd of thy sheep,
Keep thy lamb, in safety keep;
Nothing can thy power withstand,
None can pluck me from thy hand.

p 2 Loving Saviour, thou didst give
Thine own life that we might live,
And the hands outstretched to bless
Bear the cruel nails' impress.

f 3 I would praise thee every day,
Gladly all thy will obey,
Like thy blessèd ones above
Happy in thy precious love.

mf 4 Loving Shepherd, ever near,
    Teach thy lamb thy voice to hear;
    Suffer not my steps to stray
    From the straight and narrow way.

5 Where thou leadest I would go,
    Walking in thy steps below,
f   Till before my Father's throne
    I shall know as I am known.

Mrs. E. Miller†

145

1 I LOVE to hear the story
    Which angel voices tell,
  How once the King of Glory
    Came down on earth to dwell.
I am both weak and sinful,
    But this I surely know,
The Lord came down to save me,
    Because he loved me so.
        I love to hear the story, etc.

2 I'm glad my blessèd Saviour
    Was once a child like me,
To show how pure and holy
    His little ones might be;
And if I try to follow
    His footsteps here below,
He never will forget me,
    Because he loves me so.
        I love to hear the story, etc.

3 To tell his love and mercy
    My sweetest songs I'll raise;
And though I cannot see him,
    I know he hears my praise;
For he himself has promised
    That even I may go
To sing among his angels,
    Because he loves me so.
        I love to hear the story, etc.

446   *R. S. Hawker*

mf 1 SING to the Lord the children's hymn,
        His gentle love declare,
     Who bends amid the seraphim
        To hear the children's prayer.

p   2 He at a mother's breast was fed,
        Though God's own Son was he;
     He learnt the first small words he said
        At a meek mother's knee.

      3 Close to his loving heart he pressed
        The children of the earth;
     He lifted up his hands and blessed
        The babes of human birth.

mf 4 Lo, from the stars his face will turn
        On us with glances mild;
     The angels of his presence yearn
        To bless the little child.

      5 Keep us, O Jesus, Lord, for thee,
        That so, by thy dear grace,
     We, children of the font, may see
        Our heavenly Father's face.

447   *W. St. Hill Bourn*

f   1 CHRIST, who once amongst us
        As a child did dwell,
     Is the children's Saviour,
        And he loves us well;
mf   If we keep our promise
        Made him at the font,
f   He will be our Shepherd,
        And we shall not want.

mf 2 There it was they laid us
         In those tender arms,
      Where the lambs are carried
         Safe from all alarms;
      If we trust his promise,
         He will let us rest
      In his arms for ever,
         Leaning on his breast.

      3 Though we may not see him
         For a little while,
      We shall know he holds us,
         Often feel his smile;
p   Death will be to slumber
         In that sweet embrace,
f   And we shall awaken
         To behold his face.

mf 4 He will be our Shepherd
         After as before,
      By still heavenly waters
         Lead us evermore;
      Make us lie in pastures
         Beautiful and green,
      Where none thirst or hunger,
         And no tears are seen.

p   5 Jesus, our Good Shepherd,
         Laying down thy life,
      Lest thy sheep should perish
         In the cruel strife,
mf Help us to remember
         All thy love and care,
f   Trust in thee, and love thee
         Always, everywhere.

448
                                    J. M. Neale

mf 1 AROUND the throne of God a band
       Of glorious angels ever stand;
f   Bright things they see, sweet harps they hold
       And on their heads are crowns of gold.

mf 2 Some wait around him, ready still
       To sing his praise and do his will;
       And some, when he commands them, go
       To guard his servants here below.

   3 Lord, give thy angels every day
     Command to guide us on our way,
     And bid them every evening keep
     Their watch around us while we sleep.

   4 So shall no wicked thing draw near,
     To do us harm or cause us fear;
f   And we shall dwell, when life is past,
     With angels round thy throne at last.

449
                                 C. Erskine Clark

   1 O, DAVID was a shepherd lad,
       And guarded well the sheep;
     By night and day, good times or bad,
       His watch he used to keep.
     But David's less than David's Son,
       Though a Shepherd too is he;
     Through all the world his pastures run,
       And of his flock are we.

   2 O, David was a shepherd lad,
       And more he dared to do:
     Goliath all in armour clad
       With sling and stone he slew.
     But David's Son, more daring yet,
       Put weapons all away;
     All evil things with goodness met,
       And stronger was than they.

3 O, David was a shepherd lad,
   And a kingdom he attained;
And gold and glory great he had,
   And forty years he reigned.
But David's Son is rich in love,
   And reigns eternally;
For King he is in heaven above,
   And on the earth shall be.

450   *Margaret Cropper*

mf 1 O CHRIST, whom we may love and know
     And follow to the end,
   We who are friends together come
     To thee our heavenly Friend.

2 Thou who didst share our daily toil
     To make us good and free,
   Help us to share thy fiery love
     And shining purity.

3 Give us thy love, that loves us all
     And dared the glorious Cross,
   That we may love to share and know
     Each other's joy and loss.

4 Give us thy purity to shield
     Our souls in each dark place,
f   To give us wings to rise to thee,
     And power to see thy face.

451   *For young children*   *C. Wesley*

1 GENTLE Jesus, meek and mild,
   Look upon a little child;
   Pity my simplicity,
   Suffer me to come to thee.

2 Fain I would to thee be brought:
Dearest God, forbid it not;
Give me, blessed Lord, a place
In the kingdom of thy grace.

3 Hide me, from all evil hide,
Self and stubbornness and pride;
Hold me fast in thine embrace,
Let me see thy smiling face.

PART 2

4 Lamb of God, I look to thee;
Thou shalt my example be:
Thou art gentle, meek, and mild,
Thou wast once a little child.

5 Fain I would be as thou art;
Give me thy obedient heart.
Thou art pitiful and kind;
Let me have thy loving mind.

6 Let me, above all, fulfil
God my heavenly Father's will,
Never his good Spirit grieve,
Only to his glory live.

PART 3

7 Thou didst live to God alone;
Thou didst never seek thine own;
Thou thyself didst never please:
God was all thy happiness.

8 Loving Jesus, gentle Lamb,
In thy gracious hands I am:
Make me, Saviour, what thou art;
Live thyself within my heart.

9 I shall then show forth thy praise,
Serve thee all my happy days;
Then the world shall always see
Christ, the holy Child, in me.

452 *For young children*   *A. Midlane*

mf 1 THERE'S a Friend for little children
          Above the bright blue sky,
          A Friend who never changes,
          Whose love will never die:
p   Our earthly friends may fail us,
          And change with changing years;
f   This Friend is always worthy
          Of that dear name he bears.

mf 2*There's a rest for little children
          Above the bright blue sky,
          Who love the blessèd Saviour,
          And to the Father cry:
p   A rest from every turmoil,
          From sin and sorrow free,
          Where every little pilgrim
          Shall rest eternally.

mf 3 There's a home for little children
          Above the bright blue sky,
f   Where Jesus reigns in glory,
          A home of peace and joy:
mf   No home on earth is like it,
          Nor can with it compare;
f   For every one is happy,
          Nor could be happier, there.

     4*There's a crown for little children
          Above the bright blue sky,
mf   And all who look for Jesus
          Shall wear it by and by:
f   A crown of brightest glory,
          Which he will then bestow
mf   On those who found his favour
          And loved his name below.

f 5 There's a song for little children
   Above the bright blue sky,
  A song that will not weary,
   Though sung continually:
mf A song which even angels
   Can never, never sing;
  They know not Christ as Saviour,
   But worship him as King.

f 6 There's a robe for little children
   Above the bright blue sky;
  And a harp of sweetest music,
   And palms of victory.
  All, all above is treasured,
   And found in Christ alone:
p Lord, grant thy little children
   To know thee as their own.

453
         G. S. Hodge

f 1 HOSANNA we sing, like the children dear,
  In the olden days when the Lord lived here;
mf He blessed little children, and smiled on
   them,
  While they chanted his praise in Jerusalem.

f 2 Alleluia we sing, like the children bright
  With their harps of gold and their raiment
   white,
  As they follow their Shepherd with loving
   eyes
  Through the beautiful valleys of Paradise.

  3 Hosanna we sing, for he bends his ear,
  And rejoices the hymns of his own to hear;
mf We know that his heart will never wax cold
  To the lambs that he feeds in his earthly
   fold.

4 Alleluia we sing in the church we love,
  Alleluia resounds in the Church above;
  To thy little ones, Lord, may such grace be
    given,
  That we lose not our part in the song of
    heaven.

454 *W. Chatterton Dix*

1 IN our work and in our play,
    Jesus, be thou ever near,
  Guarding, guiding, all the day,
    Keeping in thy holy fear.

2 Thou didst toil, O royal Child,
    In the far-off Holy Land,
  Blessing labour undefiled,
    Pure and honest, of the hand.

3 Thou wilt bless our play-hour too,
    If we ask thy succour strong;
  Watch o'er all we say and do,
    Hold us back from guilt and wrong.

4 O, how happy thus to spend
    Work and play-time in his sight,
  Till the rest which shall not end,
    Till the day which knows not night!

455 *National* *J. M. C. Crum*

LET us thank the Christ for all who did their
    duty,
  Famous men of old and great of heart in fight;
Who fought their way and laboured for their day,
    And strove to make our England
  A happy, lovely England,
Happy in his praise and lovely in his light.

2 Now they thank the Christ who called them to be
        captains;
    Now they sing his praise in everlasting light;
  And still they pray, they pray the Lord to-day
        That he would make our England
        A happy, lovely, etc.

3 Let us pray the Christ that he would make us
        soldiers
    Truer in his ways and braver in his fight;
  That we, as they, may loyally obey,
        And help to make our England
        A happy, lovely, etc.

456　*A closing prayer*　　　　　*J. M. Neale†*
　　　　　　　Based on Adam of St. Victor

    1 JESUS, kind above all other,
        Gentle Child of gentle Mother,
        In the stable born our Brother,
            Whom the angel hosts adore:

    2 Jesus, cradled in a manger,
        Keep us free from sin and danger,
        And to all, both friend and stranger,
            Give thy blessing evermore.

FOR SCHOOL AND COLLEGE USE

457　*Beginning of Term*　　　　*H. J. Buckoll*

    1 LORD, behold us with thy blessing
        Once again assembled here:
        Onward be our footsteps pressing
            In thy love and faith and fear;
            Still protect us
        By thy presence ever near.

2 For thy mercy we adore thee,
    For this rest upon our way;
Lord, again we bow before thee,
    Speed our labours day by day;
        Mind and spirit
    With thy choicest gifts array.

3 Keep the spell of home affection
    Still alive in every heart;
May its power, with mild direction,
    Draw our love from self apart,
        Till thy children
    Feel that thou their Father art.

4 Break temptation's fatal power,
    Shielding all with guardian care,
Safe in every careless hour,
    Safe from sloth and sensual snare;
        Thou, our Saviour,
    Still our failing strength repair.

458 *End of Term* H. J. Buckoll

1 LORD, dismiss us with thy blessing,
    Thanks for mercies past receive;
Pardon all, their faults confessing;
    Time that's lost may all retrieve;
        May thy children
    Ne'er again thy Spirit grieve.

2 Bless thou all our days of leisure,
    Help us selfish lures to flee;
Sanctify our every pleasure,
    Pure and blameless may it be;
        May our gladness
    Draw us evermore to thee.

3 By thy kindly influence cherish
    All the good we here have gained;
May all taint of evil perish
    By thy mightier power restrained;
      Seek we ever‿
    Knowledge pure and love unfeigned.

4 Let thy Father-hand be shielding
    All who here shall meet no more;
May their seed-time past be yielding
    Year by year a richer store;
      Those returning‿
    Make more faithful than before.

CONFIRMATION

459
                        M. Bridges

mf 1 MY God, accept my heart this day,
    And make it always thine,
That I from thee no more may stray,
    No more from thee decline.

p 2 Before the Cross of him who died,
    Behold, I prostrate fall;
Let every sin be crucified,
    And Christ be all in all.

mf 3 Anoint me with thy heavenly grace,
    And seal me for thine own;
f   That I may see thy glorious face,
    And worship near thy throne.

mf 4 Let every thought and work and word
    To thee be ever given:
Then life shall be thy service, Lord,
    And death the gate of heaven.

f 5 All glory to the Father be,
    All glory to the Son,
All glory, Holy Ghost, to thee,
    While endless ages run.

460

Bishop C. H. Boutflower

1 O GOD, in this thine hour of grace,
   With needy heart and empty hand,
   Yet bidden of thee to seek thy face,
   For blessing at thy feet we stand.

2 Ours are the vows, the frail desires,
   The high resolve to dare and do;
   Our flickering faith to thee aspires,
   And passes like the morning dew.

3 Ours is the mighty need of thee—
   How great, thy love alone can know;
   Ours but the hunger and the plea
   That strives and will not let thee go.

4 Thy word we clasp, thy touch we wait;
   Our eyes, O God, are unto thee,
   Whose lovingkindness makes us great,
   Whose strength shall seal our victory.

461

J. M. C. Crum

1 STRONG Captain, in thy holy ranks
   We take our places now:
   Give us the mood befitting those
   Who make so great a vow.

2 For foolishness it were to come
   In hardihood of pride,
   And cowardice it were to come
   And wish to be untried.

3 We'll not mistrust our want of strength
   Nor trust our strength of will;
   Our only confidence, that thou
   Believest in us still.

4 Make, then, our task to match our strength,
   Our strength to match our task,
   And make us unafraid to do
   Whatever thou wilt ask.

462 *After the Confirmation*   *Alice M. Bode*

1 ONCE pledged by the Cross, as children of God,
  To tread in the steps your Captain has trod,
  Now, sealed by the Spirit of wisdom and might,
    Go forward, Christ's soldiers, go forward and
      fight!

2 Your weapons of war are sent from above:
  The Spirit's good sword, the breastplate of love;
  Your feet with the Gospel of peace be well shod;
  Put on the whole armour, the armour of God.

3 Full well do ye know the foe must be met,
  Full well do ye feel that Satan has set
  His powers of darkness in battle array;
  But those who are for you are stronger than they.

4 The fight may be long, but triumph is sure,
  And rest comes at last to those who endure:
  The rest that remaineth, the victory won,
  And (dearer than all things) your Captain's
    'Well done!'

5 Then, on to the fight 'gainst sin and the world!
  Stand fast in his strength, his banner unfurled;
  And, sealed by the Spirit of wisdom and might,
    Go forward, Christ's soldiers, go forward and
      fight!

The following hymns are also suitable:

156   Come, thou Holy Spirit, come.
157   Come, Holy Ghost, our souls inspire.
232   Come, gracious Spirit, heavenly Dove.
303   Soldiers of Christ, arise.
307   Stand up, stand up for Jesus.
330   Thine for ever, God of Love.
331   O Jesus, I have promised.

HOLY MATRIMONY

463   *Mrs. D. F. Gurney*

mf 1 O PERFECT Love, all human thought transcending,
  Lowly we kneel in prayer before thy throne,
 That theirs may be the love which knows no ending,
  Whom thou for evermore dost join in one.

2 O perfect Life, be thou their full assurance
  Of tender charity and steadfast faith,
 Of patient hope, and quiet brave endurance,
  With childlike trust that fears nor pain nor death.

3 Grant them the joy which brightens earthly sorrow,
p Grant them the peace which calms all earthly strife;
mf And to life's day the glorious unknown morrow
  That dawns upon eternal love and life.

464   *Bishop Mandell Creighton*

1 O THOU who gavest power to love
  That we might fix our hearts on thee,
 Preparing us for joys above
  By that which here on earth we see;

2 Thy Spirit trains our souls to know
  The growing purpose of thy will,
 And gives to love the power to show
  That purpose growing larger still:

3 Larger, as love to reverent eyes
  Makes manifest another soul,
 And shows to life a richer prize,
  A clearer course, a nobler goal.

4 Lord, grant thy servants who implore
   Thy blessing on the hearts they blend,
That from that union evermore
   New joys may blossom to the end.

5 Make what is best in each combine
   To purge all earthly dross away,
To strengthen, purify, refine,
   To beautify each coming day.

6 So may they hand in hand advance
   Along life's paths from troubles free;
Brave to meet adverse circumstance
   Because their love points up to thee.

465
C. A. Alington

1 O FATHER, by whose sovereign sway
   The sun and stars in order move,
Yet who hast made us bold to say
   Thy nature and thy name is love:

2 O royal Son, whose every deed
   Showed love and love's divinity,
Yet didst not scorn the humblest need
   At Cana's feast in Galilee:

3 O Holy Spirit, who dost speak
   In saint and sage since time began,
Yet givest courage to the weak
   And teachest love to selfish man:

4 Be present in our hearts to-day,
   All powerful to bless, and give
To these thy children grace that they
   May love, and through their loving live.

The following hymns are also suitable:

182   Father, hear the prayer we offer.
231   O Holy Spirit, Lord of grace.
311   Lead us, heavenly Father, lead us.

THE DEPARTED

466

Thomas of Celano
Tr. W. J. Irons and Compilers

Dies irae, dies illa

1 DAY of wrath! O day of mourning!
See fulfilled the prophets' warning!
Heaven and earth to ashes turning!

2 O what fear man's bosom rendeth
When from heaven the Judge descendeth,
On whose sentence all dependeth!

3 Wondrous sound the trumpet flingeth,
Through earth's sepulchres it ringeth,
All before the throne it bringeth.

4 Death amazed and nature quaking
See all creatures now awaking,
To the Judge their answer making.

5 Lo, the book exactly worded,
Wherein all hath been recorded:
Thence shall judgement be awarded.

6 When the Judge his seat attaineth,
And each hidden deed arraigneth,
Not a sin unjudged remaineth.

7 What shall I, frail man, be pleading,
Who for me be interceding,
When the just are mercy needing?

8 King of majesty tremendous,
Who dost free salvation send us,
Fount of pity, then befriend us.

9 Think, good Jesu, my salvation
Caused thy wondrous Incarnation;
Leave me not to reprobation.

10 Faint and weary thou hast sought me,
On the Cross of suffering bought me;
Shall such grace be vainly brought me?

11 Righteous Judge! for sin's pollution
   Grant thy gift of absolution,
   Ere that day of retribution.

12 Guilty, now I pour my moaning,
   All my shame with anguish owning;
   Spare, O God, thy suppliant groaning.

13 By the sinful woman shriven,
   By the dying thief forgiven,
   Thou to me a hope hast given.

14 Worthless are my prayers and sighing;
   Yet, thy mercy not denying,
   Save me from the wrath undying.

15 With the sheep vouchsafe to place me;
   Do not with the goats abase me;
   But to thy right hand upraise me.

16 While the wicked are confounded,
   Doomed to grief and loss unbounded,
   Call me with thy saints surrounded.

17 Low I kneel, with heart-submission,
   Bowed to dust in sore contrition:
   Shield me, dying, from perdition.

18 Ah, that day of tears and mourning!
   From the dust of earth returning
   Man for judgement must prepare him:
   Spare, O God, in mercy spare him!

19 Lord, all pitying, Jesu blest,
   Grant them thine eternal rest.

467   *J. Ellerton*

p   1 NOW the labourer's task is o'er,
         Now the battle day is past;
mf   Now upon the farther shore
         Lands the voyager at last:
p   Father, in thy gracious keeping
         Leave we now thy servant sleeping.

2 There the tears of earth are dried,
   There its hidden things are clear;
mf   There the work of life is tried
   By a juster Judge than here:
p   Father, in thy, etc.

3 There the sinful souls, that turn
   To the Cross their dying eyes,
mf   All the love of Christ shall learn
   At his feet in Paradise:
p   Father, in thy, etc.

mf 4 There no more the powers of hell
   Can prevail to mar their peace;
   Christ the Lord shall guard them well,
   He who died for their release:
p   Father, in thy, etc.

5 'Earth to earth, and dust to dust,'
   Calmly now the words we say,
   Leaving *him* to sleep in trust
   Till the resurrection-day:
   Father, in thy, etc.

468

R. F. Littledale and Compilers

p 1 O LORD, to whom the spirits live
   Of all the faithful passed away,
mf   Unto their path that brightness give
   Which shineth to the perfect day:
p   O Lamb of God, Redeemer blest,
   Grant them eternal light and rest.

mf 2 Bless thou the dead that die in thee;
   As thou hast given them release,
   So quicken them thy face to see,
   And give them everlasting peace:
p   O Lamb of God, etc.

mf　3 Direct us with thine arm of might,
　　　　And bring us, perfected with them,
f　　To dwell within thy city bright,
　　　　The heavenly Jerusalem:
p　　　O Lamb of God, etc.

469　　　*From the Swahili. Tr. E. S. Palmer*

Yesu Bin Mariamu

mf　1 JESU, Son of Mary,
　　　　Fount of life alone,
　　Here we hail thee present
　　　　On thine altar-throne:
　　Humbly we adore thee,
　　　Lord of endless might,
　　In the mystic symbols
　　　　Veiled from earthly sight.

PART 2

p　2 Think, O Lord, in mercy
　　　　On the souls of those
　　Who, in faith gone from us,
　　　　Now in death repose.
　　Here 'mid stress and conflict
　　　Toils can never cease;
　　There, the warfare ended,
　　　　Bid them rest in peace.

　　3 Often were they wounded
　　　　In the deadly strife;
　　Heal them, Good Physician,
　　　　With the balm of life.
　　Every taint of evil,
　　　Frailty, and decay,
　　Good and gracious Saviour,
　　　　Cleanse and purge away.

4 Rest eternal grant them,
　　After weary fight;
Shed on them the radiance
　　Of thy heavenly light.
mf　Lead them onward, upward,
　　To the holy place,
Where thy saints made perfect
　　Gaze upon thy face.

The following hymns are also suitable:

140　Jesus lives! thy terrors now.
272　Let saints on earth in concert sing.
275　Brief life is here our portion.
285　There is a land of pure delight.

EMBER DAYS

470
　　　　　　　　　　　　　　　　J. M. Neale

mf 1 CHRIST is gone up; yet ere he passed
　　From earth, in heaven to reign,
He formed one holy Church to last
　　Till he should come again.

2 His twelve apostles first he made
　　His ministers of grace;
And they their hands on others laid,
　　To fill in turn their place.

3 So age by age, and year by year,
　　His grace was handed on;
And still the holy Church is here,
　　Although her Lord is gone.

p 4 Let those find pardon, Lord, from thee,
　　Whose love to her is cold:
mf　Bring wanderers in, and let there be
　　One Shepherd and one fold.

471

Bishop J. Armstrong

mf 1 O THOU who makest souls to shine
    With light from lighter worlds above,
  And droppest glistening dew divine
    On all who seek a Saviour's love;

2 Do thou thy benediction give
    On all who teach, on all who learn,
  That so thy Church may holier live,
    And every lamp more brightly burn.

3 Give those who teach pure hearts and wise,
    Faith, hope, and love, all warmed by
        prayer:
  Themselves first training for the skies,
    They best will raise their people there.

4 Give those who learn the willing ear,
    The spirit meek, the guileless mind:
  Such gifts will make the lowliest here
    Far better than a kingdom find.

5 O bless the shepherd, bless the sheep,
    That guide and guided both be one:
  One in the faithful watch they keep,
    Until this hurrying life be done.

f 6 If thus, good Lord, thy grace be given,
    In thee to live, in thee to die,
  Before we upward pass to heaven
    We taste our immortality.

472

J. M. Neale

1 THE earth, O Lord, is one wide field
    Of all thy chosen seed;
  The crop prepared its fruit to yield,
    The labourers few indeed.

2 We therefore come before thee now
    With fasting and with prayer,
Beseeching of thy love that thou
    Wouldst send more labourers there.

3 Not for our land alone we pray,
    Though that above the rest;
The realms and islands far away,
    O let them all be blest.

4 Endue the bishops of thy flock
    With wisdom and with grace,
Against false doctrine like a rock
    To set the heart and face.

5 To all thy priests thy truth reveal,
    And make thy judgements clear;
Make thou thy deacons full of zeal,
    And humble and sincere:

6 And give their flocks a lowly mind
    To hear—and not in vain;
That each and all may mercy find
    When thou shalt come again.

473
                         J. Montgomery ‡

mf 1 LORD, pour thy Spirit from on high,
    And thine ordainèd servants bless;
Graces and gifts to each supply,
    And clothe thy priests with righteousness.

2 Within thy temple when they stand,
    To teach the truth as taught by thee,
Saviour, like stars in thy right hand
    Let all thy Church's pastors be.

3 Wisdom and zeal and faith impart,
    Firmness with meekness, from above,
To bear thy people in their heart,
    And love the souls whom thou dost love;

p   4   To watch and pray and never faint,
      By day and night their guard to keep,
  To warn the sinner, cheer the saint,
      To feed thy lambs and tend thy sheep.

mf   5   So, when their work is finished here,
      May they in hope their charge resign;
f   When the Chief Shepherd shall appear,
      O God, may they and we be thine.

FESTIVAL OF THE DEDICATION
OF A CHURCH

474   *Tr. J. M. Neale‡*

Urbs beata Jerusalem

1   BLESSÈD city, heavenly Salem,
      Vision dear of peace and love,
  Who of living stones art builded
      In the height of heaven above,
  And by angel hosts encircled
      As a bride dost earthward move!

2   Christ is made the sure Foundation,
      Christ the Head and Corner-stone,
  Chosen of the Lord, and precious,
      Binding all the Church in one,
  Holy Sion's help for ever,
      And her confidence alone.

3   To this temple, where we call thee,
      Come, O Lord of hosts, to-day;
  With thy wonted loving-kindness
      Hear thy servants as they pray;
  And thy fullest benediction
      Shed within its walls alway.

4*Here vouchsafe to all thy servants
    What they ask of thee to gain,
What they gain from thee for ever
    With the blessèd to retain,
And hereafter in thy glory
    Evermore with thee to reign.

*Note.—The complete version of the above hymn
(the several parts of which may be sung separately)
will be found in the 'Processional' section (620).*

475   *C. Guiet. Tr. I. Williams and Compilers*

Patris aeterni Suboles coaeva

f   1   O WORD of God above,
        Who fillest all in all,
    Hallow this house with thy sure love,
        And bless our festival.

mf 2   Here from the font is poured⏝
        The grace to cleanse from sin;
    Here the anointing of the Lord
        Confirms the soul within.

    3   Here Christ to faithful hearts
        His Body gives for food;
    The Lamb of God himself imparts⏝
        The chalice of his Blood.

    4   Here guilty souls that pine
        May health and pardon win;
    The Judge acquits, and grace divine⏝
        Restores the dead in sin.

    5   Yea, God enthroned on high
        Here also dwells to bless;
    Here trains adoring souls that sigh⏝
        His mansions to possess.

f   6   Against this holy home
          Rude tempests harmless beat,
      And Satan's angels fiercely come
          But to endure defeat.

      7   All might, all praise be thine,
          Father, co-equal Son,
      And Spirit, bond of love divine,
          While endless ages run.

476   *In remembrance of past worshippers*

W. H. Draper

f   1   IN our day of thanksgiving one psalm let us
          offer
      For the saints who before us have found
          their reward;

p   When the shadow of death fell upon them,
          we sorrowed,

f   But now we rejoice that they rest in the
          Lord.

mf   2   In the morning of life, and at noon, and at
          even,
      He called them away from our worship
          below;
      But not till his love, at the font and the altar,
          Had girt them with grace for the way they
          should go.

      3   These stones that have echoed their praises
          are holy,
      And dear is the ground where their feet
          have once trod;
      Yet here they confessed they were strangers
          and pilgrims,
      And still they were seeking the city of God.

f 4 Sing praise, then, for all who here sought and
      here found him,
  Whose journey is ended, whose perils are
  past:
 They believed in the Light; and its glory is
 round them,
  Where the clouds of earth's sorrow are
  lifted at last.

HOSPITALS: THE SICK

477
           G. Thring

mf 1 THOU to whom the sick and dying
  Ever came, nor came in vain,
 Still with healing word replying
  To the wearied cry of pain,
p   Hear us, Jesu, as we meet
   Suppliants at thy mercy-seat.

2 Still the weary, sick, and dying
  Need a brother's, sister's, care,
mf On thy higher help relying
   May we now their burden share,
   Bringing all our offerings meet
   Suppliants at thy mercy-seat.

3 May each child of thine be willing,
  Willing both in hand and heart,
 All the law of love fulfilling,
   Ever comfort to impart;
   Ever bringing offerings meet
   Suppliant to thy mercy-seat.

4 So may sickness, sin, and sadness
  To thy healing virtue yield,
f Till the sick and sad, in gladness,
   Rescued, ransomed, cleansèd, healed,
   One in thee together meet,
   Pardoned at thy judgement-seat.

478   *E. H. Plumptre*

f 1 THINE arm, O Lord, in days of old
        Was strong to heal and save;
      It triumphed o'er disease and death,
        O'er darkness and the grave:
p   To thee they went, the blind, the dumb,
        The palsied and the lame,
      The leper with his tainted life,
        The sick with fevered frame.

f 2 And lo, thy touch brought life and health,
        Gave speech and strength and sight;
      And youth renewed and frenzy calmed
        Owned thee, the Lord of light:
      And now, O Lord, be near to bless,
        Almighty as of yore,
      In crowded street, by restless couch,
        As by Gennesareth's shore.

mf 3 Be thou our great deliverer still,
        Thou Lord of life and death;
      Restore and quicken, soothe and bless,
        With thine almighty breath:
      To hands that work, and eyes that see,
        Give wisdom's heavenly lore,
      That whole and sick, and weak and strong,
        May praise thee evermore.

479   *Charles Kingsley*

mf 1 FROM thee all skill and science flow,
        All pity, care, and love,
      All calm and courage, faith and hope:
        O pour them from above!

     2 And part them, Lord, to each and all,
        As each and all shall need,
      To rise, like incense, each to thee,
        In noble thought and deed.

3 And hasten, Lord, that perfect day
When pain and death shall cease,

f   And thy just rule shall fill the earth
With health and light and peace;

4 When ever blue the sky shall gleam,
And ever green the sod,
And man's rude work deface no more
The paradise of God.

ALMSGIVING

480   *Bishop Chr. Wordsworth*

f   1 O LORD of heaven and earth and sea,
To thee all praise and glory be!
How shall we show our love to thee,
Who givest all?

mf 2 The golden sunshine, vernal air,
Sweet flowers and fruit, thy love declare;
When harvests ripen, thou art there,
Who givest all.

3 For peaceful homes, and healthful days,
For all the blessings earth displays,
We owe thee thankfulness and praise,
Who givest all.

p   4 Thou didst not spare thine only Son,
But gav'st him for a world undone,
And freely with that blessèd One
Thou givest all.

mf 5 Thou giv'st the Holy Spirit's dower,
Spirit of life and love and power,
And dost his sevenfold graces shower
    Upon us all.

6 For souls redeemed, for sins forgiven,
For means of grace and hopes of heaven,
Father, what can to thee be given,
    Who givest all?

f 7 We lose what on ourselves we spend,
We have as treasure without end
Whatever, Lord, to thee we lend,
    Who givest all;

8 To thee, from whom we all derive ͜
Our life, our gifts, our power to give:
O may we ever with thee live.
    Who givest all.

HARVEST

481

Sir H. W. Baker

1 PRAISE, O praise our God and King;
Hymns of adoration sing:
    For his mercies still endure
    Ever faithful, ever sure.

2 Praise him that he made the sun
Day by day his course to run:
    For his mercies, etc.

3 And the silver moon by night,
Shining with her gentle light:
    For his mercies, etc.

4 Praise him that he gave the rain
To mature the swelling grain:
    For his mercies, etc.

5 And hath bid the fruitful field
  Crops of precious increase yield:
    For his mercies, etc.

6 Praise him for our harvest-store;
  He hath filled the garner-floor:
    For his mercies, etc.

7 And for richer food than this,
  Pledge of everlasting bliss:
    For his mercies, etc.

8 Glory to our bounteous King;
  Glory let creation sing:
    Glory to the Father, Son,
    And blest Spirit, Three in One.

482

H. Alford and Compilers

f 1 COME, ye thankful people, come,
    Raise the song of harvest-home:
    All is safely gathered in,
    Ere the winter storms begin;
mf   God, our Maker, doth provide
    For our wants to be supplied:
f   Come to God's own temple, come;
    Raise the song of harvest-home.

mf 2 All this world is God's own field,
    Fruit unto his praise to yield;
    Wheat and tares therein are sown,
    Unto joy or sorrow grown;
    Ripening with a wondrous power
    Till the final harvest-hour:
p   Grant, O Lord of life, that we
    Holy grain and pure may be.

mf 3 For we know that thou wilt come,
And wilt take thy people home;
From thy field wilt purge away
All that doth offend, that day;
p And thine angels charge at last
In the fire the tares to cast,
f But the fruitful ears to store
In thy garner evermore.

mf 4 Come then, Lord of mercy, come,
Bid us sing thy harvest-home:
Let thy saints be gathered in,
Free from sorrow, free from sin;
f All upon the golden floor
Praising thee for evermore:
Come, with all thine angels come,
Bid us sing thy harvest-home.

483   *M. Claudius. Tr. Jane M. Campbell*

Wir pflügen und wir streuen

mf 1 WE plough the fields, and scatter
The good seed on the land,
But it is fed and watered
By God's almighty hand:
He sends the snow in winter,
The warmth to swell the grain,
The breezes, and the sunshine,
And soft, refreshing rain.

f All good gifts around us
Are sent from heaven above;
Then thank the Lord, O thank the
Lord,
For all his love.

mf 2 He only is the Maker
  Of all things near and far;
He paints the wayside flower,
  He lights the evening star;
The winds and waves obey him,
  By him the birds are fed;
Much more to us, his children,
  He gives our daily bread.
f   All good gifts, etc.

mf 3 We thank thee then, O Father,
  For all things bright and good,
The seed-time and the harvest,
  Our life, our health, our food.
Accept the gifts we offer
  For all thy love imparts,
And, what thou most desirest,
  Our humble, thankful hearts.
f   All good gifts, etc.

484
W. Chatterton Dix

f 1 TO thee, O Lord, our hearts we raise
  In hymns of adoration,
To thee bring sacrifice of praise
  With shouts of exultation:
Bright robes of gold the fields adorn,
  The hills with joy are ringing,
The valleys stand so thick with corn
  That even they are singing.

mf 2 And now, on this our festal day,
  Thy bounteous hand confessing,
Upon thine altar, Lord, we lay
  The first-fruits of thy blessing:
p By thee the souls of men are fed
  With gifts of grace supernal;
Thou who dost give us earthly bread,
  Give us the Bread eternal.

mf   3 We bear the burden of the day,
      And often toil seems dreary;
  But labour ends with sunset ray,
      And rest comes for the weary:
  May we, the angel-reaping o'er,
      Stand at the last accepted,
  Christ's golden sheaves for evermore
      To garners bright elected.

f   4 O blessèd is that land of God,
      Where saints abide for ever;
  Where golden fields spread far and broad,
      Where flows the crystal river:
  The strains of all its holy throng
      With ours to-day are blending;
  Thrice blessèd is that harvest-song
      Which never hath an ending.

485

Mrs. A. L. Barbauld

1 PRAISE to God, immortal praise,
  For the love that crowns our days!
  Bounteous source of every joy,
  Let thy praise our tongues employ:

2 For the blessings of the field,
  For the stores the gardens yield,
  Flocks that whiten all the plain,
  Yellow sheaves of ripened grain:

3 All that spring with bounteous hand
  Scatters o'er the smiling land;
  All that liberal autumn pours
  From her rich o'erflowing stores.

4 These to thee, my God, we owe,
  Source whence all our blessings flow;
  And for these my soul shall raise
  Grateful vows and solemn praise.

486

W. St. Hill Bourne

mf 1 THE sower went forth sowing,
  The seed in secret slept
Through weeks of faith and patience,
  Till out the green blade crept;
And warmed by golden sunshine
  And fed by silver rain,
At last the fields were whitened
  To harvest once again.

f   O praise the heavenly Sower,
     Who gave the fruitful seed,
    And watched and watered duly,
     And ripened for our need.

mf 2 Behold, the heavenly Sower
  Goes forth with better seed,
The word of sure salvation,
  With feet and hands that bleed;
Here in his Church 'tis scattered,
  Our spirits are the soil;
Then let an ample fruitage
  Repay his pain and toil.

f   O beauteous is the harvest
     Wherein all goodness thrives!
    And this the true thanksgiving—
     The first-fruits of our lives.

3 Within a hallowed acre
  He sows yet other grain,
When peaceful earth receiveth
  The dead he died to gain;
For though the growth be hidden,
mf We know that they shall rise;
Yea, even now they ripen
  In sunny Paradise.

    O summer land of harvest,
     O fields for ever white
    With souls that wear Christ's raiment,
     With crowns of golden light!

mf 4 One day the heavenly Sower
     Shall reap where he hath sown,
And come again rejoicing,
     And with him bring his own;
p   And then the fan of judgement
     Shall winnow from his floor
The chaff into the furnace⌣
     That flameth evermore.
O holy, aweful Reaper,
     Have mercy in the day⌣
Thou puttest in thy sickle,
     And cast us not away.

FOR THOSE AT SEA

487   *W. Whiting*

1 ETERNAL Father, strong to save,
Whose arm hath bound the restless wave,
Who bidd'st the mighty ocean deep
Its own appointed limits keep:
    O hear us when we cry to thee
    For those in peril on the sea.

2 O Christ, whose voice the waters heard
And hushed their raging at thy word,
Who walkedst on the foaming deep,
And calm amid the storm didst sleep:
    O hear us when we cry to thee
    For those in peril on the sea.

3 O Holy Spirit, who didst brood⌣
Upon the waters dark and rude,
And bid their angry tumult cease,
And give, for wild confusion, peace:
    O hear us when we cry to thee
    For those in peril on the sea.

4 O Trinity of love and power,
  Our brethren shield in danger's hour;
  From rock and tempest, fire and foe,
  Protect them wheresoe'er they go:
      Thus evermore shall rise to thee
      Glad hymns of praise from land and sea.

FOR ABSENT FRIENDS

488   *Isabel S. Stevenson*

mf 1 HOLY Father, in thy mercy⌣
       Hear our anxious prayer:
     Keep our loved ones, now far distant,
       'Neath thy care.

    2 Jesus, Saviour, let thy presence⌣
        Be their light and guide;
p   Keep, O keep them, in their weakness,
        At thy side.

    3 When in sorrow, when in danger,
        When in loneliness,
      In thy love look down and comfort
        Their distress.

mf 4 May the joy of thy salvation⌣
        Be their strength and stay;
      May they love and may they praise thee
        Day by day.

p   5 Holy Spirit, let thy teaching⌣
        Sanctify their life;
mf   Send thy grace, that they may conquer
        In the strife.

    6 Father, Son, and Holy Spirit,
        God the One in Three,   [them
      Bless them, guide them, save them, keep
        Near to thee.

FAREWELL SERVICES

489   *J. E. Rankin*

1 GOD be with you till we meet again;
 By his counsels guide, uphold you,
 With his sheep securely fold you:
God be with you till we meet again.

2 God be with you till we meet again;
 'Neath his wings protecting hide you,
 Daily manna still provide you:
God be with you till we meet again.

3 God be with you till we meet again;
 When life's perils thick confound you,
 Put his arm unfailing round you:
God be with you till we meet again.

4 God be with you till we meet again;
 Keep love's banner floating o'er you,
 Smite death's threatening wave before
  you:
God be with you till we meet again.

IN TIME OF WAR

490   *Sir H. W. Baker*

mf 1 O GOD of love, O King of peace,
 Make wars throughout the world to cease;
 The wrath of sinful man restrain:
p Give peace, O God, give peace again.

mf 2 Remember, Lord, thy works of old,
 The wonders that our fathers told;
 Remember not our sin's dark stain:
p Give peace, O God, give peace again.

mf 3 Whom shall we trust but thee, O Lord?
     Where rest but on thy faithful word?
     None ever called on thee in vain:
p   Give peace, O God, give peace again.

f 4 Where saints and angels dwell above,
     All hearts are knit in holy love;
     O bind us in that heavenly chain:
p   Give peace, O God, give peace again.

491
H. F. Chorley

f 1 GOD the all-terrible! King, who ordainest
     Great winds thy clarions, the lightnings
     thy sword,
mf Show forth thy pity on high where thou
     reignest:
     Grant to us peace, O most merciful Lord.

p 2 God the omnipotent! mighty avenger,
     Watching invisible, judging unheard,
     Doom us not now in the day of our danger:
     Grant to us peace, O most merciful
     Lord.

3 God the all-merciful! earth has forsaken
     Thy ways of blessedness, slighted thy
     word;
     Bid not thy wrath in its terrors awaken:
     Grant to us peace, O most merciful Lord.

f 4 So shall thy children in thankful devotion
     Praise him who saved them from peril and
     sword,
     Singing in chorus from ocean to ocean,
     'Peace to the nations, and praise to the
     Lord.'

492 *For Airmen*   *E. H. Blakeney*

mf 1 LORD of the worlds, unseen or seen,
  Whose eyes behold all things that are,
Who rulest earth and sea and air
  And guid'st the course of every star,
Look pitying from thy throne, nor cease
To draw the nations to thy peace.

2 And if, at duty's trumpet call,
  Our manhood now be summoned hence
To battle for the right, the just,
  O shield them by thy providence.
f How confident are those that stand
Beneath the shelter of thy hand!

mf 3 To all who, spurning earthly joys,
  Seek undismayed the trackless way
High in the wide expanse of heaven,
  Be thou their help, by night and day;
Through fire, through cloud, o'er land, o'er
   wave,
Still be thy presence strong to save.

p 4 But should, O God, thy sovran will
  Allow the final sacrifice,
To thee their lives are dedicate:
  Not theirs to falter at the price.
O Lord of earth and sea and air,
For those in peril hear our prayer.

mf 5 Not given in vain, these gallant lives!
  The silent passing of the years
Shall touch them not, who fought—and fell:
  They ask no tribute of our tears.
f O loyal hearts, from death set free!
Not lost, but living unto thee.

SOCIETIES, MEETINGS, ETC.

CHOIRS

493   *Sir S. H. Nicholson*

f 1 HOW joyful 'tis to sing
        To God enthroned on high,
     To raise the ancient strain
        Of tuneful psalmody
           As choristers, who thus delight
           To chant his praise by day and night!

mf 2 Yet art is not enough,
        Nor voice that charms the ear,
     Unless the heart be tuned
        And worship be sincere:
           Help us to fix our minds on thee,
           And lead us to simplicity.

     3 Should we with wandering thoughts
        Our minds allow to stray,
     Nor heed God's holy word,
        And, kneeling, fail to pray,
           Help us to serve with godly fear,
           Lest we forget thy presence near.

     4 We seek to perfect praise
        On earth, in hope that we
     Some glimpses here may gain
        Of heavenly harmony,
           Where discord ne'er shall mar the tone
           Of those that sing around the throne.

f 5 Then in the praise of God
        Let boys and men unite,
     And, mindful of our trust,
        Gird on our robes of white,
           As symbol of the purity
           That all must seek, who seek for thee.

SERVERS

494   *Adam Fox*
Based on Liturgy of Malabar

1 HANDS that have been handling
   Holy things and high
   Still, Lord, in thy service
   Bless and fortify.

2 Ears which heard the message
   Of the words of life
   Keep thou closed and guarded
   From the noise of strife.

3 Eyes whose contemplation
   Looked upon thy love,
   Let them gaze expectant
   On the world above.

4 'Holy, Holy, Holy,'
   Thee our lips confessed:
   On those lips for ever
   Let no falsehood rest.

5 Feet which trod the pavement
   Round about God's board,
   Let them walk in glory
   Where God's light is poured.

6 Bodies that have tasted
   Of the living Bread,
   Be they re-created
   In their living Head.

7*Be we all one Body,
   All our members one,
   Measured by the stature
   Of God's full-grown Son.

TEACHERS

495 *Florence Smith*

1 LORD and Master, who hast called us
   All our days to follow thee,
We have heard thy clear commandment,
   'Bring the children unto me.'

2 So we come to thee, the Teacher,
   At thy feet we kneel to pray:
We can only lead the children
   When thyself shalt show the way.

3 Teach us thy most wondrous method,
   As of old in Galilee
Thou didst show thy chosen servants
   How to bring men unto thee.

4 Give us store of wit and wisdom,
   Give us love which never tires,
Give us thine abiding patience,
   Give us hope which ay inspires.

5 Mighty Wisdom of the Godhead,
   Thou the one eternal Word,
Thou the Counsellor, the Teacher,
   Fill us with thy fullness, Lord.

BELL-RINGERS

496 *H. C. Wilder*

1 UNCHANGING God, who livest⌣
   Enthroned in realms on high,
To men the power thou givest
   Thy name to magnify.
We raise the bells for ringing
   With ready mind and will,
And come before thee, bringing⌣
   Our hearts, our strength, our skill.

2 We call, from tower and steeple,
　　Upon the day of days,
All faithful Christian people
　　To worship, prayer, and praise;
We ring with joyous gladness
　　When man and wife are blessed;
We peal in muffled sadness
　　For loved ones laid to rest.

3 By union free and willing
　　The work of God is done;
Our Master's prayer fulfilling,
　　We would in him be one:
One, as the Church our Mother
　　Would have her children stand,
Befriending one another,
　　A strong and steadfast band.

4 Our lives, like bells, while changing,
　　An ordered course pursue;
Through joys and sorrows ranging,
　　May all those lives ring true.
May we, through Christ forgiven,
　　Our faults and failures past,
Attain our place in heaven,
　　Called home to rest at last.

MEN'S SERVICES

497

Ada R. Greenaway

1 　　RISE at the cry of battle,
　　　　Arm for the coming strife;
By night and day you must fight your way
　　　　Till you pass through death to life;
　　　　Ready to face the danger,
　　　　Ready to right the wrong.
There is many a foe on the way you go:
　　　　Quit you like men, be strong!

2   Fiery and fierce the conflict,
       Daring and swift the foe;
His hosts are found on the battle ground,
     Where they wait to lay you low.
     Sharp are his darts and deadly,
      Keen is the strife and long;
Then arm for the fight in the armour of light:
     Quit you like men, be strong!

3   Strive till the strife is over,
      Fight till the fight is won;
Though sore opprest, seek not for rest
     Until the day is done.
     After the well-fought battle
      Join in the victor's song;
Your trophies bring to Christ your King:
     Quit you like men, be strong!

MOTHERS' SERVICES

498   *Christian Burke*

1 LORD of life and King of Glory,
     Who didst deign a child to be,
     Cradled on a mother's bosom,
      Throned upon a mother's knee;
     For the children thou hast given
      We must answer unto thee.

2 Since the day the blessèd Mother
     Thee, the world's Redeemer, bore,
     Thou hast crowned us with an honour
      Women never knew before;
     And that we may bear it meetly
      We must seek thine aid the more.

3 Grant us then pure hearts and patient,
     That in all we do or say
     Little souls our deeds may copy,
      And be never led astray;
     Little feet our steps may follow
      In a safe and narrow way.

4 When our growing sons and daughters
    Look on life with eager eyes,
Grant us then a deeper insight
    And new powers of sacrifice;
Hope to trust them, faith to guide them,
    Love that nothing good denies.

5 May we keep our holy calling
    Stainless in its fair renown,
That, when all the work is over
    And we lay the burden down,
Then the children thou hast given
    Still may be our joy and crown.

499   *Bishop Gilbert White*

1 'HAIL, O Mary, full of grace,
  Daughter true of David's race!
  Thou, of women first and best,
  Art beyond all others blest.

2 Fear not, thou shalt bear a Son,
  Aided by the Holy One;
  Greater than the greatest, he
  Son of God most high shall be.'

3 Thus the holy angel said.
  Blessed Mary bowed her head:
  'Lo, the handmaid of the Lord;
  With his word may all accord.'

4 So to hearts still undefiled
  Comes the promise of a child,
  Full of joy, akin to tears,
  Full of hope, yet full of fears.

5 Happy she who answers still,
   'Be it, Lord, at thy sweet will;
   All I am to thee I owe,
   All thy purpose thou dost know.

6 What thou givest to be mine,
   May it ne'er be aught but thine:
   Be it good or be it ill,
   Still be all at thy sweet will.'

7 Holy Mary, taught by thee
   Let us vain forebodings flee.
   God is giving; fears must cease:
   In his will is perfect peace.

YOUTH SERVICES

500   *B. Baron*

1 GO forth with God! the day is now
      That thou must meet the test of youth:
   Salvation's helm upon thy brow,
      Go, girded with the living truth.
         In ways thine elder brethren trod
         Thy feet are set. Go forth with God!

2 Think fair of all, and all men love,
      And with the builder bear thy part:
   Let every day and duty prove
      The humble witness of thy heart.
         Go forth! tis God bids thee increase
         The bounds of love and joy and peace.

3 Behold with thine uplifted eyes
      Beauty through all that sorrow seems,
   And make of earth a paradise,
      The substance of thy dearest dreams.
         Bring laughter to thy great employ:
         Go forth with God and find his joy.

4 Go forth with God! the world awaits
   The coming of the pure and strong;
Strike for the faith and storm the gates
   That keep the citadel of wrong.
      Glory shall shine about thy road,
      Great heart, if thou go forth with
         God!

501 *National*   *J. M. C. Crum*

1 O GOD, whose mighty works of old
   Our fathers to their sons have told,
   Be with us still from age to age,
   Our children's children's heritage.

2 Thine are the kingdoms: at thy feet
   All peoples of the earth do meet
   In equal lowliness of prayer
   To find thine equal pity there.

3 Thy strength made strong our fathers'
      hands,
   A people great on seas and lands,
   To win, till earth shall pass away,
   Such honour as the earth can pay.

4 Be with their children: give us grace
   To know, nor fear to hold, their place,
   Nor meanly shrink, nor boast at ease—
   A people great on lands and seas.

5 Keep thou our boyhood free and fair
   And quick to help and brave to dare:
   From greed and selfishness and shame
   Guard thou, O Lord, the English name.

6 Keep thou our girlhood fair and free
   In mirth and love and modesty:
   From ugly thought and deed and word
   Guard thou our English homes, O Lord.

7 O God, whose mighty works of old
   Our fathers to their sons have told,
   Be thou our strength from age to age,
   Our children's children's heritage.

REUNION GATHERINGS

502   *O. W. Holmes*

1 THOU gracious God, whose mercy lends‿
   The light of home, the smile of friends,
   Our gathered flock thine arms enfold
   As in the peaceful days of old.

2 Wilt thou not hear us while we raise
   In sweet accord of solemn praise
   The voices that have mingled long
   In joyous flow of mirth and song?

3 For all the blessings life has brought,
   For all its sorrowing hours have taught,
   For all we mourn, for all we keep,
   The hands we clasp, the loved that sleep,

4 The noon-tide sunshine of the past,
   These brief, bright moments fading fast,
   The stars that gild our darkening years,
   The twilight ray from holier spheres,

5 We thank thee, Father; let thy grace‿
   Our loving circle still embrace,
   Thy mercy shed its heavenly store,
   Thy peace be with us evermore.

SAINTS' DAYS: GENERAL

FESTIVALS OF APOSTLES

503

♭ St. Ambrose
Tr. J. M. Neale and Compilers
Aeterna Christi munera

f   1 THE eternal gifts of Christ the King,
The apostles' glory, let us sing;
And all, with hearts of gladness, raise
Due hymns of thankful love and praise.

   2 For they the Church's princes are,
Triumphant leaders in the war,
In heavenly courts a warrior band,
True lights to lighten every land.

mf   3 Theirs is the steadfast faith of saints,
And hope that never yields nor faints,
And love of Christ in perfect glow
That lays the prince of this world low.

f   4 In them the Father's glory shone,
In them the will of God the Son,
In them exults the Holy Ghost,
Through them rejoice the heavenly host.

p   5 To thee, Redeemer, now we cry,
That thou wouldst join to them on high
Thy servants, who this grace implore,
mf   For ever and for evermore.

504

Tr. Bishop R. Mant and Compilers
Exultet caelum laudibus

   1 LET all on earth their voices raise,
Re-echoing heaven's triumphant praise,
To him who gave the apostles grace
To run on earth their glorious race.

2 Thou at whose word they bore the light
Of Gospel truth o'er heathen night,
To us that heavenly light impart,
To glad our eyes and cheer our heart.

3 Thou at whose will to them was given
To bind and loose in earth and heaven,
Our chains unbind, our sins undo,
And in our hearts thy grace renew.

4 Thou in whose might they spake the word
Which cured disease and health restored,
To us its healing power prolong,
Support the weak, confirm the strong.

5 And when the thrones are set on high,
And judgement's aweful hour draws nigh,
Then, Lord, with them pronounce us blest,
And take us to thine endless rest.

505

Tr. J. M. Neale ‡

Annue, Christe

1 O CHRIST, thou Lord of worlds, thine ear to
hear us bow
On this the festival of thine apostle now,
Who taught to men thy power to free from sin's
offence
The souls of those that tread the way of peni-
tence.

2 Redeemer, save thy work, thy noble work of
grace,
Sealed with the holy light that beameth from thy
face;
Nor suffer them to fall to Satan's wiles a prey
For whom thou didst on earth death's costly
ransom pay.

3 Pity thy flock, enthralled by sin's captivity,
  Forgive each guilty soul and set the bondmen
      free;
  And those thou hast redeemed by thine own
      Passion sore
  Grant to rejoice with thee, O King, for evermore.

506   *J. B. de Santeuil. Tr. I. Williams* ‡
              Supreme, quales, Arbiter

mf 1 DISPOSER supreme, and Judge of the earth,
      Who choosest for thine the meek and the
          poor;
    To frail earthen vessels, and things of no
        worth,
      Entrusting thy riches which ay shall endure;

    2 Those vessels soon fail, though full of thy light,
      And at thy decree are broken and gone;
f   Thence brightly appeareth thy truth in its
          might,
      As through the clouds riven the lightnings
          have shone.

    3 Like clouds are they borne to do thy great will,
      And swift as the winds about the world go:
    The Word with his wisdom their spirits doth
        fill;
      They thunder, they lighten, the waters
          o'erflow.

    4 Their sound goeth forth, 'Christ Jesus the
        Lord!'
      Then Satan doth fear, his citadels fall;
    As when the dread trumpets went forth at
        thy word,
      And one long blast shattered the Canaan-
          ite's wall.

mf 5 O loud be their trump, and stirring their
        sound,
    To rouse us, O Lord, from slumber of sin!
    The lights thou hast kindled in darkness
        around,
    O may they awaken our spirits within!

f 6 All honour and praise, dominion and might,
    To God, Three in One, eternally be,
    Who round us hath shed his own marvellous
        light,
    And called us from darkness his glory to
        see.

507   *J. B. de Santeuil. Tr. Sir H. W. Baker*

          Caelestis aulae principes

f 1 CAPTAINS of the saintly band,
    Lights who lighten every land,
    Princes who with Jesus dwell,
    Judges of his Israel;

  2 On the nations sunk in night
    Ye have shed the Gospel light;
    Sin and error flee away,
    Truth reveals the promised day.

mf 3 Not by warrior's spear and sword,
    Not by art of human word,
    Preaching but the Cross of shame,
    Rebel hearts for Christ ye tame.

p 4 Earth, that long in sin and pain
    Groaned in Satan's deadly chain,
f   Now to serve its God is free
    In the law of liberty.

5 Distant lands with one acclaim
   Tell the honour of your name,
   Who, wherever man has trod,
   Teach the mysteries of God.

6 Glory to the Three in One
   While eternal ages run,
   Who from deepest shades of night
   Called us to his glorious light.

See also hymn **529** *and accompanying note.*

Note.—Hymn **602**, *parts 2 and 3, may be used on the Festivals of Apostles or Evangelists between Easter Day and Trinity Sunday.*

FESTIVALS OF EVANGELISTS

508

R. Campbell and others
Based on Adam of St. Victor

mf   1 COME, pure hearts, in sweetest measures
   Sing of those who spread the treasures
     In the holy gospels shrined:
   Blessèd tidings of salvation,
   Peace on earth, their proclamation,
     Love from God to lost mankind.

2 Thou, by whom the words were given
   For our light and guide to heaven,
     Spirit, on our darkness shine;
   Graft them in our hearts, increasing
   Faith, hope, love, and joy unceasing,
     Till our hearts are wholly thine.

3 O that we, thy truth confessing
   And thy holy word possessing,
     Jesu, may thy love adore;
f   Unto thee our voices raising,
   Thee with all thy ransomed praising
     Ever and for evermore.

509

Adam of St. Victor. Tr. Jackson Mason
Plausu chorus laetabundo

f 1 COME sing, ye choirs exultant,
    Those messengers of God,
  Through whom the living gospels
    Came sounding all abroad;
  Whose voice proclaimed salvation,
    That poured upon the night,
  And drove away the shadows,
    And flushed the world with light.

mf 2 He chose them, our Good Shepherd,
    And, tending evermore
  His flock through earth's four quarters,
    In wisdom made them four:
  In one harmonious witness
    The chosen four combine,
  While each his own commission
    Fulfils in every line.

f 3 Four-square on this foundation
    The Church of Christ remains,
  A house to stand unshaken
    By floods or winds or rains.
  O glorious happy portion
    In this safe home to be,
  By God, true Man, united
    With God eternally!

510

I. Watts

mf 1 HOW beauteous are their feet,
    Who stand on Sion's hill,
  Who bring salvation on their tongues
    And words of peace instil!

    2 How happy are our ears
    That hear this happy sound,
  Which kings and prophets waited for,
    And sought, but never found!

3   How blessèd are our eyes
     That see this heavenly light!
Prophets and kings desired it long,
     But died without the sight.

_f_ 4   The Lord makes bare his arm
          Through all the earth abroad:
     Let every nation now behold
          Their Saviour and their God.

511

C. S. Phillips

1 SPIRIT of Jesus, who didst move
        The hearts and pens of men to write
        The story of the world's true Light,
   His words of power and deeds of love;

2 We thank thee for those scribes of old
        Who, while apostles journeyed still
        Their worldwide witness to fulfil,
   Set down the glorious tale they told;

3 We thank thee for the writers three,
        Who from such fleeting records wrought
        The first three gospels, and so taught
   The truth for every age to see.

4 Then, as faith ripened, thou didst call
        A fourth evangelist, to show
        The Christ whom souls had come to know
   As Way, as Truth, as Life, for all.

5 Spirit of Jesus, give thy grace
        To us who read, that so we may
        Know him more fully day by day
   Until we see him face to face.

FESTIVALS OF THE BLESSED VIRGIN
MARY

512   *Bishop Venantius Fortunatus*
                          Tr. J. M. Neale and Compilers

Quem terra, pontus, aethera

mf 1 THE God whom earth and sea and sky
       Adore and laud and magnify,
       Whose might they own, whose praise they tell,
p   In Mary's body deigned to dwell.

mf 2 O Mother blest! the chosen shrine
       Wherein the Architect divine,
       Whose hand contains the earth and sky,
p   Vouchsafed in hidden guise to lie:

mf 3 Blest in the message Gabriel brought;
       Blest in the work the Spirit wrought;
f   Most blest, to bring to human birth
       The long Desired of all the earth.

    4 O Lord, the Virgin-born, to thee
       Eternal praise and glory be,
       Whom with the Father we adore
       And Holy Ghost for evermore.

513   *Bishop T. Ken†*

mf 1 HER Virgin eyes saw God incarnate born,
       When she to Bethlem came that happy morn:
       How high her raptures then began to swell,
       None but her own omniscient Son can tell.

p 2 As Eve, when she her fontal sin reviewed,
       Wept for herself and all she should include,
f   Blest Mary, with man's Saviour in embrace,
       Joyed for herself and for all human race.

mf 3 All saints are by her Son's dear influence
    blest;
She kept the very fountain at her breast:
The Son adored and nursed by the sweet
    Maid
A thousandfold of love for love repaid.

f 4 Heaven with transcendent joys her entrance
    graced,
Near to his throne her Son his Mother placed;
And here below, now she's of heaven possest,
All generations are to call her blest.

514

Bishop R. Heber

1 VIRGIN-BORN, we bow before thee:
Blessèd was the womb that bore thee;
Mary, Maid and Mother mild,
Blessèd was she in her Child.

2 Blessèd was the breast that fed thee;
Blessèd was the hand that led thee;
Blessèd was the parent's eye
That watched thy slumbering infancy.

3 Blessèd she by all creation,
Who brought forth the world's Salvation,
And blessèd they—for ever blest—
Who love thee most and serve thee
    best.

4 Virgin-born, we bow before thee:
Blessèd was the womb that bore thee;
Mary, Maid and Mother mild,
Blessèd was she in her Child.

515   *Sir H. W. Baker*

mf 1 SHALL we not love thee, Mother dear,
             Whom Jesus loves so well?
          And to his glory year by year
             Thy joy and honour tell?

p   2 Bound with the curse of sin and shame
             We helpless sinners lay,
mf   Until in tender love he came
             To bear the curse away.

mf   3 And thee he chose from whom to take
             True flesh his flesh to be;
p   In it to suffer for our sake,
f   By it to make us free.

p   4 Thy Babe he lay upon thy breast,
             To thee he cried for food;
          Thy gentle nursing soothed to rest
             The incarnate Son of God.

mf   5 O wondrous depth of grace divine
             That he should bend so low!
          And, Mary, O what joy 'twas thine
             In his dear love to know!

f   6 Joy to be Mother of the Lord,
             And thine the truer bliss,
          In every thought and deed and word
             To be for ever his.

mf   7 And as he loves thee, Mother dear,
             We too will love thee well;
          And to his glory year by year
             Thy joy and honour tell.

f 8 Jesu, the Virgin's holy Son,
        We praise thee and adore,
     Who art with God the Father **One**
        And Spirit evermore.

FESTIVALS OF MARTYRS AND OTHERS

516   *Tr. J. M. Neale and Compilers*

Deus, tuorum militum

FOR A MARTYR

1 O GOD, thy soldiers' great reward,
    Their portion, crown, and faithful Lord,
    From all transgressions set us free
    Who sing thy martyr's victory.

2 By wisdom taught he learned to know
    The vanity of all below,
    The fleeting joys of earth disdained,
    And everlasting glory gained.

3 Right manfully his cross he bore,
    And ran his race of torments sore;
    For thee he poured his life away,
    With thee he lives in endless day.

4 We therefore pray thee, Lord of love,
    Regard us from thy throne above;
    On this thy martyr's triumph-day
    Wash every stain of sin away.

5 All praise to God the Father be,
    All praise, eternal Son, to thee,
    Whom with the Spirit we adore
    For ever and for evermore.

517   *J. B. de Santeuil. Tr. I. Williams†*
            Ex quo salus mortalium

FOR A MARTYR

mf 1 OUR Lord the path of suffering trod;
     And, since his Blood for man hath flowed,
     'Tis meet that man should yield to God
         The life he owed. Alleluia!

2 No shame to own the Crucified!
     Nay, 'tis our immortality
     That we confess our God who died,
         And for him die. Alleluia!

p 3 Beholding his predestined crown,
     Into death's arms the martyr goes:
f   Dying, he conquers death; o'erthrown,
         O'erthrows his foes. Alleluia!

mf 4 Lord, make us thine own soldiers true;
     Grant us brave faith, a spirit pure,
     That for thy name, thy Cross in view,
         We may endure. Alleluia!

f 5 Eternal Father of the Word,
     Eternal Word, we thee adore,
     Eternal Spirit, God and Lord
         For evermore. Alleluia!

518   *St. Joseph the Hymnographer*
                Tr. J. M. Neale†
        τῶν ἱερῶν ἀθλοφόρων

FOR MARTYRS

1 LET our choir new anthems raise,
     Wake the song of gladness:
   God himself to joy and praise
     Turns the martyrs' sadness.
   Bright the day that won their crown,
     Opened heaven's bright portal,
   As they laid the mortal down
     To put on the immortal.

2 Never flinched they from the flame,
   From the torture never;
Vain the foeman's sharpest aim,
   Satan's best endeavour:
For by faith they saw the land
   Decked in all its glory,
Where triumphant now they stand
   With the victor's story.

3 Up and follow, Christian men!
   Press through toil and sorrow;
Spurn the night of fear, and then,
   O the glorious morrow!
Who will venture on the strife?
   Blest who first begin it!
Who will grasp the land of life?
   Warriors, up and win it!

519
Iste confessor

Tr. Compilers

FOR A CONFESSOR OR BISHOP

1 HE who to Jesus manfully bore witness,
He whom God's people join to-day to honour,
Now in the hidden mansions of the blessèd
      Bideth for ever.

2 With store of virtues God adorned his spirit,
Guiding his willing feet in paths of goodness,
Through all the earthly years while in his body
      Mortal breath tarried.

3 Wherefore with voices linked in happy chorus
Hymn we his praises on this holy feast-day,
Praying for grace to follow in his footsteps
      Now and hereafter.

4 Glory and honour, powèr and salvation
Be unto him, who, thronèd in the highest,
Ordereth meetly earth and sky and ocean,
      Triune, eternal.

520

C. S. Phillips

FOR DOCTORS OF THE CHURCH

1 STALWART as pillars bearing high their burden,
So do the Church's doctors stay the temple
Where truth abideth, on the one Foundation
Grounded for ever.

2 O faithful stewards in God's holy household,
Out of your treasure new and old things bringing,
Still do your writings to the Light of ages
Steadfastly witness.

3 Souls wise and loyal to the Spirit's leading,
Bravely ye battled for the faith delivered,
While of its ageless mysteries ye furnished
New understanding.

4 Now with unclouded gaze ye are beholding
Him of whose face ye strained to catch the vision;
To whom be glory, Father, Son, and Spirit,
Through endless ages.

521

? *St. Ambrose. Tr. Compilers†* (1904)
Jesu, corona virginum

FOR VIRGINS

1 O JESU, thou the virgins' crown,
Thy gracious ear to us bow down,
Born of that Virgin whom alone
The Mother and the Maid we own.

2 In thee, their Bridegroom and their Lord,
The virgins find their bright reward,
And wheresoe'er thy footsteps wend
With hymns and praises thee attend.

3 O gracious Lord, we thee implore
Thy grace into our minds to pour;
From all defilement keep us free,
And make us pure in heart for thee.

4 All praise to God the Father be,
  All praise, eternal Son, to thee,
  Whom with the Spirit we adore,
  For ever and for evermore.

522   *Bishop W. H. Frere*†

FOR MISSIONARY SAINTS

1 THE saints who toiled from place to place,
  Spreading the Gospel of God's grace,
  Now in their heavenly homeland dwell
  With Christ, whom here they served so well.

2 Alert at thy command to go,
  And everywhere thy word to sow,
  They went, O Master, far and wide,
  Eager, but yet unsatisfied.

3 Thine was the task they took in hand,
  Thine their good news for every land,
  Thine was their power, and thine again
  Their passion for the souls of men.

4 That task of thine, by them begun,
  Must now by our weak hands be done:
  Strengthen, O Lord, to work for thee
  These hands, at home and over sea.

FOR ANY SAINT'S DAY

523   *Adam of St. Victor*
                            Tr. Yattendon Hymnal
Supernae matris gaudia

1 JOY and triumph everlasting
    Hath the heavenly Church on high;
  For that pure immortal gladness
    All our feast-days mourn and sigh;
  Yet in death's dark desert wild
  Doth the mother aid her child;
  Guards celestial thence attend us,
  Stand in combat to defend us.

2 Here the world's perpetual warfare
 Holds from heaven the soul apart;
Legioned foes in shadowy terror
 Vex the Sabbath of the heart.
O how happy that estate
Where delight doth not abate!
For that home the spirit yearneth,
Where none languisheth nor mourneth.

3 There the body hath no torment,
 There the mind is free from care,
There is every voice rejoicing,
 Every heart is loving there.
Angels in that city dwell;
Them their King delighteth well:
Still they joy and weary never,
More and more desiring ever.

4 There the seers and fathers holy,
 There the prophets glorified,
All their doubts and darkness ended.
 In the Light of Light abide.
There the saints, whose memories old
We in faithful hymns uphold,
Have forgot their bitter story
In the joy of Jesus' glory.

524   *18th cent. Tr. J. H. Clark*

Pugnate, Christi milites

f 1 SOLDIERS, who are Christ's below,
Strong in faith resist the foe:
Boundless is the pledged reward
Unto them who serve the Lord.

mf 2 'Tis no palm of fading leaves
That the conqueror's hand receives;
Joys are his, serene and pure,
Light that ever shall endure.

3 For the souls that overcome
 Waits the beauteous heavenly home,
 Where the blessèd evermore
 Tread on high the starry floor.

p 4 Passing soon and little worth
 Are the things that tempt on earth;
mf Heavenward lift thy soul's regard:
 God himself is thy reward.

f 5 Father, who the crown dost give,
 Saviour, by whose Death we live,
 Spirit, who our hearts dost raise,
 Three in One, thy name we praise.

525
R. Hill and others

mf 1 LO, round the throne, a glorious band,
 The saints in countless myriads stand,
 Of every tongue redeemed to God,
 Arrayed in garments washed in Blood.

p 2 Through tribulation great they came;
 They bore the cross, despised the shame;
 From all their labours now they rest,
 In God's eternal glory blest.

mf 3 They see their Saviour face to face,
 And sing the triumphs of his grace;
f Him day and night they ceaseless praise,
 To him the loud thanksgiving raise:

 4 'Worthy the Lamb, for sinners slain,
 Through endless years to live and reign!
 Thou hast redeemed us by thy Blood,
 And made us kings and priests to God.'

mf 5 O may we tread the sacred road
 That saints and holy martyrs trod;
 Wage to the end the glorious strife,
f And win, like them, a crown of life.

526   *Bishop Chr. Wordsworth*

f 1 HARK! the sound of holy voices,
        Chanting at the crystal sea
     Alleluia, Alleluia,
        Alleluia, Lord, to thee:
     Multitude, which none can number,
        Like the stars in glory stands,
     Clothed in white apparel, holding⏝
        Palms of victory in their hands.

mf 2 Patriarch, and holy prophet,
        Who prepared the way of Christ,
     King, apostle, saint, confessor,
        Martyr, and evangelist,
     Saintly maiden, godly matron,
        Widows who have watched to prayer,
f Joined in holy concert, singing⏝
        To the Lord of all, are there.

p 3*They have come from tribulation,
        And have washed their robes in Blood,
     Washed them in the Blood of Jesus;
        Tried they were, and firm they stood:
     Mocked, imprisoned, stoned, tormented,
        Sawn asunder, slain with sword,
f They have conquered death and Satan
        By the might of Christ the Lord.

     4 Marching with thy Cross their banner,
        They have triumphed following⏝
     Thee, the Captain of Salvation,
        Thee, their Saviour and their King:
mf Gladly, Lord, with thee they suffered;
        Gladly, Lord, with thee they died,
f And by death to life immortal
        They were born, and glorified.

5 Now they reign in heavenly glory,
 Now they walk in golden light,
Now they drink, as from a river,
 Holy bliss and infinite;
p Love and peace they taste for ever,
 And all truth and knowledge see
mf In the beatific vision
 Of the blessèd Trinity.

f 6 God of God, the One-begotten,
 Light of Light, Emmanuel,
In whose Body joined together
 All the saints for ever dwell;
Pour upon us of thy fulness,
 That we may for evermore
God the Father, God the Son, and⌣
 God the Holy Ghost adore.

527
Bishop W. Walsham How

f 1 FOR all the saints who from their labours rest,
Who thee by faith before the world confessed,
Thy name, O Jesu, be for ever blest.
      Alleluia!

2 Thou wast their rock, their fortress, and their might;
Thou, Lord, their Captain in the well-fought fight;
Thou, in the darkness, still their one true Light.   Alleluia!

3 O may thy soldiers, faithful, true, and bold,
Fight as the saints who nobly fought of old,
And win, with them, the victor's crown of gold.   Alleluia!

mf 4 O blest communion, fellowship divine!
We feebly struggle, they in glory shine;
Yet all are one in thee, for all are thine.
Alleluia!

p 5 And when the strife is fierce, the warfare long.
Steals on the ear the distant triumph-song,
mf And hearts are brave again and arms are
strong. Alleluia!

6 The golden evening brightens in the west;
Soon, soon to faithful warriors comes their
rest:
p Sweet is the calm of Paradise the blest.
Alleluia!

f 7 But lo, there breaks a yet more glorious day;
The saints triumphant rise in bright array:
The King of Glory passes on his way.
Alleluia!

8 From earth's wide bounds, from ocean's
farthest coast,
Through gates of pearl streams in the count-
less host,
Singing to Father, Son, and Holy Ghost.
Alleluia!

528

I. Watts and others

f 1 HOW bright these glorious spirits shine!
Whence all their white array?
How came they to the blissful seats
Of everlasting day?

p 2 Lo, these are they from sufferings great
Who came to realms of light;
And in the Blood of Christ have washed
Those robes that shine so bright.

f   3 Now with triumphal palms they stand
      Before the throne on high,
   And serve the God they love amidst
      The glories of the sky.

mf 4 Hunger and thirst are felt no more,
      Nor suns with scorching ray;
   God is their Sun, whose cheering beams
      Diffuse eternal day.

    5 The Lamb, which dwells amidst the throne,
      Shall o'er them still preside,
   Feed them with nourishment divine,
      And all their footsteps guide.

p   6 Midst pastures green he'll lead his flock,
      Where living streams appear;
mf   And God the Lord from every eye
      Shall wipe off every tear.

f   7 To Father, Son, and Holy Ghost,
      The God whom we adore,
   Be glory, as it was, is now,
      And shall be evermore.

529

Bishop R. Heber

f   1 THE Son of God goes forth to war
      A kingly crown to gain;
   His blood-red banner streams afar:
      Who follows in his train?
   Who best can drink his cup of woe,
      Triumphant over pain,
   Who patient bears his cross below,
      He follows in his train.

mf 2 The martyr first, whose eagle eye‿
    Could pierce beyond the grave;
Who saw his Master in the sky,
    And called on him to save.
Like him, with pardon on his tongue
    In midst of mortal pain,
He prayed for them that did the wrong:
    Who follows in his train?

3 A glorious band, the chosen few
    On whom the Spirit came,
Twelve valiant saints, their hope they knew,
    And mocked the cross and flame.
They met the tyrant's brandished steel,
    The lion's gory mane;
They bowed their necks, the death to feel:
    Who follows in their train?

f 4 A noble army, men and boys,
    The matron and the maid,
Around the Saviour's throne rejoice
    In robes of light arrayed.
They climbed the steep ascent of heaven
    Through peril, toil, and pain:
O God, to us may grace be given
    To follow in their train.

Note.—Verses 1 and 4 are suitable for any saint's day. Verse 2 refers to St. Stephen, verse 3 to the apostles, and may be used with verses 1 and 4 on the festivals for which they are respectively appropriate. The whole hymn is suitable for All Saints' Day.

530
                              J. Montgomery

f 1 PALMS of glory, raiment bright,
    Crowns that never fade away,
Gird and deck the saints in light:
    Priests and kings and conquerors they.

mf 2 Yet the conquerors bring their palms
  To the Lamb amidst the throne,
f And proclaim in joyful psalms
  Victory through his Cross alone.

mf 3 Kings for harps their crowns resign,
  Crying, as they strike the chords,
f 'Take the Kingdom, it is thine,
  King of Kings and Lord of Lords.'

p 4 Round the altar priests confess,
  If their robes are white as snow,
 'Twas the Saviour's righteousness,
  And his Blood, that made them so.

mf 5 They were mortal too like us:
  O, when we like them must die,
f May our souls translated thus
  Triumph, reign, and shine on high.

531   *Bishop R. Mant and Compilers*

mf 1 FOR all thy saints, O Lord,
   Who strove in thee to live,
  Who followed thee, obeyed, adored,
   Our grateful hymn receive.

  2 For all thy saints, O Lord,
   Who strove in thee to die,
  And found in thee a full reward,
   Accept our thankful cry.

  3 Thine earthly members fit
   To join thy saints above,
  In one communion ever knit,
   One fellowship of love.

4   Jesu, thy name we bless,
         And humbly pray that we
       May follow them in holiness,
         Who lived and died for thee.

f   5   All might, all praise, be thine,
           Father, co-equal Son,
         And Spirit, bond of love divine,
           While endless ages run.

32   *Bishop R. Heber*

1 WE praise thee, Lord, for all the martyred
         throng,
   Those who by fire and sword or suffering long
   Laid down their lives, but would not yield to
         wrong:
                              Alleluia!

2 For those who fought to keep the faith secure,
   For all whose hearts were selfless, strong and
         pure,
   For those whose courage taught us to en-
         dure:
                              Alleluia!

3 For fiery spirits, held and God-controlled,
   For gentle natures by his power made bold,
   For all whose gracious lives God's love re-
         told.
                              Alleluia!

4 Thanks be to thee, O Lord, for saints unknown,
   Who by obedience to thy word have shown
   That thou didst call and mark them for thine
         own.
                              Alleluia!

SAINTS' DAYS AND OTHER HOLY DAYS: PROPER

ST. ANDREW THE APOSTLE

533   *Mrs. C. F. Alexander*

mf 1 JESUS calls us! o'er the tumult
    Of our life's wild restless sea
    Day by day his sweet voice soundeth,
    Saying, 'Christian, follow me;'

    2 As of old Saint Andrew heard it
    By the Galilean lake,
    Turned from home and toil and kindred,
    Leaving all for his dear sake.

p 3 Jesus calls us from the worship
    Of the vain world's golden store,
    From each idol that would keep us,
    Saying, 'Christian, love me more.'

mf 4 In our joys and in our sorrows,
    Days of toil and hours of ease,
    Still he calls, in cares and pleasures,
    That we love him more than these.

p 5 Jesus calls us! by thy mercies,
    Saviour, make us hear thy call,
    Give our hearts to thine obedience,
    Serve and love thee best of all.

ST. THOMAS THE APOSTLE

534   *Archbishop J. R. Darbyshire*

    1 WHO dreads, yet undismayed
    Dares face his terror;
    Who errs, yet having strayed
    Avows his error—

Him let Saint Thomas guide,
Who stirred his fellows' pride
To move to death beside
    Their Lord and Master.

2 Who longs for guidance clear
    When doubts assail him,
Nor dares to move for fear
    Lest faith should fail him—
For such let Christ's reply
To his disciple's cry,
'I am the Way,' supply
    The light in darkness.

3 Who grieves that love lies dead
    On fate's wheel broken;
And stands uncomforted
    By any token—
His faith shall be restored
By Christ's compelling word
When Thomas saw the Lord.
    And seeing worshipped.

ST. STEPHEN

535
> *Adam of St. Victor*
> *Tr. J. M. Neale and Compilers*

Heri mundus exultavit

1 YESTERDAY with exultation
Joined the world in celebration
    Of her promised Saviour's birth;
Yesterday the angel-nation
Poured the strains of jubilation
    O'er the Monarch born on earth:

2 But to-day, O deacon glorious,
  By thy faith and deeds victorious,
    Stephen, champion renowned,
Thee we hail who, triumph gaining,
Mid the faithless faith sustaining,
    First of martyr saints wast found.

3 For the crown that fadeth never
  Bear thy murderers' brief endeavour;
    Victory waits to end the strife:
Death shall be thy life's beginning,
And life's losing be the winning
    Of the true and better life.

See also hymn **529** *and accompanying note*

ST. JOHN THE EVANGELIST

536
                                    J. Keble

mf 1 WORD supreme, before creation
    Born of God eternally,
Who didst will for our salvation
    To be born on earth, and die;
Well thy saints have kept their station,
    Watching till thine hour drew nigh.

2 Now 'tis come, and faith espies thee:
    Like an eaglet in the morn,
One in steadfast worship eyes thee,
    Thy beloved, thy latest born;
In thy glory he descries thee
    Reigning from the Tree of scorn.

f 3 Lo, heaven's doors lift up, revealing
    How thy judgements earthward move:
Scrolls unfolded, trumpets pealing,
    Wine-cups from the wrath above;
p   Yet o'er all a soft voice stealing,
    'Little children, trust and love!'

f 4 Thee, the almighty King eternal,
   Father of the eternal Word,
Thee, the Father's Word supernal,
   Thee, of Both, the Breath adored,
Heaven and earth and realms infernal
   Own, one glorious God and Lord.

537   *F. B. Merryweather*

1 TO you was given, O saint beloved,
   A vision of Christ's glory
Before he lived his earthly life
   Begun with Christmas story:
The glory of the Son of God
   Before the world's creation,
In whom all things that are were made
   And have their consummation.

2 In you he found his closest friend,
   A friend though frail and mortal,
Whose love so pure gave sight so sure
   It pierced beyond heaven's portal:
So to the world you witness gave,
   With prophet's eye descrying
The life of grace and fellowship,
   The life in God undying.

3 O love of God that overflowed
   In glories of creation!
O crowning glory of all life
   In wondrous Incarnation!
All praise to God whose saint and seer
   Declared the love excelling
Now shed abroad in faithful hearts,
   Abounding and indwelling.

THE INNOCENTS' DAY

538   *Prudentius. Tr. J. M. C. Crum*

Salvete, flores martyrum

1 O MARTYRS young and fresh as flowers,
   Your day was in its morning hours
   When Christ was sought and you were found
   Like rain-strewn petals on the ground.

2 How weak to hurt you was the king!
   You are Christ's morning offering,
   His pretty lambs, his children, gay
   With martyr-crowns and palms at play.

3 And you had cheated Herod's rage,
   You little boys of Jesus' age;
   For he whom Herod sought to slay,
   Jesus, untouched escaped away.

4 Glory, O Christ the Lord, to thee,
   Child of the blessèd Virgin, be,
   Whom with the Father we adore
   And Holy Spirit evermore.

THE CIRCUMCISION

539   *S. Besnault. Tr. Compilers* (1904)

Debilis cessent elementa legis

1   THE ancient law departs,
        And all its fears remove,
   For Jesus makes with faithful hearts
        A covenant of love.

2   The Light of Light divine,
        True brightness undefiled,
   He bears for us the pain of sin,
        A holy spotless Child.

3   To-day the name is thine
At which we bend the knee;
They call thee Jesus, Child divine:
Our Jesus deign to be.

4   All praise, eternal Son,
For thy redeeming love,
With Father, Spirit, ever One,
In glorious might above.

The following hymns are also suitable:

190   To the name of our salvation.
191   Conquering kings their titles take.
192   How sweet the name of Jesus sounds.

THE CONVERSION OF ST. PAUL

540   *St. Peter Damiani. Tr. J. M. Neale* ‡

Paule, doctor egregie

1 FROM heaven's height Christ spake to call
The Gentiles' great apostle, Paul,
Whose doctrine, like the thunder, sounds
To the wide world's remotest bounds.

2 O bliss of Paul, beyond all thought,
To Paradise, yet living, caught!
He hears the heavenly mysteries there,
Which mortal tongue cannot declare.

3 The word's good seed abroad he flings;
Straightway a mighty harvest springs,
And fruits of holy deeds supply
God's everlasting granary.

4 The lamp his burning faith displays
  Has filled the world with glorious rays;
  That darkness' realm may be o'erthrown,
  And Christ may reign, and reign alone.

541   *J. Ellerton*

1 WE sing the glorious conquest
    Before Damascus' gate,
  When Saul, the Church's spoiler,
    Came breathing threats and hate;
  The ravening wolf rushed forward
    Full early to the prey;
  But lo, the Shepherd met him,
    And bound him fast to-day.

2*O glory most excelling
    That smote across his path!
  O light that pierced and blinded
    The zealot in his wrath!
  O voice that spake within him
    The calm reproving word!
  O love that sought and held him
    The bondman of his Lord!

3 O Wisdom, ordering all things
    In order strong and sweet,
  What nobler spoil was ever
    Cast at the Victor's feet?
  What wiser master-builder
    E'er wrought at thine employ
  Than he, till now so furious
    Thy building to destroy?

4 Lord, teach thy Church the lesson,
    Still in her darkest hour
Of weakness and of danger
    To trust thy hidden power:
Thy grace by ways mysterious
    The wrath of man can bind,
And in thy boldest foeman
    Thy chosen saint can find.

542   *Amy Sayle*

1 PAUL the preacher, Paul the poet,
    Fearless fighter for the truth,
Mystic, pioneer, and prophet,
    Builder of the Church's youth;

2 Foremost of Gamaliel's pupils,
    Pharisee of Christian fame,
Great apostle of the Gentiles,
    We as Gentiles bless thy name.

3 Loyal Jew, yet born a Roman,
    Citizen, yet slave of Christ,
Wealth, position, kindred, freedom,
    To thy Lord were sacrificed.

4 Still to-day we need thy teaching,
    Stern yet loving, hard yet true:
Only those who share his Passion
    Can their lives in Christ renew.

5 Paul the fiery, Paul the saintly,
    Worship with us at thy feast;
May our love to Christ be strengthened,
    And our faith through thee increased;

6 Till, when faith no more is needed,
    There where faith and sight are one,
We in heaven shall praise the Father
    In the Spirit through the Son.

PRESENTATION OF CHRIST IN THE TEMPLE

COMMONLY CALLED

THE PURIFICATION OF ST. MARY THE VIRGIN

543

J. B. de Santeuil
Tr. E. Caswall and Compilers

Templi sacratas pande, Sion, fores

1 O SION, open wide thy gates,
   Let symbols disappear:
   A Priest and Victim, both in one,
   The Truth himself is here.

2 No more the slaughtered beast must die:
   Behold, the Father's Son
   His Temple enters, soon himself
   For sinners to atone.

3 Conscious of hidden Deity,
   The lowly Virgin brings
   Her new-born Babe, with two young doves,
   Her humble offerings.

4 There waiting Simeon sees at last
   The Saviour long desired,
   And Anna welcomes Israel's Hope,
   With holy rapture fired.

5 But silent stood the Mother blest
   Of the yet silent Word,
   And, pondering in her steadfast heart,
   With speechless praise adored.

6 All glory to the Father be,
   All glory to the Son,
   All glory, Holy Ghost, to thee,
   While endless ages run.

544

J. Ellerton

f 1 HAIL to the Lord who comes,
    Comes to his Temple gate!
mf Not with his angel host,
    Not in his kingly state:
    No shouts proclaim him nigh,
    No crowds his coming wait.

p 2 But borne upon the throne
    Of Mary's gentle breast,
    Watched by her duteous love,
    In her fond arms at rest;
mf Thus to his Father's house
    He comes, the heavenly guest.

3 There Joseph at her side
    In reverent wonder stands;
    And, filled with holy joy,
    Old Simeon in his hands
    Takes up the promised Child,
    The glory of all lands.

4 Hail to the great First-born,
    Whose ransom-price they pay!
    The Son before all worlds;
    The Child of man to-day,
f That he might ransom us
    Who still in bondage lay.

mf 5 O Light of all the earth,
    Thy children wait for thee:
    Come to thy temples here,
    That we, from sin set free,
    Before thy Father's face
    May all presented be.

ST. MATTHIAS THE APOSTLE

545   *H. Alford*

1 THE highest and the holiest place
      Guards not the heart from sin:
   The Church that safest seems without
      May harbour foes within.

2 Thus in the small and chosen band
      Beloved above the rest,
   One fell from his apostleship,
      A traitor soul unblest.

3 But not the great designs of God
      Man's sins shall overthrow;
   Another witness to the truth
      Forth to the lands shall go.

4 The soul that sinneth, it shall die;
      Thy purpose shall not fail:
   The word of grace no less shall sound,
      The truth no less prevail.

5 Righteous, O Lord, are all thy ways:
      Long as the worlds endure,
   From foes without and foes within
      Thy Church shall stand secure.

THE ANNUNCIATION OF THE BLESSED
                    VIRGIN MARY

546   *Anon.* (1847)

1   PRAISE we the Lord this day,
        This day so long foretold,
   Whose promise shone with cheering ray
        On waiting saints of old.

2   The prophet gave the sign
      For faithful men to read:
  A Virgin, born of David's line,
      Shall bear the promised Seed.

3   Ask not how this should be,
      But worship and adore;
  Like her, whom heaven's majesty
      Came down to shadow o'er.

4   Meekly she bowed her head
      To hear the gracious word,
  Mary, the pure and lowly maid,
      The favoured of the Lord.

5   Blessèd shall be her name
      In all the Church on earth,
  Through whom that wondrous mercy came,
      The incarnate Saviour's birth.

6   Jesu, the Virgin's Son,
      We praise thee and adore,
  Who art with God the Father One
      And Spirit evermore.

547   *14th cent. Tr. J. M. C. Crum*

Angelus ad Virginem

1   GABRIEL to Mary came,
      She saw him in her chamber;
  Mary's heart stood still with fear,
      But gently did he greet her:
  'Thou queen of maidens, hail!' he said,
  'Thou shalt become a Mother-maid;
Thy Son shall be the Lord of earth and heaven:
      He comes to save mankind
  That men, their sins forgiven,
      The gate of heaven may find.'

2   'How can I a mother be
      That am a maid unwedded?
   How can I a mother be
      That am a maid betrothèd?'
He answered to her questioning:
   'The Holy Ghost shall do this thing.
Be not afraid, nor let thy heart be careful:
      God guards thy purity;
   His powers shall make thee joyful,
      And blessèd shalt thou be.'

3   Unto whom our Lady then
      Returned her answer meekly:
   'Here am I, the handmaiden
      Of God the Lord almighty;
O messenger of God most high,
   Revealer of this mystery,
With all my heart I long to see fulfilment⌣
      Of what I hear thee tell:
   Behold his handmaid ready⌣
      To do his holy will.'

4   Ah, thou Mother of my Lord,
      What peace through thee was given!
Thy dear Child, our Christ adored,
      Make peace in earth and heaven.
Beseech thy Son for us, that he⌣
   Would look upon us graciously,
And, all our shame and misery relieving,
      Would give us grace to come⌣
   To comfort out of grieving
      And, out of exile, home.

The following hymns are also suitable:

512   The God whom earth and sea and sky.
513   Her Virgin eyes saw God incarnate born.
514   Virgin-born, we bow before thee.
515   Shall we not love thee, Mother dear.

ST. MARK THE EVANGELIST

548   *Mrs. C. F. Alexander†*

1 FROM out the cloud of fiery light,
   Borne on the whirlwind from the north,
Four living creatures winged and bright
   Before the prophet's eye came forth.

2 The voice of God was in the four
   Beneath that awful crystal mist,
And every wondrous form they wore
   Forshadowed an Evangelist.

3 The lion-faced, he told abroad
   The strength of love, the strength of faith;
He showed the almighty Son of God,
   The Man divine who won by death.

4 O Lion of the Royal Tribe,
   Strong Son of God, and strong to save,
All power and honour we ascribe
   To thee who only makest brave.

5 For strength to love, for will to speak,
   For fiery crowns by martyrs won,
For suffering patience, strong and meek,
   We praise thee, Lord, and thee alone.

ST. PHILIP AND ST. JAMES THE APOSTLES

549   *J. B. de Santeuil*
                    Tr. J. Chandler and Compilers

Caelestis aulae principes

1 HAIL! princes of the host of heaven,
   To whom by Christ your Chief 'tis given
On shining thrones to sit on high,
   And judge the world with equity.

2 Through you was borne the Gospel light
   To those who lay in sin's dark night;
That Christ, the Life, the Truth, the Way,
   Might lead them to eternal day.

3 Not in the power of earthly sword
   Or arts of speech ye preached the Lord:
The Cross, the Cross which men despise,
   'Twas this achieved your victories.

4 And now to God, the Three in One,
   Be highest praise and glory done,
Who calls us from the gloom of night
   To share the glory of his light.

Hymn **199** *is also suitable.*

ST. BARNABAS THE APOSTLE

550   *J. Ellerton*

1 O SON of God, our Captain of Salvation,
      Thyself by suffering schooled to human grief,
We bless thee for thy sons of consolation,
      Who follow in the steps of thee their chief:

2 For all true helpers, patient, kind, and skilful,
      Who shed thy light across our darkened earth,
Counsel the doubting, and restrain the wilful,
      Soothe the sick bed, and share the children's
         mirth.

3 Such was thy Levite, strong in self-oblation
      To cast his all at thine apostles' feet;
He whose new name, through every Christian
         nation,
      From age to age our thankful strains repeat.

ST. JOHN BAPTIST

551   *Paul the Deacon. Tr. Compilers*
            Ut queant laxis Resonare fibris

1 SING we the praises of the great forerunner,
   Tell forth the mighty wonders of his story:
So may his Master cleanse our lips and make them
      Fit to extol him.

2 Lo, God's high herald, swift from heaven
    descending,
  Gives to thy father tidings of thy coming,
  Telling thy name and all the tale of marvels
      That shall befall thee.

3 Oft had the prophets in the time before thee
  Spoken in vision of the Daystar's coming; [him
  But when he came, 'twas thou that didst proclaim
      Saviour of all men.

552   *C. Coffin. Tr. I. Williams†*
          Nunc suis tandem novus e latebris

mf 1 LO, from the desert homes,
    Where he hath hid so long,
  The new Elijah comes,
    In sternest wisdom strong:
f   The voice that cries
          Of Christ from high,
          And judgement nigh
        From opening skies.

mf 2 Your God e'en now doth stand
    At heaven's opening door;
  His fan is in his hand,
    And he will purge his floor;
f   The wheat he claims
          And with him stows,
p   The chaff he throws
        To quenchless flames.

f 3 Ye haughty mountains, bow
    Your sky-aspiring heads;
mf   Ye valleys, hiding low,
    Lift up your gentle meads;
f   Make his way plain
          Your King before,
          For evermore
        He comes to reign.

mf 4 May thy dread voice around,
      Thou harbinger of Light,
   On our dull ears still sound,
      Lest here we sleep in night,
      Till judgement come,
         And on our path
         The Lamb's dread wrath
      Shall burst in doom.

   5 O God, with love's sweet might,
      Who dost anoint and arm
   Christ's soldier for the fight
      With grace that shields from harm:
f   Thrice blessèd Three,
         Heaven's endless days
         Shall sing thy praise
      Eternally.

553   *The Venerable Bede. Tr. J. M. Neale*†
         Praecursor altus luminis

   1 THE great forerunner of the morn,
      The herald of the Word, is born;
      And faithful hearts shall never fail
      With thanks and praise his light to hail.

   2 With heavenly message Gabriel came,
      That John should be that herald's name,
      And with prophetic utterance told
      His actions great and manifold.

   3 John, still unborn, yet gave aright
      His witness to the coming Light;
      And Christ, the Sun of all the earth,
      Fulfilled that witness at his birth.

   4 Of woman-born shall never be
      A greater prophet than was he,
      Whose mighty deeds exalt his fame
      To greater than a prophet's name.

5 All praise to God the Father be,
  All praise, eternal Son, to thee,
Whom with the Spirit we adore
  For ever and for evermore.

Hymn **50** *is also suitable.*

ST. PETER THE APOSTLE

554   *H. A. Martin*

1 O ROCK of ages, one Foundation
  On which the living Church doth rest—
The Church whose walls are strong salvation,
  Whose gates are praise—thy name be blest.

2 Son of the living God, O call us
  Once and again to follow thee;
And give us strength, whate'er befall us,
  Thy true disciples still to be.

3 When fears appal and faith is failing,
  Make thy voice heard o'er wind and wave;
And in thy perfect love prevailing
  Put forth thy hand to help and save.

4 And if our coward hearts deny thee
  In inmost thought, in deed or word,
Let not our hardness still defy thee,
  But with a look subdue us, Lord.

5 O strengthen thou our weak endeavour
  Thee in thy sheep to serve and tend,
To give ourselves to thee for ever,
  And find thee with us to the end.

555

Bishop W. Walsham How

1 'THOU art the Christ, O Lord,
   The Son of God most high!'
For ever be adored
   That name in earth and sky,
In which, though mortal strength may fail,
The saints of God at last prevail.

2 O surely he was blest
   With blessedness unpriced,
Who, taught of God, confessed
   The Godhead in the Christ!
For of thy Church, Lord, thou didst own
Thy saint a true foundation-stone.

3 Thrice fallen, thrice restored!
   The bitter lesson learnt,
That heart for thee, O Lord,
   With triple ardour burnt.
The cross he took he laid not down
Until he grasped the martyr's crown.

4 O bright triumphant faith,
   O courage void of fears!
O love most strong in death,
   O penitential tears!
By these, Lord, keep us lest we fall,
And make us go where thou shalt call.

Hymn 323 is also suitable.

ST. MARY MAGDALENE

556

C. S. Phillips. Based on Collaudemus
Magdalenae, *Philippe de Grève*

1 MAGDALENE, thy grief and gladness
   Voice and heart in concert sing,
Telling how the risen Saviour
   Called thee from thy sorrowing,
Tidings of his Resurrection
   To his chosen flock to bring.

2 She beheld him, yet she knew not
   In the gardener's seeming guise
Christ, who in her heart was sowing
   Seed of heavenly mysteries,
Till his voice, her name pronouncing,
   Bade her see and recognize.

3 Weep not, Mary, weep no longer!
   Now thy seeking heart may rest;
Christ the heavenly gardener soweth
   Light and joy within thy breast:
In the glowing cry 'Rabboni!'
   Be thy gratitude confest.

ST. JAMES THE APOSTLE

557   *Mrs. C. F. Alexander*

1 FOR all thy saints, a noble throng,
   Who fell by fire and sword,
Who soon were called, or waited long,
   We praise thy name, O Lord;

2 For him who left his father's side,
   Nor lingered by the shore,
When, softer than the weltering tide,
   Thy summons glided o'er;

3 Who stood beside the maiden dead,
   Who climbed the mount with thee,
And saw the glory round thy head,
   One of thy chosen three;

4 Who knelt beneath the olive shade,
   Who drank thy cup of pain,
And passed from Herod's flashing blade
   To see thy face again.

5 Lord, give us grace, and give us love,
   Like him to leave behind
Earth's cares and joys, and look above
   With true and earnest mind.

6 So shall we learn to drink thy cup,
   So meek and firm be found,
When thou shalt come to take us up
   Where thine elect are crowned.

THE TRANSFIGURATION

558
           15th cent. *Tr. Compilers* (1904)
           Caelestis formam gloriae

1 O WONDROUS type, O vision fair
Of glory that the Church shall share,
Which Christ upon the mountain shows,
Where brighter than the sun he glows!

2 The law and prophets there have place,
The chosen witnesses of grace;
The Father's voice from out the cloud
Proclaims his only Son aloud.

3 With shining face and bright array,
Christ deigns to manifest to-day
What glory shall to faith be given
When we enjoy our God in heaven.

4 And Christian hearts are raised on high
By that great vision's mystery,
For which in thankful strains we raise
On this glad day the voice of praise.

559
           St. Cosmas. Tr. J. M. Neale†
           χορὸς Ἰσραήλ

1 IN days of old on Sinai
   The Lord almighty came
In majesty of terror,
   In thunder-cloud and flame:
On Tabor, with the glory
   Of sunniest light for vest,
The excellence of beauty
   In Jesus was exprest.

2 All light created paled there,
    And did him worship meet;
The sun itself adored him,
    And bowed before his feet;
While Moses and Elijah,
    Upon the holy mount,
The co-eternal glory
    Of Christ our God recount.

3 O holy, wondrous vision!
    But O when, this life past,
The beauty of mount Tabor
    Shall end in heaven at last!
But O when all the glory
    Of uncreated light
Shall be the promised guerdon
    Of them that win the fight!

560   *J. A. Robinson*

mf 1   'TIS good, Lord, to be here!
            Thy glory fills the night;
       Thy face and garments, like the sun,
            Shine with unborrowed light.

      2   'Tis good, Lord, to be here,
            Thy beauty to behold,
       Where Moses and Elijah stand,
            Thy messengers of old.

f   3   Fulfiller of the past!
            Promise of things to be!
       We hail thy body glorified,
            And our redemption see.

mf 4   Before we taste of death,
            We see thy Kingdom come;
       We fain would hold the vision bright,
            And make this hill our home.

5   'Tis good, Lord, to be here!
     Yet we may not remain;
     But since thou bidst us leave the mount
     Come with us to the plain.

561   *F. L. Hosmer*

1 NOT always on the mount may we
   Rapt in the heavenly vision be;
   The shores of thought and feeling know
   The Spirit's tidal ebb and flow.

2 'Lord, it is good abiding here,'
   We cry, the heavenly presence near:
   The vision vanishes, our eyes
   Are lifted into vacant skies.

3 Yet hath one such exalted hour
   Upon the soul redeeming power,
   And in its strength through after days
   We travel our appointed ways;

4 Till all the lowly vale grows bright,
   Transfigured in remembered light,
   And in untiring souls we bear
   The freshness of the upper air.

5 The mount for vision: but below
   The paths of daily duty go,
   And nobler life therein shall own
   The pattern on the mountain shown.

This hymn is suitable for general use.

ST. BARTHOLOMEW THE APOSTLE

562   *C. S. Phillips*

1 NOT by far-famed deeds alone
   God's Kingdom comes to birth;
   The memory of countless saints
   Has perished from the earth.

2 John and Peter, James and Paul,
   Have left a mighty fame:
   Another of their company
   Is nothing but a name.

3 Yet for him no less the call
   And gallant course to run;
   His too to hear at journey's end
   The Master's glad 'Well done!'

Hymn **549** *may also be used.*

ST. MATTHEW THE APOSTLE

563   *W. Bright*

1 HE sat to watch o'er customs paid,
   A man of scorned and hardening trade:
   Alike the symbol and the tool
   Of foreign masters' hated rule.

2 But grace within his breast had stirred;
   There needed but the timely word:
   It came, true Lord of souls, from thee,
   That royal summons, 'Follow me.'

3 Enough, when thou wast passing by,
   To hear thy voice, to meet thine eye:
   He rose, responsive to the call,
   And left his task, his gains, his all.

4 O wise exchange! with these to part,
   And lay up treasure in thy heart;
   With twofold crown of light to shine
   Amid thy servants' foremost line.

5 Come, Saviour, as in days of old;
   Pass where the world has strongest hold,
   And faithless care and selfish greed
   Are thorns that choke the holy seed.

6 Who keep thy gifts, O bid them claim
The steward's, not the owner's, name:
Who yield all up for thy dear sake,
Let them of Matthew's wealth partake.

ST. MICHAEL AND ALL ANGELS

564 *Ascribed to Archbishop Rabanus Maurus*
Tr. Compilers

Christe, sanctorum decus angelorum

1 CHRIST, the fair glory of the holy angels,
Ruler of all men, author of creation,
Grant us in mercy grace to win by patience
Joys everlasting.

2 Send thine archangel Michael from thy presence:
Peacemaker blessèd, may he hover o'er us,
Hallow our dwellings, that for us thy children
All things may prosper.

3 Send thine archangel, Gabriel the mighty:
On strong wings flying, may he come from
heaven,
Drive from thy temple Satan the old foeman,
Succour our weakness.

4 Send thine archangel, Raphael the healer:
Through him with wholesome medicines of
salvation
Heal our backsliding, and in paths of goodness
Guide our steps daily.

5 Father almighty, Son, and Holy Spirit,
Godhead eternal, grant us our petition;
Thine be the glory through the whole creation
Now and for ever.

565

R. M. Benson

f 1 PRAISE to God who reigns above,
Binding earth and heaven in love;
All the armies of the sky
Worship his dread sovereignty.

2 Seraphim his praises sing,
Cherubim on fourfold wing,
Thrones, Dominions, Princes, Powers,
Marshalled might that never cowers.

mf 3 Speeds the Archangel from his face,
Bearing messages of grace;
Angel hosts his words fulfil,
Ruling nature by his will.

4 Yet on man they joy to wait,
All that bright celestial state,
For in Man their Lord they see,
Christ, the incarnate Deity.

5 On the throne their Lord who died
Sits in Manhood glorified;
Where his people faint below
Angels count it joy to go.

6 O the depths of joy divine
Thrilling through those orders nine,
When the lost are found again,
When the banished come to reign!

f 7 Now in faith, in hope, in love,
We will join the choirs above,
Praising, with the heavenly host,
Father, Son, and Holy Ghost.

566   *R. B.* in *Yattendon Hymnal*

f   1 ALL praise be to God,
      Whom all things obey,
From angels and men
      For ever and ay;
Who sendeth on earth
      The powers of his throne,
His providence good
      And love to make known.

2 His angels are they
      Of countenance fair,
The arm of his strength,
      His hand of kind care;
His message of peace
      To us they reveal,
His wisdom most high
      They seal or unseal.

mf   3 By martyrs of old
      They stood in the flame,
And bade them not flinch,
      But call on God's name.
Through torment, through shame,
      Through darkness of death,
They led without fear
      The sires of our faith.

f   4 They stand with the few,
      They fight for the free,
God's reign to advance
      O'er land and o'er sea;
And when the brave die
      Or fall in the fight,
Their spirits they bear
      To rest in God's sight

mf 5*For patience and toil
  A crown they prepare;
They found for the meek
  A kingdom full fair;
No famine nor plague
  'Gainst them doth prevail;
Their bread cannot lack,
  Their cruse cannot fail.

6 We pray thee, who art
  Thy angels' reward,
Thy flock to defend
  Forget not, O Lord;
But prosper their aid,
  That us they may bring
To see the true face
  Of Jesus, our King.

The following hymns are also suitable:

287 They come, God's messengers of love.
288 Stars of the morning, so gloriously bright.
448 Around the throne of God a band.

ST. LUKE THE EVANGELIST

567   *H. D. Rawnsley†*

1 SAVIOUR, who didst healing give,
  Still in power go before us;
Thou through death didst bid men live,
  Unto fuller life restore us:
Strength from thee the fainting found,
  Deaf men heard, the blind went seeing;
At thy touch was banished sickness,
  And the leper felt new being.

2 Thou didst work thy deeds of old
   Through the loving hands of others:
Still thy mercies manifold
   Bless men by the hands of brothers;
Angels still before thy face
   Go, sweet health to brothers bringing;
Still, hearts glow to tell his praises
   With whose name the Church is ringing.

3 Loved physician! for his word,
   Lo, the gospel page burns brighter:
Mission servant of the Lord,
   Painter true and faithful writer:
Saviour, of thy bounty send
   Such as Luke of Gospel story,
Friends to all in body's prison
   Till the sufferer see thy glory.

ST. SIMON AND ST. JUDE, APOSTLES
568   *J. Ellerton*

1 THOU who sentest thine apostles
   Two and two before thy face,
Partners in the night of toiling,
   Heirs together of thy grace,
Throned at length, their labours ended,
   Each in his appointed place;

2 Praise to thee for those thy champions
   Whom our hymns to-day proclaim:
One, whose zeal by thee enlightened
   Burned anew with nobler flame;
One, the kinsman of thy childhood,
   Brought at last to know thy name.

3 Praise to thee! thy fire within them
   Spake in love, and wrought in power:
Seen in mighty signs and wonders
   In thy Church's morning hour;
Heard in tones of sternest warning
   When the storms began to lower.

4 God the Father, great and wondrous
  In thy works, to thee be praise;
King of saints, to thee be glory,
  Just and true in all thy ways;
Praise to thee, from Both proceeding,
  Holy Ghost, through endless days.

ALL SAINTS' DAY

569   *18th cent. Tr. I. Williams*†

Caelestis O Jerusalem

1 O HEAVENLY Jerusalem,
    Of everlasting halls,
  Thrice blessèd are the people
    Thou storest in thy walls.

2 Thou art the golden mansion
    Where saints for ever sing,
  The seat of God's own chosen,
    The palace of the King.

3 There God for ever sitteth,
    Himself of all the crown:
  The Lamb, the Light that shineth
    And never goeth down.

4 Naught to this seat approacheth
    Their sweet peace to molest;
  They sing their God for ever,
    Nor day nor night they rest.

5 Sure hope doth thither lead us;
    Our longings thither tend:
  May short-lived toil ne'er daunt us
    For joys that cannot end.

6 To Christ the Sun that lightens
    His Church above, below,
  To Father, and to Spirit,
    All things created bow.

570   *H. T. Schenck. Tr. Frances E. Cox‡*

Wer sind die vor Gottes Throne

1 WHO are these like stars appearing,
    These, before God's throne who stand?
Each a golden crown is wearing:
    Who are all this glorious band?
        Alleluia, hark! they sing,
        Praising loud their heavenly King.

2*Who are these in dazzling brightness,
    Clothed in God's own righteousness,
These, whose robes of purest whiteness
    Shall their lustre still possess,
        Still untouched by time's rude hand?
        Whence came all this glorious band?

3 These are they who have contended
    For their Saviour's honour long,
Wrestling on till life was ended,
    Following not the sinful throng;
        These, who well the fight sustained,
        Triumph by the Lamb have gained.

4*These are they whose hearts were riven,
    Sore with woe and anguish tried,
Who in prayer full oft have striven
    With the God they glorified;
        Now, their painful conflict o'er,
        God has bid them weep no more.

5 These, the Almighty contemplating,
    Did as priests before him stand,
Soul and body always waiting
    Day and night at his command:
        Now in God's most holy place
        Blest they stand before his face.

571
I. Watts‡

mf 1 GIVE us the wings of faith to rise
    Within the veil, and see
    The saints above, how great their joys,
    How bright their glories be.

p 2 Once they were mourning here below,
    Their couch was wet with tears;
    They wrestled hard, as we do now,
    With sins and doubts and fears.

mf 3 We ask them whence their victory came:
f   They, with united breath,
    Ascribe the conquest to the Lamb,
    Their triumph to his Death.

p 4 They marked the footsteps that he trod,
    His zeal inspired their breast,
    And, following their incarnate God,
    They reached the promised rest.

f 5 Our glorious Leader claims our praise
    For his own pattern given;
    While the great cloud of witnesses
    Show the same path to heaven.

572
Archbishop W. D. Maclagan

1 THE saints of God! their conflict past
    And life's long battle won at last,
    No more they need the shield or sword,
    They cast them down before their Lord:
      O happy saints! for ever blest,
      At Jesus' feet how safe your rest!

2 The saints of God! their wanderings done,
    No more their weary course they run,
    No more they faint, no more they fall,
    No foes oppress, no fears appal:
      O happy saints! for ever blest,
      In that dear home how sweet your rest!

3 The saints of God! life's voyage o'er,
  Safe landed on that blissful shore,
  No stormy tempest now they dread,
  No roaring billows lift their head:
    O happy saints! for ever blest,
    In that calm haven of your rest.

4 The saints of God their vigil keep
  While yet their mortal bodies sleep,
  Till from the dust they too shall rise
  And soar triumphant to the skies:
    O happy saints! rejoice and sing:
    He quickly comes, your Lord and King.

5 O God of saints, to thee we cry;
  O Saviour, plead for us on high;
  O Holy Ghost, our guide and friend,
  Grant us thy grace till life shall end;
    That with all saints our rest may be
    In that bright Paradise with thee.

ST. GEORGE, PATRON OF ENGLAND

573   *F. W. Newman*

1 JESUS, Lord of our salvation,
    For thy warrior, bold and true,
  Now accept our thankful praises,
    And our strength do thou renew,
  That, like George, with courage dauntless
    We may all our foes subdue.

2 Blazoned on our country's banner
    England bears the knightly sign:
  Lord, our fatherland empower,
    That, endued with strength divine,
  She may evermore with courage
    Bear the standard that is thine.

3 Fill her youth with manly spirit,
    Patient, self-restrained, and pure,
Of thy cause the ready champions,
    Never flinching to endure
Hardness for the name of Jesus:
    So their triumph shall be sure.

4 Teach her manhood to confess thee
    As the Master, Lord, and King;
All their powers consecrated
    To thy service may men bring,
And of loyal speech and action
    Make to thee an offering.

5 Jesus, Lord, thou mighty Victor,
    Thy all-glorious name we praise:
Thou art with us, God almighty;
    'Midst our ranks thy shout we raise:
Where thy kingly war-cry soundeth,
    Lead us on through all our days.

SAINTS, MARTYRS, AND DOCTORS OF
THE CHURCH OF ENGLAND

574
                       C. A. Alington

1 GOD, whose city's sure foundation
    Stands upon his holy hill,
By his mighty inspiration
    Chose of old and chooseth still
Men of every race and nation
    His good pleasure to fulfil.

2 Here in England through the ages,
    While the Christian years went by,
Saints, confessors, martyrs, sages,
    Strong to live and strong to die,
Wrote their names upon the pages
    Of God's blessèd company.

3 Some there were like lamps of learning
    Shining in a faithless night,
Some on fire with love, and burning
    With a flaming zeal for right,
Some by simple goodness turning⌣
    Souls from darkness unto light.

4 As we now with high thanksgiving
    Their triumphant names record,
Grant that we, like them, believing⌣
    In the promise of thy word,
May, like them, in all good living
    Praise and magnify the Lord.

ST. DAVID, PATRON OF WALES

575   *E. J. Newell*

1 WE praise thy name, all holy Lord,
    For him, the beacon-light
That shone beside our western sea
    Through mists of ancient night;
Who sent to Ireland's fainting Church
    New tidings of thy word:
For David, prince of Cambrian saints,
    We praise thee, holy Lord.

2 For all the saintly band whose prayers⌣
    Still gird our land about,
Of whom, lest men disdain their praise,
    The voiceless stones cry out;
Our hills and vales on every hand
    Their names and deeds record:
For these, thy ancient hero-host,
    We praise thee, holy Lord.

3 Grant us but half their burning zeal,
 But half their iron faith,
But half their charity of heart,
 And fortitude to death;
That we with them and all thy saints
 May in thy truth accord,
And ever in thy holy Church
 May praise thee, holy Lord.

For ST. PATRICK, PATRON OF IRELAND, *see*

 162 I bind unto myself to-day.

ST. NICOLAS, PATRON OF CHILDREN
AND SAILORS

576   *W. H. Savile*

1 FAR-SHINING names from age to age
Enrich the Church's heritage,
The loyal liegemen of the Lord,
Who found in thee their great reward.

2 One name from that immortal throng
Inspires to-day our festal song:
In loving memory we hold
The bishop and the saint of old,

3 Who, far away in eastern land,
With gentle heart and open hand
Loved all things living, shared his store
With homeless men who sought his door.

4 Friend of the poor, no less was he
The guardian saint of those at sea;
O'er wave-swept rock and sheltered bay
God's churches bear his name to-day.

5 And his the skill, the tender art
That wins the trustful, child-like heart:
His dearest title to the end
'Saint Nicolas, the children's friend.'

6 To thee, O Lord, the praise be given
For this true citizen of heaven :
A star above the stormy sea
To lead the wanderer home to thee.

For ST. CECILIA, PATRONESS OF MUSIC, *see*
246 Angel-voices, ever singing.

NATIONAL

577   Anon.

mf 1 GOD save our gracious Queen,
Long live our noble Queen,
God save the Queen.
Send her victorious,
Happy and glorious,
Long to reign over us :
God save the Queen.

2*O Lord our God, arise,
Scatter our enemies,
And make them fall ;
Confound their politics,
Frustrate their knavish tricks ;
On thee our hopes we fix :
God save us all.

f 3 Thy choicest gifts in store
her be pleased to pour,
Long may she reign.
she defend our laws,
ever give us cause
ing with heart and voice,
God save the Queen.

578 *Jerusalem*   *William Blake*

1 AND did those feet in ancient time
    Walk upon England's mountains green?
And was the holy Lamb of God
    On England's pleasant pastures seen?
And did the countenance divine
    Shine forth upon our clouded hills?
And was Jerusalem builded here
    Among those dark satanic mills?

2 Bring me my bow of burning gold!
    Bring me my arrows of desire!
Bring me my spear! O clouds, unfold!
    Bring me my chariot of fire!
I will not cease from mental fight,
    Nor shall my sword sleep in my hand,
Till we have built Jerusalem
    In England's green and pleasant land.

579   *Sir Cecil Spring-Rice*

1 I VOW to thee, my country, all earthly things
    above,
Entire and whole and perfect, the service of my
    love:
The love that asks no question, the love that
    stands the test,
That lays upon the altar the dearest and the
    best;
The love that never falters, the love that pays the
    price,
The love that makes undaunted the final sacri-
    fice.

2 And there's another country, I've heard of long
   ago,
  Most dear to them that love her, most great to
   them that know;
  We may not count her armies, we may not see
   her King;
  Her fortress is a faithful heart, her pride is
   suffering;
  And soul by soul and silently her shining bounds
   increase,
  And her ways are ways of gentleness and all her
   paths are peace.

580   *Yattendon Hymnal, based on F. R. Tailour*
                          (**1615**)

1 THE Queen, O God, her heart to thee upraiseth;
  With her the nation bows before thy face;
  With high thanksgiving thee thy glad Church
   praiseth,
    Our strength thy spirit, our trust and hope thy
    grace.

2 Unto great honour, glory undeservèd,
   Hast thou exalted us, and drawn thee nigh;
  Nor, from thy judgements when our feet had
   swervèd,
    Didst thou forsake, nor leave us, Lord most
    high.

PART 2

3 In thee our fathers trusted and were savèd,
   In thee destroyèd thrones of tyrants proud;
  From ancient bondage freed the poor enslavèd;
    To sow thy truth poured out their saintly
    blood.

4 Unto our minds give freedom and uprightness;
  Let strength and courage lead o'er land and
    wave;
To our souls' armour grant celestial bright-
    ness,
  Joy to our hearts, and faith beyond the
    grave.

5 Our plenteous nation still in power extending,
  Increase our joy, uphold us by thy word;
Beauty and wisdom all our ways attending,
  Good will to man and peace through Christ
    our Lord.

581

J. R. Wreford

1 LORD, while for all mankind we pray
    Of every clime and coast,
  O hear us for our native land,
    The land we love the most.

2 O guard our shores from every foe,
    With peace our borders bless;
  With prosperous times our cities crown,
    Our fields with plenteousness.

3 Unite us in the sacred love
    Of knowledge, truth, and thee;
  And let our hills and valleys shout
    The songs of liberty.

4 Lord of the nations, thus to thee
    Our country we commend;
  Be thou her refuge and her trust,
    Her everlasting friend.

582   *Yattendon Hymnal*

1 REJOICE, O land, in God thy might;
His will obey, him serve aright;
For thee the saints uplift their voice:
Fear not, O land, in God rejoice.

2 Glad shalt thou be, with blessing crowned,
With joy and peace thou shalt abound;
Yea, love with thee shall make his home
Until thou see God's Kingdom come.

3 He shall forgive thy sins untold:
Remember thou his love of old;
Walk in his way, his word adore,
And keep his truth for evermore.

583   *Bishop J. H. B. Masterman*

1 ALMIGHTY Father, who dost give
The gift of life to all who live,
Look down on all earth's sin and strife
And lift us to a nobler life.

2 Lift up our hearts, O King of Kings,
To brighter hopes and kindlier things,
To visions of a larger good,
And holier dreams of brotherhood.

3 The world is weary of its pain,
Of selfish greed and fruitless gain,
Of tarnished honour, falsely strong,
And all its ancient deeds of wrong.

4 Hear thou the prayer thy servants pray,
Uprising from all lands to-day,
And, o'er the vanquished powers of sin,
O bring thy great salvation in!

584 *For the fallen* Sir John S. Arkwright

mf 1 O VALIANT hearts, who to your glory came
 Through dust of conflict and through battle
  flame;
 Tranquil you lie, your knightly virtue proved,
 Your memory hallowed in the land you loved.

f 2*Proudly you gathered, rank on rank, to war,
 As who had heard God's message from afar;
mf All you had hoped for, all you had, you gave
 To save mankind—yourselves you scorned to
  save.

f 3*Splendid you passed, the great surrender
  made,
 Into the light that never more shall fade;
mf Deep your contentment in that blest abode,
 Who wait the last clear trumpet-call of God.

 4 Long years ago, as earth lay dark and still,
 Rose a loud cry upon a lonely hill,
 While in the frailty of our human clay
 Christ, our Redeemer, passed the self-same
  way.

p 5 Still stands his Cross from that dread hour to
  this,
 Like some bright star above the dark abyss;
 Still, through the veil, the Victor's pitying
  eyes
 Look down to bless our lesser Calvaries.

 6 These were his servants, in his steps they
  trod,
 Following through death the martyred Son
  of God:
f Victor he rose; victorious too shall rise
 They who have drunk his cup of sacrifice.

7 O risen Lord, O Shepherd of our dead,
  Whose Cross has bought them and whose
      staff has led,
  In glorious hope their proud and sorrowing
      land
mf Commits her children to thy gracious hand.

585   *For the fallen*   Archbishop J. R. Darbyshire

1 O LORD of Life, whose power sustains
    The world unseen no less than this—
  One family in him who reigns,
    Triumphant over death, in bliss;
  To thee with thankfulness we pray
  For all our valiant dead to-day.

2 As nature's healing through the years
    Reclothes the stricken battle-fields;
  So mercy gives us joy for tears,
    And grief to proud remembrance yields,
  And mindful hearts are glad to keep
  A tryst of love with them that sleep.

3 Not names engraved in marble make
    The best memorials of the dead,
  But burdens shouldered for their sake
    And tasks completed in their stead;
  A braver faith and stronger prayers,
  Devouter worship, nobler cares.

4 O help us in the silence, Lord,
    To hear the whispered call of love,
  And day by day thy strength afford
    Our work to do, our faith to prove.
  So be thy blessing richly shed
  On our communion with our dead.

LITANIES

LITANY FOR LENT

586   *Tr. Compilers*

Attende, Domine

HEARKEN, O Lord, have mercy upon us,
 for we have sinned against thee.

1 To thee, Redeemer, King of highest heaven,
 Lift we our eyes in grief and deep abasement:
 Listen, O Saviour, to our supplications.
     Hearken, O Lord, etc.

2 Head of the Corner, right hand of the Father,
 Way of salvation, gate of life eternal,
 Wash thou away the stain of our offences.
     Hearken, O Lord, etc.

3 Lord, we beseech thee, from thy throne of glory
 Bow down thine ear to hear our cry of sorrow,
 Look down in mercy on our sore transgressions.
     Hearken, O Lord, etc.

4 All our misdoings now we lay before thee,
 Unveil with contrite heart each guilty secret:
 Saviour, in pity grant us thy forgiveness.
     Hearken, O Lord, etc.

5 Guiltless, a captive taken unresisting,
 By false accusers brought to condemnation,
 Save, Lord, and help the souls thou hast
  redeemèd.
     Hearken, O Lord, etc.

LITANY OF THE PASSION

587   *Compilers and others*

mf 1 GOD the Father, God the Son,
God the Spirit, Three in One,
Hear us from thy heavenly throne;
      Spare us, holy Trinity.

     2 Jesu, who for us didst bear
Scorn and sorrow, toil and care,
Hearken to our lowly prayer,
      We beseech thee, Jesu.

p   3 By the hour of agony
Spent while thine apostles three
Slumbered in Gethsemane,
      Hear us, holy Jesu.

     4 Jesu, by thy friend betrayed,
Jesu, sport for sinners made,
Jesu, in mock-robes arrayed,
      Hear us, holy Jesu.

     5 By the scourging meekly borne,
By the reed and crown of thorn,
By the malice and the scorn,
      Hear us, holy Jesu.

mf 6 By the outcry of the Jews,
When a murderer they would choose
And the Prince of Life refuse,
      Hear us, holy Jesu.

     7 By the horror of that cry,
'Crucify him, crucify,'
By thy going forth to die,
      Hear us, holy Jesu.

p   8 By thy nailing to the Tree,
     By the title over thee,
     By the gloom of Calvary,
          Hear us, holy Jesu.

    9 By thy seven words then said,
     By the bowing of thy head,
     By thy numbering with the dead,
          Hear us, holy Jesu.

mf 10 Jesu, who for us hast died
     And, for ever glorified,
     Reignest at the Father's side,
          Hear us, holy Jesu.

FOR ROGATIONTIDE OR OTHER OCCASIONS

588   *The Great Collect*   *Tr. J. Brownlie*

ὑπὲρ τῆς ἄνωθεν εἰρήνης

  1 LORD, to our humble prayers attend,
    Let thou thy peace from heaven descend,
    And to our souls salvation send:
         Have mercy, Lord, upon us.

  2 Rule in our hearts, thou Prince of Peace,
    The welfare of thy Church increase,
    And bid all strife and discord cease:
         Have mercy, Lord, upon us.

  3 To all who meet for worship here
    Do thou in faithfulness draw near;
    Inspire with faith and godly fear:
         Have mercy, Lord, upon us.

  4 O let thy priests be clothed with might,
    To rule within thy Church aright,
    That they may serve as in thy sight:
         Have mercy, Lord, upon us.

5 The sovereign ruler of our land
  Protect by thine almighty hand,
  And all around the throne who stand:
      Have mercy, Lord, upon us.

6 Let clouds and sunshine bless the earth,
  Give flowers and fruits a timely birth,
  Our harvests crown with peaceful mirth:
      Have mercy, Lord, upon us.

7 Let voyagers by land and sea
  In danger's hour in safety be;
  The suffering and the captive free:
      Have mercy, Lord, upon us.

8 Around us let thine arm be cast,
  Till wrath and danger are o'erpast
  And tribulation's bitter blast:
      Have mercy, Lord, upon us.

AN EVENING LITANY

589   *Litany of the Deacon*   Tr. J. Brownlie

ἀντιλαβοῦ, σῶσον, ἐλέησον

1 O GOD of grace, thy mercy send;
  Let thy protecting arm defend;
  Save us and keep us to the end:
      Have mercy, Lord.

2 And through the coming hours of night
  Fill us, we pray, with holy light;
  Keep us all sinless in thy sight:
      Grant this, O Lord.

3 May some bright messenger abide
  For ever by thy servants' side,
  A faithful guardian and our guide:
      Grant this, O Lord.

4 From every sin in mercy free;
  Let heart and conscience stainless be,
  That we may live henceforth for thee:
    Grant this, O Lord.

5 We would not be by care opprest,
  But in thy love and wisdom rest;
  Give what thou seest to be best:
    Grant this, O Lord.

6 While we of every sin repent,
  Let our remaining years be spent
  In holiness and sweet content:
    Grant this, O Lord.

7 And when the end of life is near,
  May we, unshamed and void of fear,
  Wait for the judgement to appear:
    Grant this, O Lord.

LITANY FOR CHILDREN

590   *Compilers and others*

1 GOD the Father, God the Son,
  God the Spirit, Three in One,
  Hear us from thy heavenly throne;
    Spare us, holy Trinity.

2 Jesu, Saviour meek and mild,
  Once for us a little Child
  Born of Mary undefiled,
    Hear us, holy Jesu.

3 Jesu, by that blessèd Maid
  In thy swaddling-clothes arrayed,
  And within a manger laid,
    Hear us, holy Jesu.

4 Jesu, at whose infant feet,
Bending low in worship meet,
Shepherds knelt their Lord to greet,
    Hear us, holy Jesu.

5 Jesu, to thy Temple brought,
Whom the ancient Simeon sought
By thy Holy Spirit taught,
    Hear us, holy Jesu.

6 Jesu, unto whom of yore
Wise men, hasting to adore,
Gold and myrrh and incense bore,
    Hear us, holy Jesu.

7 Jesu, who wast driven to flee
From king Herod's cruelty,
When he sought to murder thee,
    Hear us, holy Jesu.

8 Jesu, whom thy Mother found
'Mid the doctors sitting round,
Marvelling at thy words profound,
    Hear us, holy Jesu.

PART 2

9 From all pride and vain conceit,
From all spite and angry heat,
From all lying and deceit,
    Save us, holy Jesu.

10 From all sloth and idleness,
From hard hearts and selfishness,
From all lust and greediness,
    Save us, holy Jesu.

11 From refusing to obey,
From the love of our own way,
From forgetfulness to pray,
    Save us, holy Jesu.

PART 3

12 By thy birth and early years,
By thine infant wants and fears,
By thy sorrows and thy tears,
    Save us, holy Jesu.

13 By thy pattern bright and pure,
By the pains thou didst endure
Our salvation to procure,
    Save us, holy Jesu.

14 By thy wounds and thorn-crowned head,
By thy Blood for sinners shed,
By thy rising from the dead,
    Save us, holy Jesu.

15 By thy mercies infinite,
By thine all-surpassing might,
By thy glory in the height,
    Save us, holy Jesu.

PROCESSIONAL

CHRISTMAS

591

*Prudentius. Tr. J. M. Neale,
Sir H. W. Baker, and others*

Corde natus ex Parentis

1 OF the Father's love begotten
Ere the worlds began to be,
He is Alpha and Omega,
    He the source, the ending he,
Of the things that are, that have been,
    And that future years shall see,
        Evermore and evermore.

2*At his word they were created;
    He commanded; it was done:
Heaven and earth and depths of ocean
    In their threefold order one;
All that grows beneath the shining
    Of the light of moon and sun,
        Evermore and evermore.

3 O that birth for ever blessèd!
    When the Virgin, full of grace,
By the Holy Ghost conceiving,
    Bare the Saviour of our race,
And the Babe, the world's Redeemer,
    First revealed his sacred face,
        Evermore and evermore.

4 O ye heights of heaven, adore him;
    Angel-hosts, his praises sing;
Powers, dominions, bow before him,
    And extol our God and King:
Let no tongue on earth be silent,
    Every voice in concert ring,
        Evermore and evermore.

5 This is he whom seers and sages
    Sang of old with one accord;
Whom the writings of the Prophets
    Promised in their faithful word;
Now he shines, the long-expected:
    Let creation praise its Lord,
        Evermore and evermore.

6*Hail, thou Judge of souls departed!
    Hail, thou King of them that live!
On the Father's throne exalted
    None in might with thee may strive;
Who at last in judgement coming
    Sinners from thy face shalt drive,
        Evermore and evermore.

7 Now let old and young men's voices
 Join with boys' thy name to sing,
Matrons, virgins, little maidens
 In glad chorus answering;
Let their guileless songs re-echo,
 And the heart its praises bring,
  Evermore and evermore.

8 Christ, to thee, with God the Father,
 And, O Holy Ghost, to thee,
Hymn and chant and high thanksgiving
 And unwearied praises be,
Honour, glory, and dominion,
 And eternal victory,
  Evermore and evermore.

At the entrance into the Chancel:

℣. Blessed is he that cometh in the name of the Lord.

℟. God is the Lord who hath shewed us light.

592

P. Doddridge

1 HIGH let us swell our tuneful notes,
 And join the angelic throng,
For angels no such love have known
 To wake a cheerful song.

2 Good will to sinful men is shown,
 And peace on earth is given:
For, lo, the incarnate Saviour comes
 With grace and truth from heaven.

3 Justice and peace with sweet accord
 His rising beams adorn;
Let heaven and earth in concert join:
 To us a Child is born!

593   *18th cent. Tr. F. Oakeley, W. T. Brooke,*
and others

Adeste fideles

1   O COME, all ye faithful,
      Joyful and triumphant,
   O come ye, O come ye to Bethlehem;
      Come and behold him,
      Born the King of angels:
      O come, let us adore him,
      O come, let us adore him,
   O come, let us adore him, Christ the Lord!

2   God of God,
      Light of Light,
   Lo, he abhors not the Virgin's womb;
      Very God,
      Begotten, not created:
      O come, let us, etc.

3   See how the shepherds
      Summoned to his cradle,
   Leaving their flocks, draw nigh to gaze;
      We too will thither
      Bend our joyful footsteps:
      O come, let us, etc.

4   Lo, star-led chieftains,
      Magi, Christ adoring,
   Offer him incense, gold, and myrrh;
      We to the Christ-child
      Bring our hearts' oblations:
      O come, let us, etc.

5   Child, for us sinners
      Poor and in the manger,
   Fain we embrace thee with love and awe;
      Who would not love thee,
      Loving us so dearly?
      O come, let us, etc.

6   Sing, choirs of angels,
      Sing in exultation,
  Sing, all ye citizens of heaven above:
      'Glory to God
      In the highest:'
      O come, let us, etc.

7 Yea, Lord, we greet thee,
      Born this happy morning;
  Jesu, to thee be glory given:
      Word of the Father,
      Now in flesh appearing:
      O come, let us, etc.

At the entrance into the Chancel:

℣ Blessed is he that cometh in the name of the Lord.

℞. God is the Lord who hath shewed us light.

594   *G. R. Woodward*

1 SHEPHERDS, in the field abiding,
      Tell us, when the seraph bright
  Greeted you with wondrous tiding,
      What ye saw and heard that night:
      Gloria in excelsis Deo.

2 We beheld (it is no fable)
      God incarnate, King of bliss,
  Swathed and cradled in a stable,
      And the angel-strain was this:
      Gloria in excelsis Deo.

3 Quiristers on high were singing
      Jesus and his Virgin-birth;
  Heavenly bells the while a-ringing
      'Peace, goodwill to men on earth:'
      Gloria in excelsis Deo.

4 Thanks, good herdmen; true your story;
     Have with you to Bethlehem:
Angels hymn the King of Glory;
     Carol we with you and them:
          Gloria in excelsis Deo.

EPIPHANY

595   *G. Thring*

1 FROM the eastern mountains
        Pressing on they come,
   Wise men in their wisdom,
        To his humble home;
   Stirred by deep devotion,
        Hasting from afar,
   Ever journeying onward,
        Guided by a star.

2 There their Lord and Saviour
        Meek and lowly lay,
   Wondrous Light that led them
        Onward on their way,
   Ever now to lighten
        Nations from afar,
   As they journey homeward
        By that guiding star.

3 Thou who in a manger
        Once hast lowly lain,
   Who dost now in glory
        O'er all kingdoms reign,
   Gather in the heathen,
        Who in lands afar
   Ne'er have seen the brightness
        Of thy guiding star.

4*Gather in the outcasts,
   All who've gone astray;
Throw thy radiance o'er them,
   Guide them on their way:
Those who never knew thee,
   Those who've wandered far,
Guide them by the brightness
   Of thy guiding star.

5 Onward through the darkness
   Of the lonely night,
Shining still before them
   With thy kindly light,
Guide them, Jew and Gentile,
   Homeward from afar,
Young and old together,
   By thy guiding star.

6*Until every nation,
   Whether bond or free,
'Neath thy star-lit banner,
   Jesu, follow thee
O'er the distant mountains
   To that heavenly home,
Where nor sin nor sorrow
   Evermore shall come.

At the entrance into the Chancel :

℣. All nations whom thou hast made.
℟. Shall come and worship thee, O Lord.

596
Tr. C. S. Phillips

Quem pastores laudavere

1 THOU whom shepherds worshipped, hearing
Angels tell their tidings cheering,
'Sirs, away with doubt and fearing!
   Christ the King is born for all;'

2 Thou to whom came wise men faring,
   Gold and myrrh and incense bearing,
   Heartfelt homage thus declaring
      To the King that's born for all:

3 Bending low in adoration
   Thee we greet, for our salvation
   Given by wondrous Incarnation,
      King of Glory born for all.

PALM SUNDAY

597   *St. Theodulph of Orleans*
                                  Tr. J. M. Neale ‡
       Gloria, laus et honor

1 ALL glory, laud, and honour
     To thee, Redeemer, King,
   To whom the lips of children
     Made sweet Hosannas ring.

2 Thou art the King of Israel,
     Thou David's royal Son,
   Who in the Lord's name comest,
     The King and blessèd one.   All glory, etc.

3 The company of angels
     Are praising thee on high,
   And mortal men and all things
     Created make reply.   All glory, etc.

4 The people of the Hebrews
     With palms before thee went:
   Our praise and prayer and anthems
     Before thee we present.   All glory, etc.

5 To thee before thy Passion
     They sang their hymns of praise:
   To thee now high exalted
     Our melody we raise.   All glory, etc.

6 Thou didst accept their praises,
      Accept the prayers we bring,
  Who in all good delightest,
      Thou good and gracious King.   All glory, etc.

7*Thy sorrow and thy triumph
      Grant us, O Christ, to share,
  That to the holy city
      Together we may fare.   All glory, etc.

8*For homage may we bring thee
      Our victory o'er the foe,
  That in the Conqueror's triumph
      This strain may ever flow: All glory, etc.

Or

598   *St. Theodulph of Orleans*
                            Tr. J. M. Neale and Compilers

Gloria, laus et honor

1 GLORY and honour and laud be to thee, Christ,
      King and Redeemer,
  As when the children of old sang their Hosannas
      of praise.   *(Repeat)*

2 Israel's Monarch art thou, the glorious offspring
      of David,
  Thou that approachest as King, blest in the name
      of the Lord.   Glory and honour, etc.

3 'Glory to thee in the height,' the heavenly armies
      are singing;
  'Glory to thee upon earth,' men and creation
      reply.   Glory and honour, etc.

4 Bearing their branches of palm, the Hebrews
      crowded to greet thee;
  We with our prayers and our hymns now to thy
      presence draw nigh. Glory and honour, etc.

5 They came to utter thy praise as thou wentest
  thy way to thy Passion;
  We to the King on his throne lift up our jubilant
  hymn.   Glory and honour, etc.

6 Thou didst rejoice in their praise: may ours too
  by thee be accepted,
  Gracious and merciful King, who in all goodness
  art pleased.   Glory and honour, etc.

At the entrance into the Chancel :

℣. O Saviour of the world, who by thy Cross and
precious Blood hast redeemed us.

℟. Save us and help us, we humbly beseech thee,
O Lord.

599 *Adapted from Bishop Jeremy Taylor*

1 RIDE on triumphantly! Behold, we lay
  Our lusts and sins and proud wills in thy way:
  Thy road is ready, and thy paths made straight
  With longing expectation seem to wait.

2 Hosanna! Welcome to our hearts! for here
  Thou hast a temple too, as Sion dear:
  Enter, O Lord, and cleanse that holy place
  Where thou dost choose to set thy beauteous
  face.

EASTER DAY

600 *Bishop Venantius Fortunatus*
Tr. C. S. Phillips

Salve, festa dies

1 WELCOME, morning of joy, glad feast that all
  ages shall hallow,
  Day wherein, vanquishing hell, God cometh
  forth from the grave.   (*Repeat*)

2 Lo, the fresh beauty of spring, reborn from the
  womb of the winter,
  Tells how, to greet his return, nature itself is
  renewed.   Welcome, etc.

3 He who was nailed to the Cross is reigning as
    God over all things,
  While the Creator of all all things created adore.
                       Welcome, etc.

4 Now, Lord of mercy and might, of thy promise
    vouchsafe the fulfilment:
  Rise, buried Love, from the tomb; hasten, the
    third day is here.   Welcome, etc.

5 Shame would it be that thy limbs with earth's
    sorry mould should be covered,
  Or that base rock should immure him who hath
    ransomed the world.   Welcome, etc.

6*Shame that in durance should lie, close girt in the
    tomb's rocky fastness,
  He who sustains the whole world, held in the
    grasp of his hand.   Welcome, etc.

7*Fling off the clothes of the grave, leave them
    there in the sepulchre lying;
  For thou art all that we need, and without thee
    we have naught.   Welcome, etc.

8 Meekly thou stoop'st to the grave, who art
    Author of life and creation,
  Treadest the pathway of death, winning salva-
    tion for men.   Welcome, etc.

9 Give back thy face to the world, with its sun-
    shine to gladden the ages;
  Give back the light of the day, fled from our
    eyes at thy Death.   Welcome, etc.

10 Out of the prison of death thou art rescuing
    souls without number;
  Freely they press to the goal whither their
    Maker leads on.   Welcome, etc.

11 Hell's gloomy castle is stormed, unloosed are
     the chains of its captives;
 Chaos and Death flee away, cowed at the face
     of the Light.   Welcome, etc.

At the entrance into the Chancel:

℣. The Lord is risen from the grave.

℟. Who for our sakes hung on the Tree. Alleluia.

601   *Tr. Bishop Miles Coverdale†*

Christ ist erstanden

1 CHRIST is now risen again
   From his death and all his pain;
   Therefore will we merry be,
   And rejoice with him gladly. Alleluia!

2 Since he is risen indeed
   Let us love him with all speed;
   Therefore glad now will we be,
   And rejoice in him only. Alleluia!

602   *Tr. J. M. Neale and Compilers*

Aurora lucis rutilat

1 LIGHT'S glittering morn bedecks the sky;
   Heaven thunders forth its victor-cry:
                               [Alleluia!]
   The glad earth shouts her triumph high,
   And groaning hell makes wild reply:
                               [Alleluia!]

2 While he, the King, the mighty King,
   Despoiling death of all its sting,
   And trampling down the powers of night,
   Brings forth his ransomed saints to light.

3 His tomb of late the threefold guard
  Of watch and stone and seal had barred;
  But now, in pomp and triumph high,
  He comes from death to victory.

4 The pains of hell are loosed at last,
  The days of mourning now are past;
  An angel robed in light hath said,
  'The Lord is risen from the dead.'

PART 2

5 O bitter the apostles' pain
  For their dear Lord so lately slain,
  By rebel servants doomed to die
  A death of cruel agony!

6 With gentle voice the angel gave
  The women tidings at the grave:
  'Fear not, your Master shall ye see;
  He goes before to Galilee.'

7 Then, hastening on their eager way
  The joyful tidings to convey,
  Their Lord they met, their living Lord,
  And falling at his feet adored.

8 His faithful followers with speed
  To Galilee forthwith proceed,
  That there once more they may behold
  The Lord's dear face, as he foretold.

PART 3

9 That Eastertide with joy was bright,
  The sun shone out with fairer light,
  When, to their longing eyes restored,
  The glad apostles saw their Lord.

10 He bade them see his hands, his side,
    Where yet the glorious wounds abide;
    The tokens true which made it plain
    Their Lord indeed was risen again.

11 Jesu, the King of gentleness,
    Do thou thyself our hearts possess,
    That we may give thee all our days
    The tribute of our grateful praise.

*The following Doxology may be sung at the
end of any Part, or of the whole hymn:*

12 O Lord of all, with us abide
    In this our joyful Eastertide;
    From every weapon death can wield
    Thine own redeemed for ever shield.

13 All praise be thine, O risen Lord,
    From death to endless life restored;
    All praise to God the Father be
    And Holy Ghost eternally.

At the entrance into the Chancel:

℣. The Lord is risen from the grave.

℟. Who for our sakes hung on the Tree. Alleluia.

603
C. A. Alington

1 GOOD Christian men, rejoice and sing!
    Now is the triumph of our King!
    To all the world glad news we bring:
        Alleluia!

2 The Lord of Life is risen for ay:
    Bring flowers of song to strew his way;
    Let all mankind rejoice and say
        Alleluia!

3 Praise we in songs of victory
 That Love, that Life, which cannot die,
 And sing with hearts uplifted high
     Alleluia!

4 Thy name we bless, O risen Lord,
 And sing to-day with one accord
 The life laid down, the life restored:
     Alleluia!

604   *J. R. L. Stainer*

1 DAYSTAR on high, bright harbinger of gladness,
 Piercing the clouds of ignorance and error,
 Thou hast dispersed our night of sin and sadness;
  Death has no terror.
 Darkness is past, joy cometh in the morning;
 Hope springs anew for sinners without number:
 Sleepers, awake! a brighter day is dawning;
  Shake off your slumber.
   Alleluia!

2 Prophets of old spake darkly of this wonder,
 Psalmist and saints have handed on the story;
 Now he is risen, bursting bonds asunder,
  Risen to glory.
 Earth's tyrants quail; the mighty make obeisance:
 He hath preferred the innocent and lowly:
 Mercy and truth shine round about his presence:
  His name is Holy.
   Alleluia!

3 Victor he comes in majesty, revealing
Promise of life and liberty to mortals:
Heaven and earth, with hymns of triumph pealing,
    Throw wide their portals.
Praise him, ye nations, hearts and voices blending:
Raise high your song; the Conqueror advances:
Praise him with cymbals, lute and harp attending,
    Praise him with dances.
        Alleluia!

4 Hail him the Monarch, Ruler of creation;
Princes and powers, bow your heads before him;
This is the Lord, the God of our salvation;
    Let us adore him.
Lord God of Hosts, great Deity supernal,
Be thou our strength, by thee our steps be guided,
Father and Son and Spirit co-eternal,
    One undivided.
        Alleluia!

At the entrance into the Chancel:

℣. The Lord is risen from the grave.

℟. Who for our sakes hung on the Tree. Alleluia.

605   *H. Lindenborn (1741). Tr. Compilers*
           Cedant justi signa luctus

1 JESUS Christ from death hath risen!
Lo, his Godhead bursts the prison,
    While his Manhood passes free,
    Vanquishing our misery:
Risen with him to salvation
Through his self-humiliation,
    We may share his victory.

2 Far be sorrow, tears and sadness!
  See the dayspring of our gladness!
        Satan's slaves no more are we,
        Children by the Son set free:
  Rise, for Life with death hath striven,
  All the snares of hell are riven;
        Rise and claim the victory.

ROGATIONTIDE

606   *Bishop W. Walsham How*

1   TO thee our God we fly
        For mercy and for grace;
     O hear our lowly cry,
        And hide not thou thy face.
  O Lord, stretch forth thy mighty hand,
  And guard and bless our fatherland.

2   Arise, O Lord of Hosts!
        Be jealous for thy name,
     And drive from out our coasts
        The sins that put to shame.
  O Lord, stretch forth, etc.

3   Thy best gifts from on high
        In rich abundance pour,
     That we may magnify
        And praise thee more and more.
  O Lord, stretch forth, etc.

4   The powers ordained by thee
        With heavenly wisdom bless;
     May they thy servants be,
        And rule in righteousness.
  O Lord, stretch forth, etc.

5   The Church of thy dear Son
        Inflame with love's pure fire,
     Bind her once more in one,
        And life and truth inspire.
  O Lord, stretch forth, etc.

6*   The pastors of thy fold
      With grace and power endue,
   That faithful, pure, and bold,
      They may be pastors true.
O Lord, stretch forth, etc.

7   O let us love thy house,
      And sanctify thy day,
   Bring unto thee our vows,
      And loyal homage pay.
O Lord, stretch forth, etc.

8   Give peace, Lord, in our time;
      O let no foe draw nigh,
   Nor lawless deed of crime
      Insult thy majesty.
O Lord, stretch forth, etc.

9*   Though vile and worthless, still
      Thy people, Lord, are we;
   And for our God we will
      None other have but thee.
O Lord, stretch forth, etc.

At the entrance into the Chancel :

℣. The eyes of all wait upon thee, O Lord.
℟. And thou givest them their meat in due season.

607   *J. Newton†*

1   KINDLY spring again is here,
   Trees and fields in bloom appear;
   Hark! the birds with artless lays
   Warble their Creator's praise.

2   Where in winter all was snow,
   Now the flowers in clusters grow:
   And the corn, in green array,
   Promises a harvest-day.

3 On thy garden deign to smile,
   Raise the plants, enrich the soil;
   Soon thy presence will restore
   Life to what seemed dead before.

ASCENSIONTIDE

608
         Bishop Venantius Fortunatus
             Tr. C. S. Phillips
      Salve, festa dies

1 WELCOME, morning of joy, glad feast that all
    ages shall hallow,
  Day wherein, vanquishing hell, God to high
    heaven ascends.   *(Repeat)*

2 Calm is the breath of the spring that wakens
    the glory of blossom,
  Brighter the sunlight that streams forth from
    the gates of the sky.   Welcome, etc.

3 Christ hath trod under his feet the kingdom of
    torment and sadness;
  Decked is the woodland with leaves, earth
    strews her flowers at his feet.
                    Welcome, etc.

4 Trampling the powers of hell he mounts on his
    journey to heaven:
  Heaven's light hails him as God; field, sky and
    sea tell his praise.   Welcome, etc.

5 Strike off the fetters that bind the spirits that
    hell hath imprisoned,
  Call back and lift to the light souls rushing
    down to the pit.   Welcome, etc.

6*Out of the prison of death thou art rescuing
    souls without number;
  Freely they press to the goal whither their
    Maker leads on.   Welcome, etc.

7*Now may'st thou nurse in thine arms a people
    that knows no defilement,
  Bear them aloft to be given for a pure hostage
    to God.   Welcome, etc.

8 Two are the crowns that for thee the Father
    hath laid up in heaven:
  One shalt thou wear for thine own, one for a
    people redeemed.   Welcome, etc.

9 Jesu, thou Saviour of all, Creator of men and
    Redeemer,
  Only-begotten of God, sprung from the Deity's
    fount;   Welcome, etc.

10 Equal, co-eval art thou, and in fellowship one
    with the Father;
  Thine was the word of command when all
    creation began.   Welcome, etc.

11 Thou too, beholding in love the depth of
    humanity's ruin,
  Man to deliver from death, Man didst vouch-
    safe to become.   Welcome, etc.

At the entrance into the Chancel

℣. God is gone up with a merry noise.

℟. And the Lord with the sound of a trumpet.
                    Alleluia.

609
C. Wesley

1 OUR Lord is risen from the dead;
  Our Jesus is gone up on high;
  The powers of hell are captive led,
  Dragged to the portals of the sky.
             Alleluia!

2 There his triumphant chariot waits,
    And angels chant the solemn lay:
Lift up your heads, ye heavenly gates;
    Ye everlasting doors, give way.
                Alleluia!

3 Loose all your bars of massy light,
    And wide unfold the ethereal scene:
He claims these mansions as his right;
    Receive the King of Glory in.
                Alleluia!

4 Who is this King of Glory? Who?
    The Lord that all our foes o'ercame,
The world, sin, death and hell o'erthrew:
    And Jesus is the Conqueror's name.
                Alleluia!

610   *C. Wesley, T. Cotterill, and others*

1 HAIL the day that sees him rise,
            Alleluia!
To his throne above the skies;
            Alleluia!
Christ, the Lamb for sinners given,
            [Alleluia!]
Enters now the highest heaven.
            Alleluia!

2 There for him high triumph waits;
            Alleluia!
Lift your heads, eternal gates!
            Alleluia!
He hath conquered death and sin;
            [Alleluia!]
Take the King of Glory in!
            Alleluia!

3 *Circled round with angel-powers,
           Alleluia!
Their triumphant Lord and ours:
           Alleluia!
Wide unfold the radiant scene,
           [Alleluia!]
Take the King of Glory in!
           Alleluia!

4 Lo, the heaven its Lord receives,
           Alleluia!
Yet he loves the earth he leaves;
           Alleluia!
Though returning to his throne,
           [Alleluia!]
Still he calls mankind his own.
           Alleluia!

5 See! he lifts his hands above;
           Alleluia!
See! he shows the prints of love;
           Alleluia!
Hark! his gracious lips bestow
           [Alleluia!]
Blessings on his Church below.
           Alleluia!

6 Still for us he intercedes,
           Alleluia!
His prevailing Death he pleads;
           Alleluia!
Near himself prepares our place,
           [Alleluia!]
He the first-fruits of our race.
           Alleluia!

7 Lord, though parted from our sight,
　　　　　Alleluia!
Far above the starry height,
　　　　　Alleluia!
Grant our hearts may thither rise,
　　　　　[Alleluia!]
Seeking thee above the skies.
　　　　　Alleluia!

8*Ever upward let us move,
　　　　　Alleluia!
Wafted on the wings of love;
　　　　　Alleluia!
Looking when our Lord shall come,
　　　　　[Alleluia!]
Longing, sighing after home.
　　　　　Alleluia!

9*There we shall with thee remain,
　　　　　Alleluia!
Partners of thine endless reign;
　　　　　Alleluia!
There thy face unclouded see,
　　　　　[Alleluia!]
Find our heaven of heavens in thee.
　　　　　Alleluia!

At the entrance into the Chancel :

℣. God is gone up with a merry noise.
℟. And the Lord with the sound of a trumpet.
Alleluia.

611　　　　　　　　*Tr. D. T. Morgan*
Tu, Christe, nostrum gaudium

1 O CHRIST our joy, gone up on high
To fill thy throne above the sky,
　　How glorious dost thou shine!
Thy sovereign rule the worlds obey,
And earthly joys all fade away
　　In that pure light of thine.

2 Ascended up from mortal sight,
   Jesu, we praise thee in the height,
   Our joy, our great reward;
   Whom with the Father we confess,
   And with the Holy Spirit bless,
   One ever-glorious Lord.

WHITSUNDAY

612   *Bishop Venantius Fortunatus*
                           Tr. C. S. Phillips

Salve, festa dies

1 WELCOME, morning of joy, glad feast that all
     ages shall hallow,
   Day when to earth out of heaven flashed a new
     glory of grace.   (*Repeat*)

2 Flinging his torrents of fire, the sun rides high
     in the heaven;
   Forth from the ocean he comes, sinks to the
     ocean at eve.   Welcome, etc.

3 Darting his rays as he goes through the liquid
     air of the summer,
   Now doth he shorten the nights, draw out the
     length of the days.   Welcome, etc.

4 Blue is the sky by day, with crystalline radiance
     glowing;
   Night is a glory of stars, singing together for joy.
                                Welcome, etc.

5 Now doth the country rejoice in all the gay store
     of its bounty;
   Summer returns to the earth bearing her wealth
     in her hand.   Welcome, etc.

6 Flowers bespangle the field with riot and glitter
   of colour;
   White are the hedgerows with may, green grows
   the grass in the meads.   Welcome, etc.

7 One by one open their buds the blossoms of tulip
   and lily;
   Shyly smile from the grass daisies with myriad
   eyes.   Welcome, etc.

At the entrance into the Chancel :

℣. The Spirit of the Lord filleth the world.

℟. And that which containeth all things hath
knowledge of the voice. Alleluia.

613   *Frances R. Havergal*

1 TO thee, O Comforter divine,
   For all thy grace and power benign,
        Sing we Alleluia!

2 To thee, whose faithful love had place
   In God's great covenant of grace,
        Sing we Alleluia!

3 To thee, whose faithful power doth heal,
   Enlighten, sanctify, and seal,
        Sing we Alleluia!

4 To thee, our teacher and our friend,
   Our faithful leader to the end,
        Sing we Alleluia!

5 To thee, by Jesus Christ sent down,
   Of all his gifts the sum and crown,
        Sing we Alleluia!

614

W. Hammond†
Based on Veni, creator Spiritus

1 HOLY Spirit, gently come,
  Raise us from our fallen state,
Fix thy everlasting home
  In the hearts thou didst create,
    Gift of God most high!
  Visit every troubled breast,
Light and life and love supply,
  Give our spirits perfect rest.

2 Heavenly unction from above,
  Comforter of hearts that faint,
Fountain, life, and fire of love,
  Hear and answer our complaint:
    Thee we humbly pray,
  Finger of the living God,
Now thy sevenfold gift display,
  Shed our Saviour's love abroad.

3 Now thy quickening influence bring,
  On our spirits sweetly move,
Open every mouth to sing
  Jesus' everlasting love:
    Lighten every heart;
  Drive our enemies away,
Joy and peace to us impart,
  Lead us in the heavenly way.

4 Take the things of Christ and show
  What our Lord for us hath done;
May we God the Father know
  Only in and through the Son:
    Nothing will we fear,
  Though to wilds and deserts driven,
While we feel thy presence near,
  Witnessing our sins forgiven.

5 Glory be to God alone,
    God whose hand created all!
Glory be to God the Son,
    Who redeemed us from our fall!
      To the Holy Ghost
      Equal praise and glory be,
When the course of time is lost,
    Lost in wide eternity!

At the entrance into the Chancel :

℣. The Spirit of the Lord filleth the world.

℟. And that which containeth all things hath knowledge of the voice. Alleluia.

615
                              J. Montgomery

1   LORD God the Holy Ghost,
      In this accepted hour,
As on the day of Pentecost,
    Descend in all thy power.

2   The young, the old, inspire
      With wisdom from above;
And give us hearts and tongues of fire,
    To pray and praise and love.

3   Spirit of truth, be thou
      In life and death our guide;
O Spirit of adoption, now
    May we be sanctified.

TRINITY SUNDAY

616
                              H. A. Martin

1 SOUND aloud Jehovah's praises,
    Tell abroad the aweful Name!
Heaven the ceaseless anthem raises;
    Let the earth her God proclaim,
God, the hope of every nation,
God, the source of consolation,
    Holy, blessèd Trinity.

2 This the Name from ancient ages
　　Hidden in its dazzling light;
This the Name that kings and sages
　　Prayed and strove to know aright,
Through God's wondrous Incarnation
Now revealed the world's salvation,
　　　Ever blessèd Trinity.

3 Into this great Name and holy
　　We all tribes and tongues baptize;
Thus the Highest owns the lowly,
　　Homeward, heavenward, bids them rise,
Gathers them from every nation,
Bids them join in adoration
　　　Of the blessèd Trinity.

4 In this Name the heart rejoices,
　　Pouring forth its secret prayer;
In this Name we lift our voices,
　　And our common faith declare,
Offering praise and supplication
And the thankful life's oblation
　　　To the blessèd Trinity.

5 Still thy Name o'er earth and ocean
　　Shall be carried, 'God is Love,'
Whispered by the heart's devotion,
　　Echoed by the choirs above,
Hallowed through all worlds for ever,
Lord, of life the only giver,
　　　Blessèd, glorious Trinity.

At the entrance into the Chancel:

℣. Let us bless the Father and the Son and the Holy Ghost.

℟. Let us praise and exalt him for ever.

617   *Tr. J. D. Chambers and Compilers*
Ave, colenda Trinitas

1 ALL hail, adorèd Trinity!
  All hail, eternal Unity!
  O God the Father, God the Son,
  And God the Spirit, ever One.

2 To thee upon this festal day
  We offer here our thankful lay:
  O let our work accepted be,
  That blessèd work of praising thee.

3 Three Persons praise we evermore,
  One only God our hearts adore:
  In thy sure mercy ever kind
  May we our strong protection find.

4 O Trinity! O Unity!
  Be present as we worship thee;
  And with the songs that angels sing
  Unite the hymns of praise we bring.

DEDICATION FESTIVAL

618   *c. 13th cent. (York Processional)*
                             Tr. C. S. Phillips
Salve, festa dies

1 WELCOME, morning of joy, glad feast that all
    ages shall hallow,
  Day when the Bride of the Lamb joyfully wed-
    deth her Spouse.   *(Repeat)*

2 This is the palace of God, the dwelling of peace
    and refreshing:
  Hither the poor may repair, winning a Solomon's
    wealth.
        Welcome, etc.

3 True Son of David is he who hath knit us up into
his Body;
Here in your mother-home, hail him as God and
as Man.
Welcome, etc.

4 Linked by a heavenly bond are ye in the grace of
the Spirit,
If ye will honour your troth, seek to be brothers
in heart.
Welcome, etc.

5 New-made from heaven descends Jerusalem's
mystical city,
Decked with a glory that flows straight from the
fountain of light.
Welcome, etc.

6 Here at the laver of grace the King of goodness
eternal
Cleanses with water from heaven souls that
approach him in faith.
Welcome, etc.

7 Here David's Tower standeth sure: on hasting
feet run to its stronghold;
Stored up within ye shall find pledges of
heavenly bliss.
Welcome, etc.

8 This is the Ark of the Lord that succour affords
to the faithful,
Carrying safe into port them that were tossed on
the sea.
Welcome, etc.

9 Ladder of Jacob is here, the ladder that bringeth
  to heaven
Those who with faith for their guide follow the
  path of the just.
        Welcome, etc.

    At the entrance into the Chancel:

  ℣. Blessed are they that dwell in thy house.
  ℟. They will be always praising thee.

619
W. Drennan

1 THE heaven of heavens cannot contain
    The universal Lord;
Yet he in humble hearts will deign
    To dwell and be adored.

2 Where'er ascends the sacrifice
    Of fervent praise and prayer,
Or in the earth or in the skies,
    The heaven of God is there.

3 His presence there is spread abroad
    Through realms, through worlds unknown;
Who seeks the mercies of his God
    Is ever near his throne.

620
Tr. J. M. Neale and Compilers
Urbs beata

1 BLESSED city, heavenly Salem,
    Vision dear of peace and love,
Who of living stones art builded
    In the height of heaven above,
And, with angel hosts encircled,
    As a bride dost earthward move!

2 From celestial realms descending,
    Bridal glory round thee shed,
Meet for him whose love espoused thee,
    To thy Lord shalt thou be led;
All thy streets and all thy bulwarks
    Of pure gold are fashionèd.

3 Bright thy gates of pearl are shining,
    They are open evermore;
And by virtue of his merits
    Thither faithful souls do soar,
Who for Christ's dear name in this world
    Pain and tribulation bore.

4 Many a blow and biting sculpture
    Polished well those stones elect,
In their places now compacted
    By the heavenly Architect,
Who therewith hath willed for ever
    That his palace should be decked.

PART 2

5 Christ is made the sure Foundation,
    Christ the Head and Corner-stone,
Chosen of the Lord, and precious,
    Binding all the Church in one,
Holy Sion's help for ever,
    And her confidence alone.

6 All that dedicated city,
    Dearly loved of God on high,
In exultant jubilation
    Pours perpetual melody,
God the One in Three adoring
    In glad hymns eternally.

PART 3

7 To this temple, where we call thee,
    Come, O Lord of Hosts, to-day;
With thy wonted loving-kindness
    Hear thy servants as they pray,
And thy fullest benediction
    Shed within its walls alway.

8 Here vouchsafe to all thy servants
   What they ask of thee to gain,
What they gain from thee for ever
   With the blessèd to retain,
And hereafter in thy glory
   Evermore with thee to reign.

*The following Doxology may be sung at the
end of any Part, or of the whole hymn:*

9 Laud and honour to the Father,
   Laud and honour to the Son,
Laud and honour to the Spirit,
   Ever Three, and ever One,
Consubstantial, co-eternal,
   While unending ages run.

At the entrance into the Chancel:

℣. Blessed are they that dwell in thy house.
℞. They will be always praising thee.

621   *I. Watts and J. Wesley*

1 ETERNAL Power, whose high abode
Becomes the grandeur of a God,
Infinite lengths beyond the bounds
Where stars revolve their little rounds;

2 Thee while the first Archangel sings,
He hides his face behind his wings,
And ranks of shining Thrones around
Fall worshipping and spread the ground.

3 Lord, what shall earth and ashes do?
We would adore our Maker too:
From sin and dust to thee we cry,
The great, the holy, and the high!

THANKSGIVING FOR THE INSTITUTION
OF HOLY COMMUNION

622

St. Thomas Aquinas
Tr. C. S. Phillips and others

Lauda, Sion, Salvatorem

1 PRAISE, O Sion, praise thy Master,
　Praise thy Saviour, praise thy Pastor,
　　In a joyous melody:
　Put forth all thy strength to sing him,
　For the best that thou canst bring him
　　Cannot ever worthy be.

2 Tell, O tell in praises glowing
　　How the living, life-bestowing
　　Bread from heaven is given to thee:
　Bread which Christ, before he suffered,
　At the sacred banquet proffered
　　To the Twelve in company.

3*Lift thy voice in tuneful chorus,
　Joyfully in strain sonorous
　　Be thy heart's delight outpoured;
　While this solemn day we celebrate
　How the Saviour first did consecrate
　　For his guests the mystic board.

4*Here, our new King's table gracing,
　This new Passover's new blessing
　　Hath fulfilled the older rite:
　Here is new to old succeeding,
　Truth its shadow superseding,
　　Darkness swallowed up in light.

5 What he did at supper seated
　Christ ordained to be repeated
　　In his memory divine;
　Wherefore we, his precept heeding,
　And his saving Offering pleading,
　　Consecrate the bread and wine.

6 'Tis the truth to Christians given,
  Bread becomes his Flesh from heaven,
    Wine becomes his holy Blood:
Here, where sight is unavailing,
Faith may seize with grasp unfailing
    What can ne'er be understood.

7 'Neath these diverse signs are hidden
  Priceless things to sense forbidden,
    Outward signs are all we see:
Bread for eating, wine for drinking,
Yet, in ways beyond all thinking,
    Christ in each doth deign to be.

8*Whoso of this feast partaketh,
  Christ divideth not nor breaketh—
    He is whole to all that taste:
Whether one this bread receiveth
Or a thousand, still he giveth
    One same food that cannot waste.

9*Good and bad alike are sharing
  One repast, a doom preparing
    All unlike—'tis life or death:
Each a destiny is making—
See ye of the one partaking
    How the issue differeth!

10*When this Sacrament is broken,
  Doubt not in each severed token,
    Hallowed by the blessing spoken,
      What is veiled doth whole abide:
Though the sign is broken duly,
Christ himself remaineth truly
All unbroken; present fully
    Here abides the Signified.

PART 2
Ecce, Panis angelorum

11 Lo, the angels' food is given
    To the pilgrim who hath striven;
    See the children's Bread from heaven,
        Which on dogs may ne'er be spent:
    Christ the old types is fulfilling,
    Isaac bound, a Victim willing,
    Paschal Lamb its life-blood spilling,
        Manna to the fathers sent.

At the entrance into the Chancel :

℣. I am the true Bread of Life.
℟. He that cometh to me shall never hunger.

PART 3
Bone, Pastor, Panis vere

12 O true Bread, Good Shepherd, tend us,
    Jesu, of thy love befriend us,
    Thou refresh us, thou defend us,
    Let thy goodness here attend us
        Till the land of life we see;
    Thou who all things canst and knowest,
    Who such food on earth bestowest,
    Make us, where thy face thou showest,
        'Mid thy saints, though least and lowest,
        Guests and fellow heirs with thee.

Note.—*This hymn in its several parts (but omitting
the starred verses) is suitable for general use at Holy
Communion.*

SAINTS' DAYS

623   *'F. B. P.'* (c. 1600)

1 JERUSALEM, my happy home,
       When shall I come to thee?
   When shall my sorrows have an end?
       Thy joys when shall I see?

O happy harbour of the saints!
    O sweet and pleasant soil!
In thee no sorrow may be found,
    No grief, no care, no toil.

2 There lust and lucre cannot dwell;
    There envy bears no sway;
There is no hunger, heat, nor cold,
    But pleasure every way:
Thy walls are made of precious stones,
    Thy bulwarks diamonds square;
Thy gates are of right orient pearl,
    Exceeding rich and rare.

3 Ah, my sweet home, Jerusalem,
    Would God I were in thee!
Would God my woes were at an end,
    Thy joys that I might see!
Thy saints are crowned with glory great,
    They see God face to face;
They triumph still, they still rejoice:
    Most happy is their case.

4 Thy vineyards and thy orchards are
    Most beautiful and fair,
Full furnishèd with trees and fruits
    Most wonderful and rare;
Thy gardens and thy gallant walks
    Continually are green;
There grow such sweet and pleasant flowers
    As nowhere else are seen.

5 Quite through the streets with silver sound
    The flood of life doth flow,
Upon whose banks on every side
    The wood of life doth grow:
There trees for evermore bear fruit,
    And evermore do spring;
There evermore the angels sit,
    And evermore do sing.

6*There David stands with harp in hand
  As master of the choir;
Ten thousand times that man were blest
  That might this music hear:
Our Lady sings Magnificat
  With tune surpassing sweet,
And all the virgins bear their parts,
  Sitting about her feet.

7*Te Deum doth Saint Ambrose sing,
  Saint Austin doth the like;
Old Simeon and Zachary
  Have not their songs to seek:
There Magdalene hath left her moan,
  And cheerfully doth sing
With blessèd saints, whose harmony
  In every street doth ring.

8 Jerusalem, my happy home,
  Would God I were in thee!
Would God my woes were at an end,
  Thy joys that I might see!
Jerusalem, Jerusalem,
  God grant I once may see
Thy endless joys, and of the same
  Partaker ay to be!

At the entrance into the Chancel :

℣. Be glad, O ye righteous, and rejoice in the Lord.
℟. And be joyful, all ye that are true of heart.

624
C. Wesley

1 THE Church triumphant in thy love,
  Their mighty joys we know;
They sing the Lamb in hymns above,
  And we in hymns below.

2 Thee in thy glorious realm they praise,
    And bow before thy throne;
We in the kingdom of thy grace:
    The kingdoms are but one.

3 The holy to the Holiest leads:
    From hence our spirits rise,
And he that in thy statutes treads
    Shall meet thee in the skies.

625
                    Ascribed to Thomas à Kempis
                        Tr. J. M. Neale†

In domo Patris

1 OUR Father's home eternal,
    O Christ, thou dost prepare
With many divers mansions,
    And each one passing fair:
They are the victors' guerdon
    Who, through the hard-won fight,
Have followed in thy footsteps
    And reign with thee in light.

2 Amid the happy number
    The virgins' crown and queen,
The ever-Virgin Mother,
    Is first and foremost seen:
Her one and only gladness,
    That undefilèd one,
To gaze in adoration,
    The Mother, on the Son.

3*There Adam leads the chorus,
    And tunes the joyous strain
Of all his myriad children
    That follow in thy train:
Victorious over sorrow,
    The countless band to see,
Destroyed through his transgression,
    But raised to life through thee.

4 The patriarchs in their triumph
    Thy praises nobly sing,
Of old their promised offspring.
    And now their Victor-King:
The prophets harp their gladness
    That, whom their strains foretold,
In manifested glory
    They evermore behold.

5 And David calls to memory
    His own especial grace
In such clear prophet-vision
    To see thee face to face:
The apostolic cohort,
    Thy valiant and thine own,
As royal co-assessors
    Are nearest to thy throne.

6 Thy martyrs reign in glory
    Who triumphed as they fell,
And by a thousand tortures
    Defeated death and hell;
And every patient sufferer,
    Who sorrow dared contemn,
For each especial anguish
    Hath one especial gem.

7*The valiant-souled confessors
    Put on their meet array,
Who bare the heat and burden
    Of many a weary day:
The scorners of life's pleasures,
    Their self-denial ceased,
Sit down with thee and banquet
    At thy eternal feast.

8*The virgins walk in beauty
 Amidst their lily-bowers,
The coronals assuming
 Of never-fading flowers;
And innocents sport gaily
 Through all the courts of light,
To whom thou gav'st the guerdon
 Before they fought the fight.

9 The soldiers of thine army,
 Their earthly struggles o'er,
With joy put off the armour
 That they shall need no more:
For these, and all that battled
 Beneath their Monarch's eyes,
The harder was the conflict
 The brighter is the prize.

10 The penitent, attaining
 Full pardon in thy sight,
Leave off the vest of sackcloth
 And don the robe of white:
The bondsman and the noble,
 The peasant and the king,
All gird one glorious Monarch
 In one eternal ring.

At the entrance into the Chancel :

℣. Be glad, O ye righteous, and rejoice in the Lord.

℟. And be joyful, all ye that are true of heart.

626

J. Austin †

1 HAIL, glorious spirits, heirs of light,
 The high-born sons of fire, [bright:
Whose souls burn clear, whose flames shine
 All joy, yet all desire.

2 Hail, all you happy souls above,
 Who make that glorious ring
About the sparkling throne of love,
 And there for ever sing.

627   *J. M. C. Crum*

1 LET love arise and praise him
   Who came as Light from heaven,
And shines as light reflected
   In souls of men forgiven:
      Through the dimness of our shadows,
      Through the mist he came;
   For the souls of them that see him
      Blessèd be his name.

2 He cometh as the morning,
   The light of day arisen,
To them that sit in darkness,
   The souls of men in prison:
      Blessèd Light that deigns to visit
      Man in his distress!
   Welcome with thy wings of healing,
      Sun of Righteousness!

3 Behold the sky at evening,
   When day on earth is ending,
What clouds are seen at sunset
   Upon the sun attending:
      Where our sun is sinking from us
      Into skies unknown,
   All the clouds aflame with glory
      Where he passes on.

4 So, where our Christ advances,
   The Lord of Life undying,
He goes with flashing trumpets
   And pomp of banners flying;
      Not in unattended glory,
      Nor in lonely might:
   Multitudes that none can number
      Answer back his light.

5 A burning mist around him,
　　A flock of souls unending,
A cloud of flying spirits,
　　Ascending and descending,
　　　　Swimming on in light below him,
　　　　Soaring on above,
　　　　Who are these that move in rapture
　　　　Round about his love?

6 O these are souls that pitied,
　　Because they knew his pity,
And found him in their neighbour
　　And met him in their city;
　　　　These are they whose life among us
　　　　Won the weak from vice;
　　　　These are they who, little knowing,
　　　　Shared his sacrifice.

7 Through them he healed our wounded,
　　Through them he led our blindness,
Redeemed our unbelieving,
　　Atoned for our unkindness.
　　　　Therefore in the light they follow
　　　　Where the Lamb doth go;
　　　　Therefore shines their dazzling raiment
　　　　White as glistening snow.

8 So Christ his temple enters,
　　The Priest that was so wounded,
And makes a new atonement
　　As Love by love surrounded:
　　　　Love amazing that transfigures
　　　　Where its light has shone,
　　　　Love that burns upon the altar,
　　　　Love that mounts the throne.

At the entrance into the Chancel:

℣. Be glad, O ye righteous, and rejoice in the Lord.
℟. And be joyful, all ye that are true of heart.

628

C. *Wesley*†

1 COME, let us join our friends above
　　That have obtained the prize,
And on the eagle wings of love
　　To joy celestial rise.

2 E'en now by faith we join our hands
　　With those that went before,
And greet our Captain's ransomed bands
　　On the eternal shore.

GENERAL

629

S. *Baring-Gould*

1 ONWARD, Christian soldiers!
　　　Marching as to war,
With the Cross of Jesus
　　　Going on before.
Christ the royal Master
　　　Leads against the foe;
Forward into battle,
　　　See, his banners go!
　　　　Onward, Christian soldiers!
　　　　　Marching as to war,
　　　　With the Cross of Jesus
　　　　　Going on before.

2 At the sign of triumph
　　　Satan's host doth flee;
On then, Christian soldiers,
　　　On to victory!
Hell's foundations quiver
　　　At the shout of praise;
Brothers, lift your voices,
　　　Loud your anthems raise.
　　　　Onward, etc.

3 Like a mighty army
    Moves the Church of God;
Brothers, we are treading
    Where the saints have trod:
We are not divided,
    All one body we,
One in hope and doctrine,
    One in charity.
        Onward, etc.

4 Crowns and thrones may perish,
    Kingdoms rise and wane,
But the Church of Jesus
    Constant will remain:
Gates of hell can never
    'Gainst that Church prevail;
We have Christ's own promise,
    And that cannot fail.
        Onward, etc.

5 Onward, then, ye people,
    Join our happy throng,
Blend with ours your voices
    In the triumph song:
Glory, laud, and honour
    Unto Christ the King,
This through countless ages
    Men and angels sing.
        Onward, etc.

At the entrance into the Chancel:

℣. Be strong and of a good courage.
℞. And the Lord, he it is that doth go before thee.

630

I. Watts

1 FROM all that dwell below the skies
    Let the Creator's praise arise:
    Let the Redeemer's name be sung
    Through every land by every tongue.

2 Eternal are thy mercies, Lord;
  Eternal truth attends thy word:
  Thy praise shall sound from shore to shore,
  Till suns shall rise and set no more.

631 *T. Olivers. Based on the Hebrew Yigdal*

1 THE God of Abraham praise
  Who reigns enthroned above,
  Ancient of everlasting Days,
    And God of love:
  Jehovah, great I AM,
  By earth and heaven confest;
  We bow and bless the sacred name
    For ever blest.

2* The God of Abraham praise,
  At whose supreme command
  From earth we rise, and seek the joys
    At his right hand:
  We all on earth forsake,
  Its wisdom, fame, and power;
  And him our only portion make,
    Our Shield and Tower.

3 Though nature's strength decay,
  And earth and hell withstand,
  To Canaan's bounds we urge our way
    At his command:
  The watery deep we pass,
  With Jesus in our view;
  And through the howling wilderness
    Our way pursue.

4 The goodly land we see,
  With peace and plenty blest:
  A land of sacred liberty
    And endless rest;

There milk and honey flow,
And oil and wine abound,
And trees of life for ever grow,
With mercy crowned.

5   There dwells the Lord our King,
The Lord our Righteousness,
Triumphant o'er the world of sin,
The Prince of Peace:
On Sion's sacred height
His Kingdom he maintains,
And glorious with his saints in light
For ever reigns.

6★   He keeps his own secure,
He guards them by his side,
Arrays in garment white and pure
His spotless Bride:
With streams of sacred bliss,
Beneath serener skies,
With all the fruits of Paradise,
He still supplies.

7★   Before the great Three-One
They all exulting stand,
And tell the wonders he hath done
Through all their land:
The listening spheres attend,
And swell the growing fame,
And sing in songs which never end
The wondrous name.

8★   The God who reigns on high
The great archangels sing,
And 'Holy, Holy, Holy,' cry,
'Almighty King!
Who was, and is the same,
And evermore shall be:
Jehovah, Father, great I AM,
We worship thee.'

9   Before the Saviour's face
     The ransomed nations bow,
O'erwhelmed at his almighty grace
       For ever new;
     He shows his prints of love—
     They kindle to a flame,
And sound through all the worlds above
       The slaughtered Lamb.

10   The whole triumphant host
     Give thanks to God on high;
'Hail! Father, Son, and Holy Ghost,'
       They ever cry;
     Hail! Abraham's God, and mine!
     (I join the heavenly lays)
All might and majesty are thine,
       And endless praise.

At the entrance into the Chancel:

℣. They will go from strength to strength.

℟. And unto the God of gods appeareth every
one of them in Zion.

632

E. Osler

1 WORSHIP, honour, glory, blessing,
    Lord, we offer to thy name;
Young and old, thy praise expressing,
    Join their Saviour to proclaim.
As the saints in heaven adore thee,
    We would bow before thy throne;
As thine angels serve before thee,
    So on earth thy will be done.

633

G. W. Kitchin and M. R. Newbolt

1 LIFT high the Cross, the love of Christ pro-
    claim
Till all the world adore his sacred name.

2 Come, brethren, follow where our Captain
    trod,
  Our King victorious, Christ the Son of God.
                    Lift high the Cross, etc.

3 Led on their way by this triumphant sign,
  The hosts of God in conquering ranks combine.
                    Lift high the Cross, etc.

4 Each new-born soldier of the Crucified
  Bears on his brow the seal of him who died.
                    Lift high the Cross, etc.

5 This is the sign which Satan's legions fear
  And angels veil their faces to revere.
                    Lift high the Cross, etc.

6 Saved by this Cross whereon their Lord was
    slain,
  The sons of Adam their lost home regain.
                    Lift high the Cross, etc.

7 From north and south, from east and west they
    raise
  In growing unison their song of praise.
                    Lift high the Cross, etc.

8 O Lord, once lifted on the glorious Tree,
  As thou hast promised, draw men unto thee.
                    Lift high the Cross, etc.

9 Let every race and every language tell
  Of him who saves our souls from death and
    hell.
                    Lift high the Cross, etc.

10 From farthest regions let them homage bring,
And on his Cross adore their Saviour King.
> *Lift high the Cross, etc.*

11 Set up thy throne, that earth's despair may cease
Beneath the shadow of its healing peace.
> *Lift high the Cross, etc.*

12 For thy blest Cross which doth for all atone
Creation's praises rise before thy throne.
> *Lift high the Cross, etc.*

At the entrance into the Chancel :

℣. God forbid that I should glory.
℟. Save in the Cross of our Lord Jesus Christ.

634
I. Watts

1 'TWAS by thy Blood, immortal Lamb,
Thine armies trod the tempter down;
'Twas by thy word and powerful name
They gained the battle and renown.

2 Rejoice, ye heavens! let every star
Shine with new glories round the sky;
Saints, while ye sing the heavenly war,
Raise your Deliverer's name on high.

635
E. H. Plumptre

1 REJOICE, ye pure in heart!
Rejoice, give thanks, and sing;
Your festal banner wave on high,
The Cross of Christ your King:
Still lift your standard high,
Still march in firm array,
As warriors through the darkness toil
Till dawns the golden day.

2   Yes onward, onward still,
      With hymn and chant and song,
Through gate and porch and columned aisle
      The hallowed pathways throng:
      With all the angel choirs,
      With all the saints on earth,
Pour out the strains of joy and bliss,
      True rapture, noblest mirth.

3   Your clear Hosannas raise,
      And Alleluias loud;
Whilst answering echoes upward float,
      Like wreaths of incense cloud:
      With voice as full and strong
      As ocean's surging praise,
Send forth the hymns our fathers loved,
      The psalms of ancient days.

4   Yes on, through life's long path,
      Still chanting as ye go,
From youth to age, by night and day,
      In gladness and in woe:
      At last the march shall end,
      The wearied ones shall rest,
The pilgrims find their Father's house,
      Jerusalem the blest.

5   Then on, ye pure in heart!
      Rejoice, give thanks, and sing;
Your festal banner wave on high,
      The Cross of Christ your King.
      Praise him who reigns on high,
      The Lord whom we adore,
The Father, Son, and Holy Ghost,
      One God for evermore.

At the entrance into the Chancel :

℣. Let thy priests be clothed with righteousness.
℟. And thy saints sing with joyfulness.

636   *J. Newton*

1 MAY the grace of Christ our Saviour,
    And the Father's boundless love,
  With the Holy Spirit's favour,
    Rest upon us from above.

2 Thus may we abide in union
    With each other and the Lord,
  And possess, in sweet communion,
    Joys which earth cannot afford.

ALPHABETICAL INDEX

A

B

C

D

E

F

G

H

I

J

L

M

N

O

U

V

W